Rural Studies Series

Series Editors

Charles Watkins, *Department of Geography, University of Nottingham*
Michael Winter, *Countryside & Community Research Unit, Cheltenham*

As a consequence of the explosion of interest in environmental matters, the phenomenon of counter-urbanization and the successive crises of the Common Agricultural Policy, rural studies has expanded rapidly in the past decade. With roots in geography and sociology, as well as in the new subjects of environmental studies and countryside management, this series is based on inter-disciplinary perspectives.

Rights of Way

Policy, Culture and Management

Edited by
Charles Watkins

PINTER

First published 1996 by
Pinter
A Cassell Imprint
Wellington House, 125 Strand, London WC2R 0BB, England
215 Park Avenue South, New York, New York 10003, USA

British Library Cataloguing in Publication Data
Rights of way : policy, culture and management. – (Rural
  studies series)
  1. Recreation areas – Access   2. Recreation areas – Management
  3. Land use, Rural   4. Rights of way
  I. Watkins, Charles
  333.7'6'17

ISBN 1–85567–390–8   *1947995*

Library of Congress Cataloging-in-Publication Data
Rights of way : policy, culture, and management / edited by Charles Watkins.
    p.   cm. – (Rural studies series)
  Includes bibliographical references and index.
  ISBN 1–85567–390–8
  1. Recreation areas – Great Britain – Access.   2. Recreation areas – Public use – Great Britain.   3. Right of way – Great Britain.   4. Wilderness areas – Great Britain.   I. Watkins, Charles, 1955–   II. Series: Rural studies series (New York, N.Y.)
  GV75.R54   1996
  333.78' 0941 – dc20
                                                                      95–47479
                                                                          CIP

Printed and bound in Great Britain by Biddles Limited, Guildford and King's Lynn

Contents

List of illustrations   vii
List of contributors   ix
Acknowledgements   xiv
Introduction CHARLES WATKINS   1

Part I: *Policy*

1   Robbers v. Revolutionaries: What the Battle for Access Is Really All About   11
MARION SHOARD

2   Access: Policy Directions for the Late 1990s   24
NIGEL CURRY

3   New Access Initiatives: The Extension of Recreation Opportunities or the Diminution of Citizen Rights?   35
NEIL RAVENSCROFT

4   Is the Right to Roam Attainable? An Aspiration or a Pragmatic Way Forward?   49
DEBORAH PEARLMAN AND J.J. PEARLMAN

5   Countryside Stewardship and the Consumer–Citizen   69
GAVIN PARKER

Part II: *Culture*

6   'Bradford-on-Avon but Shell on the Road': The Heyday of Motor Touring through Britain's Countryside   89
BARBARA ROSCOE

7   Educated Access: Interpreting Forestry Commission   100
     Forest Park Guides
     GEORGE REVILL AND CHARLES WATKINS

8   Access and Alignment: A Passport to Rutlandshire   129
     SIMON RYCROFT

9   Accessing the Attractive Coast: Conflicts and Co-operation 142
     in the Swedish Coastal Landscape during the Twentieth
     Century
     BJÖRN SEGRELL

10   Conflict and Co-operation over Ethnic Minority Access   162
     to the Countryside: The Black Environment Network and
     the Countryside Commission
     PHIL KINSMAN

11   Trespassing Against the Rural Idyll: The Criminal Justice 179
     and Public Order Act 1994 and Access to the Countryside
     KEITH HALFACREE

     Part III: *Management*

12   Game Management and Access to the Countryside   197
     GRAHAM COX, CHARLES WATKINS AND MICHAEL
     WINTER

13   Access Opportunities in Community Forests: Public   213
     Attitudes and Access Developments in the Marston Vale
     CHRIS BULL

14   Developing Market Approaches to the Provision of Access 226
     BOB CRABTREE

15   Local Countryside = Accessible Countryside? Results   238
     from a Countryside Recreation Survey in Wakefield
     Metropolitan District
     MEL JONES AND LYNN CROWE

16   Sustaining Enjoyment of the Countryside: The Challenge   254
     and Opportunities
     KEVIN BISHOP

     Bibliography   272
     Index   294

List of Illustrations

4.1 It's okay – we're all conservationists. Cartoon from
    On More Feet and Fingers by Jim Watson   61

6.1 'Shell Counties' painting of Derbyshire by Stanley Roy
    Badmin (© Shell-Mex and BP Co Ltd)   91

6.2 Wall-chart *Shell Guide to Cambridgeshire*, showing the numbered
    elements in the text and on the map. Painting by
    John Nash (© Shell-Mex and BP Co Ltd)   94

6.3 Cover of the *Shilling Guide for Berkshire*. Painting by
    Barbara Jones (© Shell-Mex and BP Co Ltd)   96

6.4 Publicity for Shell *Shilling Guides* aimed at Shell and BP
    dealers, showing the range of marketing approaches (BP
    Archive Reference B2632. © Shell-Mex and BP Co Ltd).   98

7.1 Walkers and a new Forestry Commission village (© Crown
    Copyright. Reproduced by permission of the Controller of
    HMSO and the Forestry Commission)   111

7.2 Cover of *North Yorkshire Forests* guide (© Crown Copyright.
    Reproduced by permission of the Controller of HMSO and
    the Forestry Commission)   113

7.3 New plantation (© Crown Copyright. Reproduced by
    permission of the Controller of HMSO and the Forestry
    Commission)   115

7.4 Planting gang (© Crown Copyright. Reproduced by permission
    of the Controller of HMSO and the Forestry Commission)   116

7.5 Visitors at Loch Voil (© Crown Copyright. Reproduced by
    permission of the Controller of HMSO and the Forestry
    Commission)   117

7.6 'In the Sprucewoods' (© Crown Copyright. Reproduced by

permission of the Controller of HMSO and the Forestry
Commission)   120

7.7   Loch Achrae and Ben Venue near Brig o'Turk (© Crown
       Copyright. Reproduced by permission of the Controller of
       HMSO and the Forestry Commission)   125

7.8   Cairngorm scene: crag, loch, pinewood, capercailzie and
       roe deer (© Crown Copyright. Reproduced by permission
       of the Controller of HMSO and the Forestry Commission)   127

9.1   Summer house expansion in Sweden, 1957–90   145

9.2   Swedish coastal areas classified as being of national
       importance (*riksintressen*) because of considerable natural
       and cultural values, according to the Natural Resource Act 146

9.3   Proposed national park area in the Sankt Anna
       Archipelago, according to the national park plan   155

10.1   BEN's discursive environment in relation to the
       Countryside Commission   163

10.2   From *Pastoral Interludes* by Ingrid Pollard © 1984   165

10.3   Section 2(2) of the 1968 Countryside Act (emphasis added) 167

10.4   Proposals for comment from Countryside Commission
       (1991c) p. 14 (emphasis added)   169

10.5   Countryside 'must welcome blacks' (Moore, 1991)   170

10.6   Julian Agyeman's closing words from *Countrywide*, BBC2,
       1 August 1992   171

10.7   *Why bother?* the Countryside Commission's position on
       ethnic minority attitudes to the countryside (Countryside
       Commission 1989a, 5–6; emphasis added)   172

10.8   Reasons for the withdrawal of the 1 per cent employment
       goal (Personal correspondence with Peter Ashcroft,
       8 January 1993, emphasis added)   174

10.9   Other advice to the Countryside Commission on the
       recruitment of staff to environmental organizations
       (Cloke 1990, 19; emphasis added)   177

13.1   Marston Vale Community Forest   217

15.1   Wakefield Metropolitan District   242

15.2   The rationale for the Wakefield Metropolitan District
       countryside recreation study   243

15.3   The Walking Women's Network   252

16.1   The Policy Interpretations of Sustainability by British
       Countryside Agencies   257

16.2   Dimensions of Sustainable Enjoyment   258

16.3   Sporting Land Use Categories (Sports Council, 1990)   259

List of Contributors

The Editor

Charles Watkins is Senior Lecturer in Geography at the University of Nottingham. His main research interests are in land management, landscape history and rural and cultural geography. His books include *Woodland Management and Conservation* (David and Charles 1990) and *Ecological Effects of Afforestation* (CAB International 1993). He is co-author of *Justice Outside the City: Access to Legal Services in Rural Britain* (Longman 1991) and *Church and Religion in Rural England* (Clark 1991) and co-editor of *The Picturesque Landscape* (1994).

List of Contributors

Kevin Bishop is Lecturer in Countryside and Environmental Planning at the University of Wales, Cardiff. He read Geography at Reading University, where he subsequently completed a PhD in land management, and is a qualified town planner. He has recently completed a research project on protected areas in the UK, which will form the basis of a book to be published by Routledge. He is currently pursuing research interests in sustainable agriculture and countryside recreation.

Chris Bull is Principal Lecturer and Director of the Centre for Tourism and Leisure Studies in the Department of Geography at Canterbury Christ Church College. He has undertaken research on various aspects of countryside recreation and conservation including farm-based recreation, the voluntary conservation movement and public perceptions of community forests. His current research interests include the tourist potential of community forests and the role of voluntary groups in sustainable leisure projects.

Graham Cox is Senior Lecturer in Sociology in the School of Social Sciences at the University of Bath. He has researched extensively on agricultural and environmental change and is currently working on the politics of rural leisure activities and property rights in the country-side.

Bob Crabtree is Head of the Environmental and Socio-economics Group at the Macaulay Land Use Research Institute. His research is focused on the analysis of land use policies directed towards producing benefits to the environment and local economies. He is a consultant to OECD, central government and countryside agencies and is currently involved in the evaluation of schemes to promote sustainable management of land. Previous work on public access includes a study for Scottish Natural Heritage of the costs to farmers and landowners of public access to open land in Scotland.

Lynn Crowe is a Senior Lecturer in the School of Leisure and Food Management at Sheffield Hallam University and is course leader for the BSc in Countryside Recreation Management. She formerly worked with the Countryside Commission and with local authorities in the Yorkshire and Humberside region. Her research interests include countryside recreation planning and management and access issues.

Nigel Curry is Professor of Countryside Planning and Head of the Countryside and Community Research Unit at the Cheltenham and Gloucester College of Higher Education. His current research interests relate to agricultural knowledge systems and the structure of the rural economy. His book *Countryside Recreation, Access and Land Use Planning* was published by Chapman and Hall in 1994.

Keith Halfacree is a Lecturer in the Department of Geography at the University of Wales, Swansea. His research interests include rural social geography, social theory, population migration and political geography. More specific interests include the imaginative geographies of space, in particular, those held by 'radical' alternative groups.

Mel Jones is a Principal Lecturer and Head of Academic Resources in the School of Leisure and Food Management at Sheffield Hallam University. His research interests include landscape history, the management of historic landscapes, recreation in the urban fringe, and urban greenspace management. He has carried out research for a wide variety of clients including the Peak Park Planning Board, the South Yorkshire Community Forest and Severn Trent Water.

Phil Kinsman is a Research Officer in the Department of Geography, University of Nottingham, working on an ESRC funded project on the National Farm Survey records in the PRO, Kew. From 1991 to 1993 he was a postgraduate student in the same department, researching issues of race, landscape and national identity, particularly as seen through the images of the photographer Ingrid Pollard and the work of the pressure group, the Black Environment Network.

Gavin Parker is a researcher at the Countryside and Community Research Unit in Cheltenham, where he is reading for his doctorate in countryside policy. His research interests include countryside recreation planning and policy, the politics of planning, citizenship and rights, minority groups in the countryside, countryside access and public participation in planning. He holds degrees in Land Economy and Town Planning.

Deborah Pearlman is a Senior Lecturer in Environmental Studies in the Division of Environmental Sciences, University of Hertfordshire. Her teaching interests include countryside recreation, planning in the countryside, visitor interpretation and social issues in the environment. Her research interests include countryside access issues, walking and rambling, and recreation and minority ethnic groups. She is also involved in various teaching and learning research projects within the Division.

Jerry Pearlman is a practising solicitor in Leeds whose main interests and activities are in respect of rights of way, commons and town and villages greens, access to the countryside and other related topics. He is Honorary Solicitor to the Ramblers' Association, was a ministerially appointed member of the Yorkshire Dales National Park Committee and was Chairman of the Open Spaces Society. He has written technical articles on the law relating to these subjects.

Neil Ravenscroft is Reader in Land Management, Head of Rural Studies and Director of the Centre for Environment and Land Tenure Studies in the Department of Land Management and Development at the University of Reading. His research interests are predominantly concerned with rural recreation and he has worked on projects funded by the Countryside Commission, the Department of the Environment and the Ramblers' Association. Dr Ravenscroft has written a number of papers, lectured widely on rural recreation and is author of *Recreation Planning and Development* (Macmillan 1992).

George Revill lectures in Geography at Oxford Brookes University. His main research interests are in cultural and historical geography. He has a particular interest in industrialized landscapes in the UK. He is an editor of *The Place of Music* (Guilford/Longman 1997) and co-author of *Representing the Environment* (Routledge 1997).

Barbara Roscoe works as a freelance researcher in the field of cultural geography. She has recently completed research on a four-country, EU funded project, based at Royal Holloway, University of London, entitled 'Nature, Environment, Landscape: European Attitudes and Discourses in the Modern Period (1920–1970)', with particular reference to water regulation. Her main interests lie in the exploration of twentieth-century images, perceptions and values related to the natural environment.

Simon Rycroft is a Lecturer in Human Geography based in the School of Cultural and Community Studies at the University of Sussex. His research interests include the geographies of British and American counter-cultures in the post-war period with particular reference to the Underground Press in London and Los Angeles; the geographies of Modernity and the literature of the 1950s and 1960s, and the European semiotics of landscape, nature and environment in the Modern period.

Björn Segrell is Senior Lecturer in the Department of Geography, Linkoping University, Sweden. His main research interests are in resource conflicts in areas of attractive countryside, the Swedish coastal landscape as an area of such conflict and issues regarding public access to the countryside.

Marion Shoard is a writer and lecturer on environment matters. She has been assistant secretary of the Council for the Protection of Rural England and currently lectures in countryside planning at University College, London. She has written articles for many publications including *The Times, New Statesman and Society* and *The Geographical Magazine.* Her two books are *The Theft of the Countryside* (1980) and *This Land is Our Land* (1987).

Michael Winter is Professor of Rural Economy and Society in the Countryside and Community Research Unit at the Cheltenham and Gloucester College. His research interests include agricultural and environmental policy and politics, the sociology of agriculture and the sociology of religion. He is currently directing a project on the impact of reform of the Common Agricultural Policy on the British country-side. His most recent book is *Rural Politics: Policies for Agriculture and the Environment* (Routledge 1996).

Acknowledgements

This book is based on a selection of papers presented at the conference *Accessing the Countryside* together with commissioned chapters. The conference was held in September 1994 at Hugh Stewart Hall, University of Nottingham, and was the September meeting of the Rural Geography Study Group of the Institute of British Geographers. I would like to thank Dr Susanne Seymour for her help and assistance with the conference organization. I would also like to thank Stephen Daniels, Marion Shoard, Nigel Curry, Graham Cox, Susanne Seymour and Paul Johnson for chairing sessions at the conference; the authors of the chapters for their patience in dealing with queries; Gregor Douglas for compiling the index; Jim Watson for allowing Figure 4.1 to be reproduced; Shell-Mex and BP Co Ltd for allowing Figures 6.1–6.4 to be reproduced; the Forestry Commission for allowing Figures 7.1–7.8 to be reproduced; Mr Christopher Lewis for drawing Figures 9.2, 9.3, 13.1 and 15.1; Ingrid Pollard for allowing Figure 10.2 to be reproduced; and several anonymous referees for their comments on chapters. Finally I would like to thank Veronica Higgs of Pinter for her assistance and encouragement.

Charles Watkins
Nottingham, July 1995

Introduction

CHARLES WATKINS

This book explores the theme of public access to the countryside through the eyes of a variety of commentators and researchers. The authors come from different backgrounds and have differing approaches and views. Some are keen to make polemical points, others to analyse policy developments. Some explore theoretical approaches, others assess the results of empirical studies. The authors come from a range of academic disciplines including geography, rural land management, sociology and economics. One thing they would probably all agree on, however, is that the issue of public access to the countryside is currently the subject of great debate and that there is a considerable body of recent research, some reported in this volume, which provides new approaches to the issue.

There are several factors which imply that we may be approaching a sea-change in access to the countryside. These include the current need to find new uses for agricultural land, the social change taking place in rural areas, much of which stems from continuing counter-urbanization, and the growing demand for the consumption of the rural heritage. Nigel Curry (1994) goes so far as to suggest that the recognition of the agricultural land surplus within the EU:

> provides a whole new canvas upon which to develop market policies for countryside recreation and public policies for the citizens rights of access, central to the economic activities of the farmer and landowner, that has never been available before (p. 231).

Certainly government departments and agencies over the last few years have developed an astonishing array of schemes to develop new forms of access to the countryside. These include, taking England as an example, the Countryside Premium Scheme (1989–92), which was designed to increase the benefits to the public under the set-aside scheme in a group of eastern counties; Countryside Stewardship, run by the Countryside Commission from 1991–96 (from April 1996 run by the Ministry of Agriculture, Fisheries and Food (MAFF), which endeavours to combine nature conservation and public access on private land; MAFF's Countryside Access Scheme; the access element for Environmentally Sensitive Areas (ESA); and access to woodlands encouraged by schemes run by the Forestry Commission and the Countryside Commission. All these schemes, of course, are voluntary. In addition, the Countryside Commission (1992) has developed policies to encourage the repair and management of footpaths and bridleways and hopes that all such rights of way will be fully usable by the year 2000.

Hidden under these trends, however, and yet at the same time underpinning them, is the ancient and fundamental conflict between landowners and others. Owners enjoy the right of excluding others as an essential part of their right of ownership; many of the others see the right to walk in the countryside as a right of citizenship. Clark *et al.* (1994) describe this conflict as one of the 'cultural tensions' that will 'stand to be intensified if the major expansions of tourism in the countryside now envisaged come about' (p. 59). In this book the complex of issues that has become known as the access debate is discussed in three main sections: policy, culture and management.

Policy

Marion Shoard's chapter calls attention to the small number of access agreements made under the 1949 Act and the fact that few landowners have opened up their land to walkers. She argues that the time has come 'to abandon the notion that reasoned discussion will open our countryside and to try something else instead'. There is a need for a new law providing general right of access to the countryside. She argues that this should include 'field edge, farm road and forest and estate track' as well as 'open country', taking Sweden's *allemansrätten* as a model.

Access policies are reviewed by Nigel Curry. He considers that there is a need to reinforce existing legal rights of access and improve policies for access to open and enclosed land. He emphasizes the need to make a distinction between open and enclosed land. On the former, he argues that although new legislation might be introduced to allow wider public access, some kind of financial incentive to farmers and landowners should be made by the government. On enclosed land, payment should be made by the consumer to the owner. He argues that access management should be carried out by a single authority. Until very recently most public access policies have been developed by the Countryside Commission, but the movement of Countryside Steward-ship from CC to MAFF in 1996, together with the development of an access tier for ESAs and the Countryside Access Scheme, has massively strengthened the role of MAFF in the management of public access.

Neil Ravenscroft argues that prior to industrialization, enclosure and the associated privatization of property rights, there was a much greater *de facto* freedom to roam than exists today. He explores the way in which competing claims over the ownership and use of rural land have been regulated by a partnership between the state and landowners. This partnership has, he argues, involved the use of the seemingly benevo-lent protection of traditional access rights in the concealment of the continuing hegemony of private property. He develops this argument by examining the way in which the claimed right to roam over private land, which could formerly be interpreted as a counter-hegemonic strategy, has recently been reconstructed into a commodified form that can be purchased by the state for consumption by the citizen.

The practical attainment of the 'right to roam' in open country has long been one of the principal aims of the Ramblers' Association. Deborah and Jerry Pearlman explore the historical and legal back-ground of the right to roam. Jerry Pearlman is Honorary Solicitor to the Ramblers' Association and the chapter clearly states the Association's position on the right to roam as laid out in their policy document *Harmony in the Hills* (Ramblers' Association, 1993) and analyses con-trasting responses to it from various organizations.

In the final chapter of the policy section, Gavin Parker evaluates the various concepts of citizenship implicit within recent policies to im-prove access to the countryside in England. He examines the Country-side Commission's Countryside Stewardship Scheme and shows how particular modes of regulation and commodification of certain coun-tryside goods are imbued with values that reflect a neo-Liberal political philosophy. He contextualizes this view within theoretical debates concerning rural economy and society.

Culture

This section contains six chapters, which explore cultural aspects of access to the countryside. Going for a drive is one of the most popular forms of accessing the countryside, yet little research has been carried out to explore the development of this activity. Barbara Roscoe explores the rise of mass motoring in Britain. She concentrates on the way in which oil companies such as Shell appropriated representations of Britain and its landscapes to market their products and how such advertising constructed visions of Britain in the 1950s and 1960s, a crucial period in the history of changing access to the countryside.

George Revill and Charles Watkins examine the development of the Forestry Commission's National Forest Parks in the 1930s. Their chapter explores the way in which the National Forest Park Guides were designed to integrate the economic and amenity values of Forestry Commission land and encourage public appreciation of huge new afforestation schemes. They argue that the design and content of the guides reflect an ambiguity in the Forestry Commission's view of the types of people visiting their woods and forests.

The importance of socio-cultural dimensions of access to nature, landscape and the countryside are explored by Simon Rycroft in his chapter, which makes use of a case study of Rutland and Rutland Water. He emphasizes the changing cultural politics of access in the post-war period and explores how discourses of local and iconic national identity have affected the grounds of access.

In the Policy section Marion Shoard and Deborah and Jerry Pearlman frequently refer to the Swedish system of *allemansrätten*. Björn Segrell's chapter shows how access to the Swedish coastal landscape has been affected by increased demand for access from non-local urban-based interests. He explores how the right of public access (*allemansrätten*) and planning legislation have been used by authorities to balance various interests and demands for access.

The Black Environment Network (BEN) is an organization trying to increase the level of involvement by ethnic minorities in the countryside and to improve the environments in which these groups live. Phil Kinsman's chapter describes BEN's engagement with the Countryside Commission, the pressure applied to them through public criticism and a parallel development of co-operation in specific projects and financial support. He reveals the untidy and not necessarily tightly controlled nature of the negotiation of the meaning of issues such as participation in the environmental movement and the countryside as a signifier of national identity.

Keith Halfacree examines the attitude of the state towards specific sub-groups within the population and of the appropriate use of rural space by exploring the measures introduced by the Criminal Justice and Public Order Act 1994. He argues that the state has limited the access of travellers, ravers and environmental protesters to the English and Welsh countryside because these groups pose a threat to the pre-dominant representation of the countryside: the rural idyll.

Management

Rambling and shooting are frequently seen as activities competing for rural land. Participants are assumed to come from different cultural and social backgrounds. David O'Connor's cover design for Marion Shoard's *This Land is Our Land* (1987) shows a rambler and a sports-man, identifiable by their distinctive clothes, glaring at each other and grasping an heraldic device representing the countryside. Graham Cox, Charles Watkins and Michael Winter present results from the Game Management Project, which show the attitudes of farmers and land-owners to public access and demonstrate the way in which different intensities of game shooting and public access are managed.

A policy development which has received a lot of publicity over the past five years has been the introduction of Community Forests within the rural–urban fringe. One of their principal aims is to improve the extent of public access to the countryside. Chris Bull examines public attitudes to the Marston Vale Community Forest Project, situated on the outskirts of Bedford, and surveys access developments in the Vale. Although the public response is generally positive, he concludes that local people do not expect radical changes in the extent and quality of public access as a result of the establishment Community Forest.

Bob Crabtree's chapter on developing market approaches to the provision of public access explores the payments of farmers for the provision of additional access on their properties from the perspective of an economist. He considers three aspects: the reasons for increased public intervention to provide access, the instruments by which access may be provided and the effectiveness of the schemes that have so far been introduced. He points out that with most of the schemes the use benefits from access are seen as complementary to the largely non-use benefits from investment in conservation.

The chapter by Mel Jones and Lynn Crowe reports on a research study carried out for the City of Wakefield Metropolitan District Coun-cil in West Yorkshire, which attempted to identify shortcomings in countryside recreation provision in the District. A household survey of 1000 individuals revealed, as expected, a strong relationship between levels of participation in countryside recreation and socio-economic status. This simple relationship was complicated, however, by the important influence of residential location, the irregular distribution of managed sites, low levels of awareness of public provision, and lack of confidence in using 'the ordinary countryside' for recreation.

In the final chapter Kevin Bishop explores the issue of increased access to the countryside within the context of sustainable development. He outlines the way in which different British countryside agencies have interpreted sustainability in terms of their policies and goes on to examine the way in which concepts such as 'carrying capacity', 'limits to acceptable change' and the 'recreation opportunity spectrum' can be used to assess the likely environmental effects of recreational developments. He concludes by discussing the way in which different agencies are attempting to deliver sustainable recreation policies.

Conclusion

The sixteen chapters in this volume provide a commentary on the considerable range of research being undertaken on the issue of access to the countryside. The book does not claim to provide comprehensive coverage of recent research. Many issues, such as the possible conflict between increased access and nature conservation, the management difficulties posed by different types of visitor, such as horseriders and four-wheel-drive vehicle enthusiasts, using the same routes and the increasing provision of access by organisations such as the County Wildlife Trusts, the Woodland Trust, the Royal Society for the Protection of Birds, the National Trust and private owners, are not explored in detail. It does, however, demonstrate the value of employing different approaches to researching the issue.

The book also points to the need for additional research on this topic. There is clearly considerable room to develop some of the theoretical issues discussed in the Policy section. Work on cultural aspects of accessing the countryside is developing into a fruitful area of research and there is, moreover, still an enormous amount to learn about ways of managing the countryside to improve levels of public access. Jenny Deaville's (1995) research project, for example, is demonstrating the considerable variation in the extent of footpaths and bridleways both at the regional level and within individual counties. She has also shown the tremendous regional variation in the distribution of schemes such as Countryside Stewardship, Tir Cymen and the Countryside Access Scheme. Such research indicates the need for higher quality information, perhaps through the implementation of Geographical Information Systems as used in counties such as Gloucestershire and Hampshire, for the management of public access to the countryside.

In many parts of Britain the combination of agricultural intensification and increased traffic on roads means that there are now few pleasurable or safe places to walk in the average stretch of countryside. Walking along country lanes, formerly perhaps the most usual way of enjoying the amenities of the countryside, is no longer a pleasure and is indeed positively dangerous, owing to the massive increase in the use of cars. There has, of course, been an increase in the number of country parks and other recreational facilities in recent years, but one has to drive to these, and the experience gained there is not equivalent to walking through open and managed countryside. This loss of access comes at a time of a growing trend to live in the countryside. Part of the demand for rural living stems from strong images of country life derived through literature, photographs and advertising, much of which is derived from the period of agricultural decline and rural depopulation, when walking along lanes and footpaths was possible and normal. The expectations of such new rural residents are such that calls for better access to the countryside can only grow stronger.

Part I

Policy

1

Robbers v. Revolutionaries: What the Battle for Access Is Really All About

MARION SHOARD

For most of the past half-century, those who have wanted more access to Britain's countryside have believed that the way to get it is through reasoned discussion with those who withhold it. In a typically British way, it has been assumed, walkers, landowners, farmers, sportsmen, canoeists and fishermen need to sit down together, talk it all through and arrive at arrangements with which all can be content. Walkers should explain their needs. Landowners should explain their problems. In a spirit of mutual goodwill the two sides should then thrash matters through. Graham Cox, Charles Watkins and Michael Winter's sterling attempt to show that walking is compatible with game rearing in woodland (see Chapter 12) is a typical contribution to this process. After half a century of this thoroughly reasonable approach it is, however, time to assess the results. Of course there have been advances. Access agreements appear to be a good example. Available for nearly fifty years to open up stretches of mountain, moor, heath, down, cliff and foreshore and available for nearly thirty years to open up woodland and waterside, they seem to show what negotiation can achieve. The Peak Park Planning Board has entered into access agreements ensuring that the public will not be treated as trespassers over 81 square miles of open country. In 1990 the Duke of Bedford entered into an access agreeement with Bedfordshire County Council over 800 acres of woodland on his Woburn estate. Yet over most of the countryside, access agreements are scarce indeed. Less than half of one per cent of the land surface of England and Wales as a whole is covered by them (Rossiter, 1972; Shoard, 1987, pp. 371–85).

The failure of access agreements to materialize is symptomatic of the wider failure of reasonable discussion of the kind to which Graham Cox and Charles Watkins are so keen to contribute to achieve its purpose. Private landowners, on the whole, have not opened their holdings to walkers, even when it has been pointed out to them that the objections they present are groundless. It is my contention that there are deep-rooted reasons why this is so and that the forces which lead landowners to resist the reasonable request for access are becoming stronger, not weaker, and that the time has therefore come to abandon the notion that reasoned discussion will open our countryside and to try something else instead.

It is understandable that walkers should have relied on reason. Landowners appear to put forward reasonable objections, such as the suggestion that game may be disturbed. Several authors have pursued these objections and demonstrated that the conflicts that can arise between public access on the one hand and the rearing and shooting of pheasants, grouse and deer, forestry operations, angling, nature conservation and farming activities on the other either have little substance or can be overcome relatively easily (Sidaway, 1988; Shoard, 1987, pp. 282–314; Ratcliffe, 1992, p. 7). But these arguments have not changed landowners' minds or their behaviour. For they already know that their concern about the sensitivities of their deer and pheasants is bogus. They are well aware that on estates like Blenheim, Arundel or Burghley the rearing and shooting of a large number of pheasants goes hand in hand with a considerable measure of public access and has done so for decades. They are well aware that many landowners encourage the hunt to crash through their pheasant coverts a few days before a shoot in order to make the birds more jumpy and increase the fun of the sport. They are probably well aware that landowners in several parts of northern Europe, such as southern Sweden and much of Denmark, rear and shoot thousands of pheasants while having to accommodate the public wandering around and enjoying their woods at the same time. Yet, in Britain, most of the woodland which is in private ownership remains closed to the general public.

The fact is that when landowners present reasonable objections to greater access they are not the real reasons. They are a front for real reasons that sound less attractive and are less susceptible to being reasoned away.

Seventy per cent of Britain's land is owned by 1 per cent of the population (Norton-Taylor, 1982, p. 23), who see themselves as a race apart – not surprisingly, since many of those who own large stretches of our countryside are amongst our most privileged citizens. Titled aristocrats together with the Queen, for instance, own just under one-third of

Britain's rural land – and this group does not include the many untitled families who own large estates and who frequently intermarry with the titled owners (Shoard, 1987, pp. 127–43). Together they form an exclusive club and, for them, access to the rural land they control is a key part of their privilege and their sense of being separate from the rest of the population. Not surprisingly, as Charles Watkins and Graham Cox show, farmers are in general antipathetic to access whether they use their land for shooting or not. It is not the activities in which they engage that are important, but the attitudes of the owners of rural land in Britain.

Britain's landowners are different from many of those elsewhere in Europe in that they take their privileges for granted. Their counterparts in Sweden, Norway, Denmark, France, Germany, Russia, China, Egypt, Japan and Mexico, for example, have all witnessed land reform in which traditional, usually large-scale landowners have been dispossessed and their land handed over to much smaller-scale private owners, or in some cases on to co-operatives or the state (Shoard, 1987, pp. 20–8). Even where they have not been dispossessed completely, landowners in many other countries have also seen measures that cut into their power in a fundamental way, for instance through upper ceilings on the amount of land any one person can own or the imposition of technical qualifications before a person is allowed to own farmland (Shoard, 1987, p. 489). But not ours. The last serious piece of land reform in Britain happened in 1066. Its beneficiaries have forgotten that their legitimacy, like that of many other landowners, stems from an act of robbery and is therefore open to question. The only substantial reduction in size of our large estates which date back to Norman times was the sale usually of outlying portions to former tenants in the early 1900s. True, the people through their government agencies and local councils now own at most 13 per cent of Britain's land (Shoard, 1987, pp. 119–21). But those who control the remaining 87 per cent are probably feeling as secure today as they have ever felt. The most worrying threat to their position this century – Lloyd George's proposed land taxes – was made in 1909, and even then never carried out (Shoard, 1987, pp. 92–5). Since then landowners have shown themselves extremely skilful at turning what might be challenges to their wealth and power – such as inheritance tax – into devices which guarantee their position even more securely (Shoard, 1987, pp. 453–60; Pearlman, 1992).

Today's rulers of Britain's rural land can look back on a long and developing tradition of exclusive control of the countryside. The Norman kings and barons, who seized the land by conquest, did not go as far as claiming the actual space – the woods, the fields and so on – as a chattel. They concerned themselves in particular with the exclusive possession of its game, and the first set of their laws expropriating the rest of us was concerned only with wild animals. A confident absolutism nonetheless prevailed from the outset. The Black Act of 1723, to name but one of the game laws of the last ten centuries, made even the killing of one fish, rabbit or deer a criminal offence punishable by death. It is easy to understand how the cheery self-confidence implied by such a measure led those behind it to feel they might as well extend their attitude to wild creatures towards the space that they inhabited.

The Norman barons and kings soon came to think it natural to regard rural land, which the Saxons had largely treated as a resource for all, as their own private pleasure ground. A visitor to England from France in 1549 reported incredulously that a great part of England consisted not of cornfields but of what he dubbed 'waste, desert and savage ground' given over to deer, so that he reckoned there must be as many deer in England as there were people in France (quoted by Hoskins, 1976). The devotion of such large areas of the country to deer while so much remained untilled and people went hungry promoted rural protests such as those of the Diggers in 1642. Despite a civil war which resulted in the decapitation of the monarch, these protests left landowners untroubled (Shoard, 1987, pp. 29–115). Today, the countryside remains a fiefdom of the few, with bloodsports playing a far greater part in determining its make-up than is often appreciated. The exclusive proprietorship of the space which game inhabit might actually seem a little excessive to the average Norman baron.

Today's owners of Britain's woods are well aware that most of us are not so hungry that we are out to poach their pheasants like our forebears. They keep us out of the pheasant woods because, even more than the Normans, they want to feel that their domains are exclusively theirs. Whatever they do in their woods – whether it be shooting, allowing others to engage in paintball games, or simply strolling around – they want to do it in private. If they choose to visit their estates only rarely, they still want to think that they are lying far away, exclusively theirs. I think this attitude springs from a combination of wanting to establish a feeling of superiority to the rest of society and feeling that 'their' land is an integral part of this separateness. They do not see 'their' land as part of a common environment. Ask a Swedish landowner about possession and he will talk about his garden as a private possession but the woods beyond as part of Nature, in which all are entitled to walk and which should be shared by all. But ask a British landowner and if you are lucky enough to get a candid response rather than a smokescreen answer about disturbing nesting grouse or saving the countryside from rampaging picnickers, then you get something very different. In 1987, in a television documentary called *Power in the Land*, I asked the Hertfordshire landowner Lord Brocket what he considered to be the main advantages of being a landowner. He replied: 'I think firstly because of the privacy it offers. People like to feel that they are nice and private in the middle of their patch, whatever size their patch is. Secondly, it offers them a security for the future because land ownership has always proved over the last few hundreds of years a good investment for the future and something that people tend to hold on to through its ups and its downs in its value, and land and bricks and mortar are always the things that people shout about. And I suppose there's a third thing for some people: it's like, I think for some people, and I hope not myself, like owning a Rolls Royce. It makes a statement. It says "I have arrived"' (*Power in the Land*, 1987).

Much of Lord Brocket's estate is out of bounds to the general public. I asked him how he would react if he had to allow ordinary people to wander freely in it. He replied: 'If you had an extreme socialist government in power or Marxist, then this would be fine. It would be exactly what they are looking for. But the problem is that England is a democracy and there is such a word as "freehold", and freehold has certain benefits attached to it and one of those benefits is that you can say that it's yours and that you can use it whenever you want and it's just yours, it's exclusively yours. Now if everyone else is going to use it, then it's not your freehold' (*Power in the Land*, 1987).

Britain's landowners have succeeded in co-opting the law to enforce ideas like these, just as their medieval predecessors used the law to enforce their expropriation of wild animals through the game laws. The existence of the laws they have demanded now reinforces their belief that their attitudes are not just fair, but somehow inevitable.

In Britain today, anybody setting foot on land where no legal right of way exists and where no special provision provides for access is a law-breaker. Though trespassers cannot normally be prosecuted, in spite of all those notices, landowners know they can use 'reasonable force' to eject trespassers who decline to leave, they can sue them for damages and can secure court injunctions against persistent transgressors, which then expose them to the risk of imprisonment. The law allows land-owners to erect barriers around their land of any kind up to 6 feet high without even applying for planning permission. They may top their walls or fences with broken glass or iron spikes so long as these do not interfere with lawful uses of adjoining land, such as the grazing of animals or the passage of people along a highway. They are free to deter trespassers by allowing savage dogs to roam freely. Only in the case of commercial property must they secure dogs and display notices warning of their presence. Surely, landowners feel, the fact that all this is the law of the land only goes to show that their instinctive desire to exclude is entirely right and proper.

Elsewhere, laws can be very different. In Scandinavia, for instance, our trespass law is essentially turned on its head. Instead of the landowner possessing a right to exclude, the general public have a right to walk and the onus is on the landowner to demonstrate why this freedom should be suspended. The owner's privacy is safeguarded through restrictions on access close to dwellings, and access over fields of growing crops and military installations is forbidden. But people may walk more or less anywhere else. If a landowner wishes to exclude people, he has to apply to so do. Landowners have to fit their activities around the public right of access. Doubtless this legal reality also feeds into the more liberal attitude to access of Scandanavian landowners (Shoard, 1995).

Our landowners' hostility to access does not, however, stem only from an attachment to privacy backed up by the sense that the law endorses this. They have also come to associate the right of exclusion with the profitability of their holdings. Medieval landowners whose fields, if not their deer parks, were thronged with country people saw the economic value of their land as tied up in what it produced. In the nineteenth century, however, this started to change when landowners in England started selling the right to shoot pheasants or fish for salmon and trout, and their counterparts in Scotland started charging rich men to stalk deer or to shoot grouse. As these pursuits became favoured activities for the privileged it became important that they were exclusive (Shoard, 1987, pp. 99–103). People paying large sums for the privilege of shooting a stag on some duke's land would surely not want to have to mix with Highland peasantry or members of the urban working class out on a picnicking trip from Glasgow or Aberdeen. Without anybody realizing what was happening, rural solitude became not only something landowners desired for themselves, but an asset they could use to enhance their wealth and one they would therefore be foolish to give away for nothing.

Powerful forces are therefore buttressing the desire to exclude on which British landowners insist and with which those seeking to negotiate public access must engage. But that is not all. The forces I have identified are not merely firmly entrenched. For a variety of reasons, they are growing more, not less, pervasive.

The lure of privacy is certainly not diminishing. As the world grows more crowded and unruly, private space is more and more highly valued. Around the estates of the privileged, the walls are getting higher, the fences are multiplying and the razor-wire is spreading.

The trespass law, which both provides landowners with the means of exclusion and bolsters their sense of its legitimacy, is also growing stronger, not weaker. Whether or not the government intends that this should be so, the Criminal Justice and Public Order Act 1994 not only hit new age travellers, squatters and demonstrators, but also provides a generalized strengthening of the landowner's right of exclusion. Before Mrs Thatcher came to power, criminal sanctions against trespass applied only in respect of railway lines and embankments, military land covered by special bylaws, aerodromes and certain ornamental grounds in towns, although trespass with intent to poach game was also criminal.

Landowners secured their first advance on this situation in 1986 on the back of Michael Fagan's well-publicized entry into the Queen's bedroom and the encampment by a group of hippies in a Somerset farmer's field. A Public Order Act of that year criminalized trespass to the following extent: if a senior police officer believes two or more people are trespassing and that they plan to reside on the land in question 'for any period' and if the occupier of the land has asked them to leave and any of the alleged trespassers have caused damage to property on the land or have used threatening or insulting words towards the land occupier or his agent, the police officer may direct those people to leave the land. If they fail to leave, or having left, return within three months, they are committing a criminal offence and can be imprisoned and/or fined up to £2,500.

Progress for landowners – but not immediately very threatening to ramblers, you may think. Now, however, things are more serious. The 1994 Criminal Justice and Public Order Act, primarily aimed at hunt saboteurs and other protestors on land without the owner's consent, criminalizes an assembly on land without the landowner's consent if the chief police officer considers that such an assembly might result in serious disruption to the life of the community or significant damage to land or a building of historical, architectural, archaeological or scientific importance. This too may appear to have little to do with ordinary walkers, although criminalization of trespass of any kind subtly undermines the idea that anyone has any right to go on to private land. Some aspects of this Act, however, are likely to threaten walkers more directly. The Act introduces the criminal offence of so-called 'aggravated trespass'. Section 68 provides that if any person trespasses on land in the open air and does anything intended by him to obstruct, or disrupt some lawful activity or intimidate any person so as to deter him from engaging in that activity he may, if found guilty, be imprisoned for up to three months and/or be fined a maximum of £2,500. A policeman who reasonably suspects that a person is committing such an offence has the power to arrest him without a warrant. The police have powers to get rid of people committing aggravated trespass. They can direct such people to leave the land; if they fail to do so or having left return within seven days, they can be arrested without warrant, or prosecuted and fined or imprisoned for up to three months.

How would this affect walkers? The 'intent' on the part of trespassers to obstruct lawful activity, which the Act criminalizes, might be deemed to amount to no more than possessing awareness of the probable consequences of the trespasser's acts. A landowner who put up signs telling people that their presence might disturb deer-stalking, pheasant-rearing, lambing, forestry operations or whatever else he liked to specify, would then be able to claim that a walker who must have seen his notice but still went on to his land 'intended' to disrupt the named activity and was therefore guilty of the new offence. He would then be in a position to call the police.

Already walkers in the Highlands frequently see notices like the following, from Strathconan, west of Inverness, in 1994: 'Deer in these hills are shot from mid-August to February for sport, meat and Government control policy. Walkers are therefore warned that rambling on high ground at this time can seriously upset large areas for deer stalking and can be dangerous' (Hansard, 5 April 1994, column 367). Imagine the difference if the notice was re-worded as follows: 'Walking in these hills may be punishable by a fine of up to £2,500 or three months imprisonment or both.'

During the Bill's passage through Parliament, a tabled amendment stated that 'a person exclusively exercising his rights as a *bona fide* rambler, hill-walker or other recreational user of the countryside shall not commit an offence under this Act'. For the Government, Earl Ferrers retorted: 'The law should apply equally to everyone. Where ramblers, hill-walkers and others behave offensively – if they do – it is right that aggravated trespass should apply to them' (Hansard, 24 May 1994, column 712).

The success of the prosecution of a rambler who merely ignored a sign warning that deer-stalking was in progress would doubtless turn on legal argument about the meaning of 'intent'. But the mere possibility that such a prosecution might succeed would enormously strengthen the landowner's armoury against the walker. Signs announcing that trespass is a criminal offence under the Criminal Justice and Public Order Act 1994 punishable by imprisonment would be quite an improvement, from their point of view, on the vague and hitherto unfounded threat that 'trespassers will be prosecuted'. We can expect landowners not only to take advantage of the provisions of the Act but to see them as further entrenching the legitimacy of their right to exclude.

Insofar as the pursuit of profit has strengthened the landowners' desire to exclude, this factor is also growing stronger rather than weaker as landowners discover that renting shooting and fishing rights is not the only profitable activity that is enhanced by the right to exclude. As more people visit the countryside for more purposes, landowners are beginning to see that they have barely begun to exploit the financial potential of their right to exclude. Not only are they finding more uses for their land, for example war-gaming, which depend on excluding non-participants, but they are also starting to charge people directly to visit waterfalls, parks, nature trails or other places where people want to go. You have to pay to visit the West Lyn valley near Lynmouth, Ingleton Falls and Clapham Beck in the Yorkshire Dales, Swallow Falls in Snowdonia, High Force in Teesdale or the Doone Valley on Exmoor (Shoard, 1989; 1992a). What is certain is that we are going to have to get used to paying more and more often if we want to visit such places in future.

Landowners are well aware that as the world gets more crowded and people have more money, their right to exclude can increasingly be turned into cash. Canoeing, motorbike scrambling, landscape painting, climbing, caving, rambling, birdwatching and visiting stately homes will become more and more popular. The right of exclusion gives landowners the choice of resisting these activities and preserving their privacy, or charging those who engage in them, and is thus doubly valuable.

It is important to make clear that the right of exclusion is not the same thing as the right to charge for inclusion. To bar people from your land is one thing; to use your land as an opportunity to turn people into a cash crop, without any pretence that your control of their movements is necessitated by the needs of other activities like farming, is to go a stage further.

Customers for the entrepreneurs of entry need not only be individuals. The state is consenting to pay its Danegeld to the robber barons building their turnstiles through our countryside. Increasingly government schemes are providing financial compensation to landowners in return for allowing public access.

One of the first schemes was the set-aside top-up scheme, under which farmers in the east of England who agreed to allow people to stroll on land under which they were already getting set-aside payments could receive an extra payment for allowing access to it. Countryside Stewardship, and in Wales Tyr Cymen, have extended the notion to lowland heathland, coastal land, watersides, uplands, chalk and limestone grassland, historic landscapes, woodland in the twelve community forests, old orchards and old meadow and pasture in north Devon and Hereford and Worcester (Countryside Commission, 1994a). More recently, the agri-environment package of the 1992 CAP Reform has led to the introduction of financial rewards for permitting access to land on which landowners are already receiving payments under the Environmentally Sensitive Areas scheme (ESA) and under Non-Rotational Set-Aside (NRSA).

Farmers now get £274 per mile per year merely for allowing people to walk along access strips ten metres wide along the sides of or across fields in ESAs and £145 under NRSA (MAFF 1994, 6–7). The landowners of the past who established the idea of a right of exclusion would be amazed to learn the size of the potential bounty they have created for their descendants.

The right of exclusion is being increasingly used to turn access into a tradeable asset. The government's endorsement of the right of the landowner to charge others to set foot on his or her land puts the official seal of approval on the notion that access to the countryside is a commodity to be bought from landowners rather than a free public good. This is like bestowing on one group a whole new form of wealth. I believe this is against the public interest since it is in the public interest that public goods like this should remain publicly owned.

Our landowners, then, do not just remain attached to the right of exclusion for strong reasons. Their reasons are growing stronger, so is their attachment to them and so are the laws which underwrite and legitimize them. It is therefore not surprising that they have been showing little reason to give away access rights in the course of polite discussion. On the contrary we must expect landowners to grow ever more resistant to requests for public access, for reasons which from their point of view make excellent sense.

If that means that those of us who want to open up our countryside cannot depend on reasoned dialogue, how should we seek to progress our cause? Some maintain that it does not matter if the law stays unchanged because if enough of us break it then it will wither on the vine. You sometimes hear people saying that they wander around on private land all the time, so why cannot everyone else do likewise? In fact, plenty of people do get thrown off private land. The situation on the ground is messy to be sure – in some places a considerable amount of trespass is tolerated as *de facto* access; elsewhere it is not. The characteristics of the trespasser also make a difference. A respectable-looking tweedy gentleman out training gun-dogs might encounter fewer difficulties than a rambler from town, clad in anorak and woolly hat. In any case, most Britons are law-abiding people. The adult men in Jacqui Burgess's survey of access to woodland (Countryside Commission, 1994) were extremely worried about accidentally trespassing. British people do not like sneaking around doing something they know to be unlawful, and many think trespassing is wrong because it is against the law. In any case, they do not want their presence in the countryside to be disquietingly provisional, their enjoyment tinged with the possibility of an ugly scene with a shotgun-wielding farmer or landowner. The experience is changed by this element, unacceptably so for many people.

The only honest and effective way of opening the countryside to the people is to require landowners to relinquish some of the rights in their asset which they are otherwise bound to defend and exploit. We must get to the heart of the matter and attack the right of exclusion itself. This is not such an unthinkable undertaking. Take the situation in the former West Germany. Traditionally, Germans had enjoyed a measure of access to forests but owners were free to curtail it, for instance for hunting. During the 1960s conflicts grew between huntsmen and walkers in forests near to towns where landowners attempted to bar access with fences and other structures. Matters came to a head in the countryside around Bonn and were resolved by the regional authority of North Rhine Westphalia, which drafted a legal right of access to forest and forced it through in the face of considerable opposition. This law became the prototype for the federal Forest Law of 1975, which gave West Germans the right to wander freely at their own risk in all woodland, large or small, whether publicly or privately owned. Landowners may apply to a forest authority for this general right to be suspended for specific reasons, for instance to prevent danger to walkers when trees are being felled, to protect sensitive wildlife or to allow forestry operations to take place. Hunting activities have to be made to fit in with the demands of walkers – unlike the situation in Britain, where the supposed requirements of pheasant rearing and shooting are used to justify the exclusion of the public from much of the woodland of lowland England.

The extension of access rights in Germany beyond forests has been achieved gradually with a body of access rights consolidated in West Germany's Nature Conservation Act of 1987. Now Germans in what used to be the Federal Republic enjoy a right of passage along all roads and paths except those which pass close to a dwelling, and in practice this opens up most riverbanks and lakesides. There is a right of access to uncultivated areas (such as heaths and sand dunes) and to fields which are not in use. Arrangements in what used to be East Germany are being brought more or less into line. The overall effect is to create a country fundamentally opened to walkers, albeit without the blanket provisions of Norway or Sweden (Shoard, 1991, p. 91, Chapter 9).

In Denmark, where the 1992 Nature Protection Act stopped private landowners from restricting access in woods of more than five hectares, Danes already had the right to roam over uncultivated, unfenced areas such as heathland and over the beach and foreshore (Shoard, 1992). The citizens of Switzerland have had the right to wander over woodland and grazing pasture since the turn of the twentieth century (Shoard, 1992, p. 36; Scott, 1991).

We in Britain ought to have a similar new law, ideally for a general right of access to the countryside of the kind that exists in Norway and Sweden. A régime similar to Norway's Outdoor Recreation Act of 1957 or Sweden's *allemansrätt* would give people a right to walk almost anywhere except fields of growing crops, military installations and land close to dwelling houses. I can see no valid reason why a right to roam in Britain should not give walkers access not only to mountain, moor, heath and down, but also to woodland, lakeside, riverbank, coastline, field edge, farm road and forest and estate track as well. As in Scandinavia, temporary exemptions could be made to meet the needs of nature conservation or other incompatible land-use activities. Failing this, we should push for such partial moves in this direction as we can achieve, with a view to gradually building up rights of access. Moorland and woodland present obvious early targets.

Such an approach is, however, not compatible with some moves now being made which appear progressive to some people. If we are going to insist on access as of right, we cannot afford to rejoice when a private landowner opens up a hitherto inaccessible beauty spot so he can charge walkers to visit it; still less can we afford to welcome government schemes that subsidize landowners who grant access. Both effectively buttress the landowner's right to exclude and put back efforts to erode it.

Not all those who want to walk in the countryside may be happy to turn their back on what may appear to be advances. However, as a possible change of government comes closer, this is the time to make clear what we really want. Neither turnstiles on the trails nor government subsidies to landowners can open our countryside to its people. All they will do is sustain those whose predecessors robbed ordinary people of the right to walk in the countryside. As revolutionaries we may liberate our countryside. As reformers we are certain to fail.

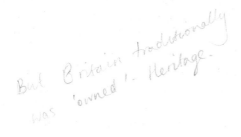

But Britain was 'owned' traditionally. Heritage.

2

Access: Policy Directions for the Late 1990s

NIGEL CURRY

Introduction

A wide range of policy proposals for a number of components of rural leisure has been put forward during the early 1990s, by the government (Department of the Environment, 1992a, 1992b), its agencies (Countryside Commission, 1991c, 1992; Sports Council, 1992) and a range of interest groups and professional bodies (Ramblers' Association, 1993a; Country Landowners' Association, 1992). These have covered issues embracing sport, recreation and tourism as well as access, and have addressed matters of national policy, statutory planning, informal strategic planning, community involvement and relations between participants and landowners. The broader implications of these proposals have been discussed fully by the author elsewhere (Curry, 1994). This chapter develops a number of possible policy options specifically relating to access to the countryside as a subset of these broader proposals for rural leisure. Such access proposals are important for at least two reasons. Firstly, national recreation data (Countryside Recreation Network Newsletter, 1994) suggests that the majority, some 75 per cent, of trips to the countryside are for the consumption of the wider unmanaged countryside for which access is the principal vehicle, rather than to managed facilities. Access therefore may be construed as a principal means through which rural leisure consumption is facilitated. Secondly, access policies have perennially been the most controversial in terms of national provisions for rural leisure.

The chapter considers such access policy options for the late 1990s in four groups: firstly, the need to reinforce existing legal rights; secondly, policies for access to open country; thirdly, access to enclosed land; and finally, some policies for the management of access to the countryside.

Reinforcing Legal Rights

Quite clearly, there is an existing body of legislation, since the 1949 National Parks and Access to the Countryside Act, that defines legal or *de jure* rights of access to the countryside in England and Wales. This provides the starting-point for any development of access policies for the late 1990s, since only when existing legal rights are fully defined and understood, will policies for improving access opportunities be able to be developed on a firm and unambiguous footing. Yet one of the hallmarks of existing rights is a lack of understanding of them on the part of the public and the landowner alike. A first element of policy, therefore, should be to seek to clarify the existing legal framework. Firstly, as has been suggested by the Common Land Forum (Countryside Commission, 1986), there is the possibility of introducing consolidating legislation to clarify such rights. But the history of the Common Land Forum's deliberations (Curry, 1994) and of attempts during the 1980s to pass Private Members' Bills relating to access (for example the Access to Commons and Open Country Bill, the Walkers (Access to the Countryside) Bill and the Definitive Map Modification Bill), none of which proceeded to Acts, suggests that new legislation, which attempts simply to consolidate and clarify, is unlikely to be a particular priority of government.

More pragmatically, policy should concentrate on clarifying access rights through less formal means. History suggests that if this is done only at the national level, it is likely to meet with less than total success. The Access Charter (Countryside Commission, 1985b) did little to ameliorate the limited understanding of access rights on the part of either the public or the landowner.

Most productively, perhaps, a better public understanding of access rights could be imparted through county councils as part of an orchestrated set of policies for access. These might embrace the review and completion of the definitive map, maintenance obligations, legal disputes, Public Path Orders, Definitive Map Modification Orders and so on, as well as providing clear information for the public and the landowner over legal rights. A consolidation of this county-level service might also allow statements to be made about the nature of *de facto* access in particular areas, something that would be impossible within consolidating legislation. The Countryside Commission (1992) is now committed to this less formal approach, and proposes the introduction of integrated information services that are both practical and accessible and are produced at a local level.

Improving Access to Open Country

If *existing* rights of access to the countryside can be made more clear in this way, *enhancing* access opportunities can proceed on a sounder basis. Access to open country is the conventional battleground for increasing access opportunities and two policy options are available in this context. The perennial one, since James Bryce's Access to Mountains (Scotland) Bill of 1884, is, of course, legislation. Notwithstanding the practical difficulties in introducing consolidating legislation, let alone new statutory proposals in the area of access, this option has always sought to increase the inherent freedoms of the citizen, i.e. to enhance legal rights. Such legislation may have one, or both, of two elements: the first is that of extending the definition of open country. This has been suggested a number of times in the past, for example to include parkland (Shoard, 1978 and Chapter 1), but more recently it has been reconsidered in the context of the New National Forest, community forests and a range of farm woodland schemes. Where the state has a significant stakeholder interest in such developments, redefining open country to embrace them does merit some consideration, particularly as they would extend open country to lowland England and Wales where the greatest demand is manifest but where open country is largely absent. But such developments are likely to ensue only as part of some bargaining process, through grant aid and other provisions, or through planning obligations (Curry, 1993), and such legislative bargaining could therefore be construed as paying for access in some way, even though by indirect means.

A second element to new legislation for access to open country would be to change provisions relating to the definition of trespass. Although again an enduring feature of proposed legislative reform, it has been most recently mooted by the Ramblers' Association (1993) with a claimed consensus from the Country Landowners' Association, the National Farmers' Union, English Nature and others. Drawing on the findings of the Common Land Forum, for open country it calls for a change in the law on trespass to reverse the presumption of trespass unless permission had been gained from the landowner. Instead, it calls for a freedom to roam in open country where trespass within that freedom is restricted to damage and wilful interference.

With an economic crisis in upland agriculture the time may be right for such legislation to succeed, but this is principally because the Ramblers' Association is proposing a number of 'sweeteners' in exchange for such enhanced rights. These include a suspension of access for such periods as game shooting and lambing and financial considerations to farmers for the protection of various habitats and wildlife, for environmental custodianship, for wardening and for compensation for any economic loss.

But these proposals, although construed as new legislation, are in fact again likely to succeed, if indeed they do, only because of the financial considerations proposed for farmers and landowners. Both possible areas of new legislation are therefore inextricably linked with financial incentives. This places an emphasis on the second policy option for improving access to open country, which is through some form of payment. Of crucial importance here, in policy terms, is the appropriateness of who should pay. Four payment mechanisms are possible. Firstly, the consumer paying direct; secondly, the taxpayer paying through direct cash transfers from the state; thirdly, the taxpayer paying through fiscal concessions to the farmer or landowner; and fourthly, the direct purchase of the land by the state. In the case of open country any of the latter three mechanisms is appropriate. Because access to open country is characterized by a sufficient degree of externalities, manifest in the fact that it is difficult to exclude people from such access opportunities, it is appropriate for the state to make such payments or expenditure. Effectively, access to open country has a number of characteristics of a 'public good'.

A number of these 'payment schemes' have been available for a considerable time, but have a number of enduring shortcomings. In terms of state cash transfers, local authorities have had powers to secure Access Agreements and Orders, through payments, since the 1949 National Parks and Access to the Countryside Act. Management agreements under the 1981 Wildlife and Countryside Act also allow transfer payments for recreation purposes, including those on open country. But the shortcoming of these particular schemes is that they have rarely been used, except in the Peak District, because of their cost and cumbersome legal form. Many of the new agri-environment policies, for example the Countryside Premium Scheme, the Countryside Stewardship Scheme, Environmentally Sensitive Areas and the Woodland Grant Scheme, do contain provisions for State cash transfers for access, to the extent that they can be exploited in open country, but again, these schemes are voluntary and therefore relegate the opportunities for new access through them to the vagaries of the farmers' personal preferences.

Fiscal concessions for new access opportunities also can be exploited. Some, such as tax breaks for entering into community forest agreements (Bishop, 1991), are unlikely to pertain to open country unless its definition is changed in law, but exemptions from inheritance tax under the 1975 Finance Act (Countryside Commission, 1990b), in exchange for new access opportunities on individual estates of particular scenic quality, do include open country. This provision would appear to have been used quite widely and it is estimated that some 150 private estates covering some 134,000 hectares have taken advantage of it at a cost to the taxpayer of £140 million (Curry, 1994). This arrangement has two significant shortcomings for improving access, particularly to open country. Firstly, the requirement for fiscal concessions is that access to the land is adequate, rather than necessarily increased. Such access also does not have to be *de jure*, and may proceed only on a permissive basis. Secondly, tax matters are confidential and, despite pressure from the Ramblers' Association and some concern from the Countryside Commission, the Treasury has resisted giving publicity to the estates for which exemptions have been made. Since 1991, the Commission has been notified of such exemptions, but essentially it is difficult to find out where these new access arrangements are (*Daily Telegraph*, 1992).

Direct land purchase for the purposes of increasing access to open country has been available to local authorities since the 1949 National Parks and Access to the Countryside Act, and can be compulsory where deemed necessary, and has been available to the Countryside Commission, for experimental purposes, since the 1968 Countryside Act. The use of these powers by local authorities is rare, often because of a fear of loss of goodwill, and because of the difficulty of drawing up legal agreements. Tamesdown Metropolitan Borough purchased Hobson Moor Quarry in 1983 for climbing purposes, and a number of parish councils have set up trusts to purchase local areas of open land (although invariably not legally defined open country), but other examples are hard to find. The Countryside Commission has never exercised its powers despite the fact that they could be used in the development of novel (and therefore experimental) mechanisms for improving access to open country.

For open country, although some consideration might be given to new legislation that seeks to extend the definition of open country and reinterpret the definition of trespass, history would suggest that it is unlikely without some form of financial incentive or compensation. It is these financial measures that would appear to offer the greatest potential for improving access opportunities to open country. Because such access has a number of 'public good' attributes, principally non-excludability, payment for increased opportunities by the state may be justified. Provisions exist for all three mechanisms open to the state, but each suffers from a number of operational problems. Policy priorities should therefore be, firstly, to make the payment of state cash transfers more systematic both in terms of which type of scheme is used (local authority or agri-environmental scheme) and the geographical distribution of such payments collectively. Unless payments are co-ordinated across all available schemes, their distribution is likely to be patchy.

For fiscal concessions, the principal policy priority should be to make them better known to the consuming public. Without such knowledge, they will not constitute increased opportunities. Direct land purchase, although more difficult in capital budget terms, does offer the cheapest solution to state-funded access to open country in the longer term, since it obviates the need for annual payments and their periodic re-negotiation. Encouragement should be given to the increased use of these powers, since at the extreme they can be imposed compulsorily.

Improving Access to Enclosed Land

Improving access to enclosed land is a different matter than for open country. Few have suggested that, realistically, legislative compulsion for such access is either feasible or desirable. Rather, the focus has been on some form of transfer payment mechanism, or access payment scheme, for the enhancement of such opportunities (Countryside Commission, 1994a). The potential for this policy option is rather different than for open country in terms of the payment mechanisms available. Whereas payment to the farmer or landowner by the state can be justified on grounds of externalities and specifically non-excludability for open country, this is not the case for enclosed land. By definition, excludability is likely to be attainable for this type of countryside. In this case, the logic behind state payment for such access is weak. Excludability gives access to enclosed land the characteristics of a market commodity, and there is therefore sound reason for the consumer paying directly. Indeed, such systems of private access tolls have been instituted for bridleways, an initiative from the Groundwork Trust, endorsed by the British Horse Society (Lowe, Clark and Cox,

1991). They have been introduced, for example, in Essex, Berkshire and Cheshire and link up *de jure* bridleways to avoid roads, creating a more comprehensive system of access on horseback. This, it is claimed, can lead to a reduction in trespass as currently defined in law and allow field boundaries, along which these 'private' bridleways pass, to remain uncultivated.

Thus, direct consumer payment for improved access, which must be considered as only one of the four possible means of payment for access considered in the previous section, is certainly feasible. But a number of other arguments support this notion of direct consumer payments for access to enclosed land. Firstly, the consumption of access of all types is overwhelmingly triggered by market demands. A number of authors have sought to measure the strength of a variety of influences over rural leisure participation (e.g. Roberts 1979; Benson and Willis, 1990) and have constantly identified income, car ownership and educational attainment as the strongest. These all reflect both a willingness and ability to pay (a market demand) for consumption. If a desire to consume is market demand driven, then there is a logic for the supply of this type of access also to be market driven, since this will be more economically efficient. Secondly, there are adverse equity impacts in state payments, since the observed social structure of participation in walking in the countryside, particularly for longer walks, is skewed in a pronounced way towards the more affluent (Fitton 1978; Reiling *et al.*, 1983; Gratton and Taylor, 1985; Harrison, 1991; Countryside Commission, 1992). Direct state subsidies for such access, since they will benefit the more affluent more than proportionately than the less affluent, will clearly be socially regressive. Direct consumer payments are therefore also more socially equitable.

Thirdly, they shift the burden of cost on to the consumer (rather than the taxpayer) and are therefore also cheaper in exchequer cost terms. They also shift the responsibility of income generation on to the supplier and, with it, responsibilities for revenue costs, capital costs, risk and so on, away from the public authority. Fourthly, treating access opportunities on enclosed land as market commodities also allows state control over the quality of such developments to be less ambiguous. If they are considered to constitute development, or the state wishes them to be through changes to the General Development Order, then regulatory controls can be imposed through the development plan system and development control, which can be enforced through legal mechanisms. This offers a simplification to the policing process, which is otherwise tied up with a range of other (usually discretionary) incentives.

In addition, direct consumer payments offer a number of advantages in respect of a range of issues concerned with the operation of such access payment schemes that have preoccupied the Countryside Commission (1994a). Firstly, the need for (possibly costly) monitoring would be obviated, since there would be minimal stakeholder interest on the part of the state in the operation of the scheme. Whether or not the scheme is effective in public cost terms would be less important than whether or not the scheme was viable from the standpoint of the operator. Secondly, issues of how these schemes should be prioritized amongst individual applicants, who should be eligible and how long they should last would become less important than the individual farmer's or landowner's decision to offer access through the market place. Again, the viability of such potential schemes would rest with the individual entrepreneur. Thirdly, the issue of who should have the responsibility for administering and managing these schemes would cease to be important. State interest could be confined to issues of regulation over the control of development, and state expenditure on management would not be necessary. Finally, and perhaps most importantly, the difficult issue of how much farmers and landowners should be paid to run such schemes would also not arise. The individual landowner would take responsibility for the basis upon which payments are derived, either through cost plus or opportunity cost approaches.

Thus, the current government preoccupation with access payment schemes for enclosed land, where the state foots the bill, can be seen to be both inefficient and inequitable as well as providing a large number of problems and costs relating to their institution and management. The notion of such payments coming from the consumer direct, it must be stressed specifically for enclosed land, is more efficient and equitable, has a much reduced exchequer cost, and can be controlled if desired through regulatory planning mechanisms. In short, policies for improved access to enclosed land should concentrate on direct consumer payments, the 'turnstiles at the gate' approach that effectively considers such access as a market commodity.

Improving the Management of Access

Perhaps not surprisingly, public policy priorities for the management of access should concentrate on both ensuring access rights, through keeping paths open, resolving legal disputes and through completions of the definitive map, and enhancing access opportunities beyond this statutory framework, particularly for open country. In view of significant problems in both of these areas, a priority for management should be the allocation of additional resources to allow these functions to be executed more effectively, a central tenet of recent proposals from the Country Landowners' Association (1992). This is not an unrealistic proposition, since spending on legal obligations in respect of public rights of way doubled in cash terms (a 50 per cent increase in real terms) between 1987 and 1991 (Countryside Commission, 1993d), and significant additional public expenditure is proposed for access payment schemes (Countryside Commission, 1994a).

Resources notwithstanding, there is still a need to clarify management responsibilities for access. Two problems need addressing in this respect. Firstly, a number of authorities have a stakeholding in the maintenance and furtherance of access rights and opportunities. The Ministry of Agriculture, the Forestry Authority, the Countryside Commission and the Treasury all have an interest in access payment schemes, yet local authorities have principal responsibility of the administration of access rights. Enhancing access opportunities generally, whether through law or payment, is likely to be most effective if administered through a single authority. The county council (or where appropriate, the national park authority) is the most likely contender here, but currently, the effectiveness in implementing access policies within counties has been inhibited by their being part of the portfolio of highways departments. This is merely an historical accident, since in law there are no statutory rights for recreation *per se*, but only for rights of passage. Access provisions have thus become a very small appendage to a very much larger body of highways legislation and the implementation of them correspondingly a residual priority within highways departments. Since planning departments invariably have responsibility for all other aspects of countryside recreation, it is quite likely that the management of access arrangements would be more effectively executed if these responsibilities were transferred to them. In addition, if regulatory planning mechanisms are introduced to provide environmental controls over private access payment schemes, these can be better co-ordinated with legal responsibilities if administered by a single department.

Whichever statutory body should hold a clear responsibility for managing access, a number of recent management initiatives have served to dissipate the force of the management function. Firstly, the contracting-out of management work to farmers and landowners, for example through Environmental Land Management Services (ELMS) agreements, presents problems of policing and, except in the case of statutory access rights, may be ambiguous. For access that has been paid for by the state in open country, such sub-contracting may be appropriate because of the non-excludability considerations discussed above. In this context, grant aid should be extended within agricultural improvement schemes. But for enclosed land, where access opportunities have all the hallmarks of market commodities, there is little logic in state payments for their maintenance. Such works should be left to farmers and landowners themselves, within their responsibilities to any regulatory planning controls.

Secondly, government initiatives such as the Parish Paths Partnership scheme (Department of the Environment, 1992c) have shifted the burden of management for local improvement schemes on to voluntary parish council effort and the good offices of local interest groups, specifically with the intention of relieving local highways authorities of an element of their burden of responsibility. This has a number of shortcomings. Quite obviously, it is passing the proper responsibility of the authority on to a third party, allowing authorities a greater opportunity to fail to execute their own undertakings. It also perpetuates the 'management on the cheap' characteristics of many countryside management initiatives of the 1960s and 1970s, which were always vulnerable, being dependent on the good offices and enthusiasms of particular individuals. It is essentially non-accountable, too, and may result in very variable outcomes in different parts of the country. In addition, in seating management responsibilities with parishes there is a natural disposition that access opportunities will be for the local population. Since the majority of access consumption is migratory in nature, it is questionable that the maintenance of paths by local people for use by non-local people will sustain a strong commitment of locals for very long. The notion of villages and parishes providing better information services about local countryside access opportunities (Countryside Commission, 1992) may also meet with limited success if its principal effect simply is to encourage use by non-locals. Finally, this pragmatic approach will always leave a lot of questions unanswered as to what will happen to the management of access responsibilities if and when such schemes as the Parish Paths Partnership come to an end.

Thirdly, the development of access liaison groups, or Countryside Recreation and Access Groups as the Country Landowners' Association (1992) terms them, whilst providing consensual forums for the debate of access issues, also, if vested with management responsibilities, again both shifts and dissipates the management function.

Rather than diffusing management responsibilities in these ways, access policies for the late 1990s should seek to consolidate them. It is management that lies at the cutting edge of provision and it has developed in an ad hoc way despite, rather than because of, legislative provision. There is a case for the management of access to be placed of a firmer footing, if not through legislation, then through government circulars or planning policy guidance. Above all, power should be vested in a single administering authority.

Conclusions

Access policies for the late 1990s thus have four strands. Firstly, the legal rights of access to the countryside, chiefly through the system of public rights of way, should be vigorously defended, clarified and made more widely known to the public, whose right it is to exploit them. Any attempts to compromise these rights through any form of payment scheme should be vigorously resisted. Secondly, improving access to open country might possibly be enhanced by new legislation that alters the definitions of open country and trespass in favour of the public at large, but is more likely to be successful if instituted through some kind of financial incentives to farmers and landowners for improved access. Because of the non-excludability characteristics of open country, such incentives are most appropriately provided by the state either through direct cash transfers, fiscal incentives or land purchase. These should be pursued in concert and with full geographical co-ordination, and should be made fully known to the public.

Thirdly, improving opportunities for access to enclosed land, on the other hand, should be pursued through direct payments from the consumer to the farmer and landowner since, in the absence of non-excludability, this is both more efficient and more equitable. Environmental controls over this 'market' should be imposed through the regulatory planning system. Finally, systems for the management of both access rights and improved access opportunities should be administered through a single authority that has both the power and the resources to integrate access provision in its many facets. Only through these orchestrated measures will access to the countryside of England and Wales be anything other than the source of conflict and confusion that it has been for more than one hundred years.

3

New Access Initiatives: The Extension of Recreation Opportunities or the Diminution of Citizen Rights?

NEIL RAVENSCROFT

Introduction

The question of access to the countryside of England and Wales for the pursuit of informal recreation activities such as rambling and walking has, over the last century and a half, never moved far from the political agenda. Not only does the countryside enjoy a unique cultural significance (see, for example, Clark *et al.*, 1994; Archbishops' Commission on Rural Areas, 1990; Pye-Smith and Hall, 1987; or Shoard, 1980), but walking in it is one of the most popular forms of active recreation in Britain. Indeed, about 80 per cent of the population venture into the countryside at least once a year (Countryside Commission, 1991c) while nearly half the population are considered by the Sports Council to be frequent walkers (McInnes, 1993).

At the centre of the political debate have been arguments about the accessibility, in legal and social terms, of the countryside for an ever more urban population (Newby, 1986). While it is argued in managerial terms that walkers have never enjoyed a greater range of opportunities for legal access (Royal Institution of Chartered Surveyors, 1989), it is clear that in most respects the actual, socially constructed, experience has declined, with much greater *de facto* freedom to roam prior to nineteenth-century industrialization, land enclosure and the associated 'privatization' of property rights (Bonyhady, 1987). This argument is taken up by Hill (1980), who suggests that the issue came to the fore as industrialization limited available urban green space, thereby increasingly forcing people into an already enclosed countryside:

If the Industrial Revolution unlocked a new horn of plenty, it did so at tremendous human cost for the mass of the people. Through

> technology, it undoubtedly laid the basis for big all-round increases in living standards; but it exacted a price, not the least of which was the loss of leisure, which for some had been a marked feature of earlier societies.
> (Hill, 1980, p. 113)

Since that time the rhetoric surrounding the trends in the demand for access to the countryside has been unrelenting, particularly with respect to the unwelcome influence of the motor car (Curry, 1994). This is exemplified by assertions such as Joad's, that the ' ... invasion of the country by the towns ... ' would be prevented by ' ... nothing short of the exhaustion of the world's supply of petrol ... ' (1945, p. 22). There has undoubtedly been a significant growth in demand (Newby, 1986), but prophecies such as Joad's of a post-World War II 'explosion' in countryside recreation have proved ill-founded (Blunden and Curry, 1988; Harrison, 1991), although certainly effective in maintaining caution in rural policy issues and thereby the unchallenged supremacy of agriculture and existing rural landowners and users.

Although it is convenient to implicate the enclosure of rural land with the growing dysfunction between ownership and usage, the issue is both more complex and ultimately less instrumental. For rather than the regulation of access being of incidental concern to the 'serious' business of rural landownership and management, it has been a central element of its very legitimation, principally in distinguishing the rights of the rural-landed from the 'mere' claims of the rural-landless. As such, Thompson (1993) has argued, access has been located as an allowance or dispensation granted by an alliance of ruling interests to those 'disqualified' from rural property ownership or usage, thereby indicating a regard for their 'custodial responsibilities'. The dichotomy itself is therefore less about the ownership of property *per se*, than it is about the relationship between the ownership and control of certain sorts of property (rural land) and the governance of certain sorts of people ('alien others', whether property owners or not).

What emerges, therefore, is a judicial/administrative 'partnership', comprising the state and landowners, seemingly (and somewhat curiously) seeking to protect certain 'rights', or at least 'values' of the non-landed. Rather than being of a formally juridical construction, however, this partnership is rooted in custom and incorporates the non-landed as well. Equally, rather than the protection of non-landed 'rights' *per se*, this public/private partnership is based on the synchronous legitimatory needs of landowners and the state. Thus landownership, as a societal construct, relies for its legitimation upon the sanction of the state (Harrison, 1987), which in turn demands support for its strength and stability to act as a vehicle for that legitimation (Shivji, 1989). Rather than being incidental, the role of the third party, the non-landed, is arguably the most significant of the three. In assuming the character of 'other', the alter-ego of the landed, the non-landed effectively legitimate both their state-sponsored 'protection' and the paternal sensibility and responsibility of the landed.

The basis of this public/private partnership is essentially, therefore, the regulation of competing claims over the ownership and use of rural land, with an outward show of benevolence, in terms of the protection of certain access rights, attempting to conceal the continuing expropriation and alienation of rural landownership. Rather than the rhetorically implied market failure of neo-classical economics discourse, therefore, the situation is more accurately represented as an enduring site of class struggle and stratification (Whatmore, Munton and Marsden, 1990), with the state providing a context within which the 'non-landed' have sought to establish their moral 'right' to roam in contra-distinction to the 'landed', who have sought to maintain the hegemony of private property.

This struggle has traditionally been one-sided, reflecting the nexus between private property and the state. Rather than representing the dichotomy between individualism and commonality, therefore, the public/private partnership has been firmly located within the individualized mercantile discourse of profitability and power. Indeed, the partnership has, since the Agriculture Act 1947, assumed corporatist proportions in involving directly the landowning and farming community in the generation and implementation of rural policy (see Cox, Lowe and Winter, 1988).

However, a number of factors have recently coincided to cause a reassessment of the situation. On the one hand, there has been growing 'citizen' support for the extension of the corporatist partnership to include non-farming and landowning interests. With respect to access this has included calls for a general right to roam over open, uncultivated country (Blunden and Curry, 1990), culminating in official support by the Countryside Commission (1991a). On the other hand, there has been a significant downturn in farming fortunes, causing farmers to seek alternative sources of income. Thus, although still remaining vigorously opposed to any increase in citizens' formal rights of access (Country Landowners' Association, 1991), farmers and landowners are now facing the unsavoury prospect of needing both the money and, increasingly, the political support of those citizens. This chapter therefore seeks to analyse the changing nature of the public/

private/state partnership, particularly with respect to the ways in which it has been appropriated to underwrite the 'depoliticization' of relative values in favour of a positivist form of 'rational' empiricism. Within this rationality, not only has market discourse been exploited for the continued legitimation of private property rights, but its metaphorical opposite, market failure, has been used to underpin the extension of 'non-market' recreation opportunities through the effective appropriation of the popular cultural affirmation of *de facto* 'rights'. Where once the claimed 'citizen right' to roam over private land was essentially a counter-hegemonic strategy, therefore, it has now been reconstructed into a commodified form suitable for purchase (by the state) and consumption (by the citizen), thereby reaffirming the dominance of private property ownership and the subservience of non-property rights.

Access, Rights and the Law

Given its heredity, it is inescapable that countryside recreation in England and Wales should be defined in any terms other than law (Harrison, 1991). However, rather than the common law signifying a common interest, this legality has been interpreted as the protection of private property (Lewis, 1993), although often by the activity of the judiciary rather than by Parliament. The rights of citizens are thereby relegated to the merely public: essentially highways and other rights of passage expressly 'gifted' by landowners (Bonyhady, 1987). However, while a narrow view might have been taken on the creation of legal rights, both Parliament and the courts have sought to maintain the public's *de facto* rights, both by refusing to criminalize simple trespass and by awarding minimal damages when such cases came to court. However, as Bonyhady points out:

> *De facto* rights are ... inherently a partial and unreliable substitute for public rights of access ... The problem is that these 'rights' are no more than a result of Parliament and the courts denying landowners an effective remedy for trivial wrongs. (1987, p. 16)

While not necessarily reflecting people's needs, the rights of way network remains at the core of provision for informal access to the countryside. This is based upon what Clark *et al.* (1994) describe as the Countryside Commission's bias towards constructing people's needs around a quiet, informal experience of the countryside. In addition to legal rights of passage, therefore, a variety of contractual arrangements providing conditional access to private land has also been encouraged.

Regardless of any rights rhetoric, however, none of these latter contractual arrangements provides more than short term licences, under-
lining the 'gift' nature of the public/private partnership rather than
the extension and protection of recreation opportunities.

The legal construction of countryside recreation is thus much more
closely associated with a 'civilizing' mission than it is with the narrower
legal definition of rights of access. In emphasizing Marx's 'juridical
illusion of existing property relations', this construction effectively
defines those 'demanding' greater rights of access as alien or deviant,
while also defining any attempts to question the morality of private land
ownership as efforts to overturn the supposed natural order of the
market. In effect, therefore, the power relations inherent in the public/
private partnership decentralize the debate from one of equity or
equality, in terms at least of individual choice (LeGrand, 1991), to one
of expropriation and personal liberty: the expropriation of property;
and the personal liberty of the landed. Any claim for increased public
access to private land is therefore constructed by landowners (and
legitimated by the state) as an encroachment on their libertarian
freedom, only to be secured under a market-defined 'voluntary' arrangement of public recognition and compensation for their loss.

Instead of being primarily associated with the distribution of rights in
property, therefore, the access 'problem' is part of a deeper debate
about the very significance of property and its associated rights. As
Baudrillard (1981) suggests, this centres on new forms of discrimination, which go beyond mere possession into social organization and
usage. Where once it was sufficient for landowners and farmers simply
to own land, it is now a significant element of social classification to be
able to demonstrate control over it, as Williamson pointed out at the
First Countryside Recreation Network conference, on access:

> In the good old days when ramblers wore cloth caps and carried their
> lunch in an old gas mask bag, the issues seemed clearer. It was 'them and
> us', the 'haves and the have-nots'. Now there are rural 'haves' and urban
> 'haves' still arguing about the same problems, still presenting the same
> polarised views, and tending to forget both the urban and rural 'have-
> nots'. (1992, p. 87).

In the place of the class-associated rights debate has come a landowner-
sponsored, state-regulated focus on power. As Foucault (1980) suggests, territoriality becomes a metaphorical arena in which the effects of
power, given a corporeal dimension, can be analysed and determined.

Central to this arena has been the depoliticization of ownership in favour of a concentration on status and signification, an issue taken up by Crouch (1992) in his work on the meaning of 'rural'. Farmers and landowners have therefore stressed their attachment to 'traditional' ways of life and their evident custodianship of the rural when compared to the naivety, or wilful lack of concern, exhibited by others, regardless of their pedigree or residence:

> The laws which restrict where we can go in the countryside are founded on the belief that the vast mass of Britain's inhabitants, once off the roads and out of their cars will follow a course of selfish destruction ... (Pye-Smith and Hall, 1987, p. 5)

This concern for people's behaviour once 'let loose' in the country is reminiscent of Foucault's (1984) notion of surveillance, where those in authority focus on the safety of the inexperienced and the unaware, as well as on the degree to which, in this case, owners and farmers have been, and continue to be, responsible managers of the countryside. Thus, it is suggested that most access 'problems' are more perceived than actual (Clarke, 1992); that landowners and farmers are able to accommodate visitors, but through management rather than as a result of 'uncontrolled' free access (Clifton-Brown, 1992). This is nothing less than a politically-legitimized appropriation of power relations, with property ownership, the ultimate validation of capitalist values posited, in accordance with Donzelot's (1980) tutelary complex, as a responsibility unsuited to the evident ephemerality of 'ordinary' people. Those in a position of power within the public/private partnership are therefore able to maintain the status quo by ensuring, as far as they can, that these 'ordinary' people are unable to gain any sense of belonging in the countryside. In so doing they are effectively signifying a cultural commodification that at once ties people into the socio-economic imperatives of ownership while systematically denying them any wider political debate over the future of the countryside.

Recent Initiatives in the Provision for Public Access

It is no mean achievement for farmers and landowners to have been able to exert such a strong and continuing influence on the social status quo. The last decade and a half has witnessed a somewhat contradictory situation in both British and European countryside policy where, on the one hand, growing environmentalism has begun to challenge post-World War II agricultural fundamentalism while, on the other hand, state support for farmers has been continually reconfirmed. Although the power of the farming lobby should not be underestimated, the primary reason for continued support is probably more a question of timing, with the European Commission's need to reduce food surpluses having had a higher priority than the dismantling of the corporatist government machine in Britain.

Indeed, rather than recognizing that what Cox, Lowe and Winter (1988, p. 332) refer to as 'state nurtured productionist pressures' had caused farmers to degrade consistently the rural environment, the Wildlife and Countryside Act 1981 reinforced corporatist notions of the responsible autonomy and, thereby, the continuing power of farmers. Indeed, it is clear that the Wildlife and Countryside Act 1981 effectively signalled a return to the pre-twentieth century notions of public/ private partnership, with a renewed emphasis on the eminence of property owners, particularly in protecting the countryside from the evident deviancy of the non-landed. A current example of this rhetoric is contained in Gregory's recent book on conservation law:

> ... in the end the welfare of the countryside depends upon the stewardship of its owners and occupiers. That stewardship exists and has always existed. The character of the countryside that we know and love is mostly man-made. It is sculpted by those who make their living from the land, those who own it and those who live in it. They have created the rural landscape – the harmonious pattern of fields, woodlands, hedgerows, ditches, farm steadings, hamlets, parks, paddocks and dwellings, fine or humble, with grazing livestock and pastoral artefacts enhancing the general effect. They see that the country flows with milk and honey instead of becoming the wilderness of thicket and swamp which only extreme environmentalists would have. (Gregory, 1994, p. 144)

The early-1980s review of the European Common Agricultural Policy (CAP), which led to a reduction in food support prices and the introduction of levies and quotas, focused attention on helping those same farmers replace agricultural income with money from other sources (Ravenscroft, 1992). Recreation was seen as a primary source of new income for farmers, with the UK government's Farm Diversification Grant Scheme and a number of Department of the Environment planning circulars encouraging the development of non-agricultural enterprises on farms (Byrne and Ravenscroft, 1989). To this was added conservation, both in the form of agreements for the management of Sites of Special Scientific Interest under the Wildlife and Countryside Act 1981 and, increasingly, of new land designations and objectives for farming. Apart from the introduction of Set-aside, together with its

Countryside Premium Scheme, one of the most significant designations of land was under the Environmentally Sensitive Area (ESA) Scheme, which provided one of the first models of non-production financial support for farmers.

Quite apart from support for ESAs from within the farming community (see, for example, Country Landowners' Association, 1991, and Naish, 1993), the construction of farmer as custodian has found a wider acceptance, with assertions such as those of Glyptis (1992) that farmers should be encouraged to 'care' for the countryside, becoming increasingly common. However, rather than expecting this care to be an integral part of a package of price support and structural grant aid, and notwithstanding the damage inflicted by the farmers themselves, the domain assumption, underwritten by the government (see, for example, Countryside Commission, 1994a), has been that such compliance with public 'demands' should be further compensated from the public purse. In contra-distinction to the situation under urban development control, therefore, farmers have been able to establish that any 'encroachment' upon their autonomous rights of land use, as in the case of conservation or access, should, as a matter of public policy, be accompanied by appropriate compensation. This has not only maintained their claim of responsible custodianship and their willingness to compromise business interests for the good of the public, but it has also underwritten the power of their property. Unlike the owners of 'other' types of property, who cannot, in general, claim compensation for public restrictions on their rights, farmers have been able to prove that they represent a 'special' case; that theirs is a way of life rather than a job and, consequently, that the public have a 'duty' to compensate them for any undue interference (McEachern, 1992), or 'compensation blight' (Cox, Lowe and Winter, 1988).

The Countryside Commission has undoubtedly found itself in a difficult position in this process. Having focused its attention on meeting its perception of people's needs for quiet enjoyment of the countryside, the chance to increase recreation opportunities, if not rights, could hardly be rejected. Rather than seek to promote and protect the interests of recreationists, however, what the Commission appears to have done is to lend its tacit support to farmers and private landowners, both by endorsing the concept of state aid for conservation and amenity works by farmers (Countryside Commission, 1991a) and by developing the Countryside Stewardship Scheme (CSS), with its overtones of tutelary responsibility and surveillance:

Countryside Stewardship aims to demonstrate that conservation and public enjoyment of the countryside can be combined with commercial land management through a national system of incentives. The long-term objective is to develop a basis for a comprehensive scheme to achieve environmental and recreational benefits as an integral part of agricultural support. (Countryside Commission, 1991b, 1)

Not unsurprisingly, the CSS has proved particularly popular with many farmers and rural landowners, with over 25,000 hectares being brought into the scheme in its first year of operation, of which about one-quarter had provision for new access (Knightbridge and Swanwick, 1993). There is, however, already concern that not all of the access payments have secured 'new' opportunities, while many open access areas have proved difficult to locate (Pond, 1993).

Having fought hard to avoid the dissipation of the agricultural policy community, particularly from organizations interested in the wider countryside, farmers have thus apparently been only too ready to welcome them in when there is money on offer. While relieving the public of this money, however, the farming community has been careful to maintain its distance, relying on the mercantile basis of the public/private partnership in reasserting the farmers' role as business people, as well as reinforcing the link between profitable agriculture and the environmental improvement of the countryside (Naish, 1993, p. 7).

In line with the general 'Europeanization' of agricultural policy over the last three decades, the position regarding grant aid for non-agricultural production and land use has recently been overhauled in the latest reform of the CAP. Under Council Regulation (EEC) 2078/92, the 'agri-environment regulation', member states have been charged with establishing methods of agricultural production that can protect the environment and maintain the countryside, with public access being a legitimate measure, even if its relationship with the environment is less than clear. The UK's response (Ministry of Agriculture, Fisheries and Food, 1993a) revolves around five schemes, four of which provide for 'improved' access to the countryside. These are: the new Countryside Access scheme for Set-aside land, based on the previous Countryside Premium scheme, but not now limited solely to the Eastern counties of England (Ministry of Agriculture, Fisheries and Food, 1993b, 1993d and 1993e); a new option for public access to land in the ESA scheme (Ministry of Agriculture, Fisheries and Food, 1993c); the Countryside Stewardship scheme, to be taken over from the Countryside Commission (Ministry of Agriculture, Fisheries and Food,

1993a); and a new Farm Woodland Premium Scheme (Ministry of Agriculture, Fisheries and Food, 1993a), now incorporating discretionary capital payments to enhance the quality of private woodlands for environmental and recreational purposes. In all of the cases the intention is to provide new opportunities for walking and other forms of quiet recreation in areas already subject to grant aid for environmental management and improvement (Ministry of Agriculture, Fisheries and Food, 1993c). The extra grant paid is supposed to cover the costs incurred in making the land available for access, including signposting and publicity, with selection criteria designed to ensure that the new opportunities will enhance existing access, either by linking rights of way, providing new circular routes close to urban areas or providing access to previously inaccessible features such as vantage points.

Although hailed by Reynolds (1992) as a major advancement in promulgating public access as a legitimate objective of agricultural policy, these new proposals really do little more than confirm the continuation of traditional values; the asymmetric position of public subsidy for the maintenance of the libertarian freedom of farmers and landowners. Indeed, it is evident that the UK's response to the agri-environment regulations amounts to a reaffirmation of the central purpose of the public/private partnership; the legitimation of the authority of property power. Having supported, certainly in financial terms, the destruction of the countryside and its subsequent reinstatement, the public is now being committed to pay yet again for the privilege of viewing what all its subsidies have achieved; a legal means of diverting public funds into the income and capital worth of landowners and some farmers. There has been no discussion of citizen rights nor, apparently, any consideration of what the public might reasonably have expected, in addition to cheap food, from its vast investment in farming businesses and, ultimately, the land. Instead, the very expressions of demand for improved access by organizations such as the Ramblers' Association (1993a) have been interpreted against them, through the effective privatization of their erstwhile 'public' rights.

Rather than rights, therefore, the public has gained little more than short-term contractual obligations; firstly, to pay farmers and landowners, in recognition of their generosity in temporarily foregoing some of their traditional freedom; secondly, to make use of the new opportunities in order to establish the legitimacy of their access claims; and thirdly, to ensure that they are 'responsible' in their use of this private land, thereby rebutting farmers' fears of vandalism and, in the process, hopefully ensuring that new contracts will be entered into.

Paradoxically, therefore, rather than extending recreation opportunities these contractual arrangements effectively diminish the rights of citizens. Even the Countryside Commission (1994a) recognizes that the 'short-termism' implicit in these initiatives could diminish opportunities in the longer term. More pervasively, however, access 'rights' are further undermined by granting the legal, and thus the moral, highground to farmers and landowners. This highground is itself now being reinforced further through the criminalization of trespass contained in the Criminal Justice and Public Order Act 1994. Although ostensibly designed to streamline the eviction from private property of squatters, new age travellers and other 'undesirables', the legislation will, as Fairlie (1994b) suggests, apply to any 'assembly' of trespassers failing to comply with police requests to vacate property to which they do not have a legal right of access (see also Chapters 1 and 11).

Rather than signifying the acceptance of public rights in the countryside as a legitimate aim of public policy, therefore, the dualism of purchased access 'rights' to pre-determined areas combined with punitive consequences for those who fail to adhere to the new market imperative, is more redolent of a return to the property-dominated class schisms of the past. In common with the short-lived Access to Mountains Act 1937 and, to a lesser extent, the National Parks and Access to the Countryside Act 1949, public access to the countryside has been appropriated by public policy and packaged as an enhanced citizen 'right', while actually reaffirming the hegemonic power of property and its owners at the expense of the wider citizenry.

Conclusion

What is apparent in the analysis of the issues associated with access to the countryside is that the construction of the 'problem' and, hence, the solution, is very much determined by the nature of the parties to the 'partnership'. The dominant construction, cited by a wide range of interests in the debate, is concerned with values; that differences can be explained by reference to relative values, as Glyptis has noted:

> The whole access issue has to do with values accorded to areas by those who do not own them, and to do with the values and attitudes of the parties involved towards each other, be it the planner's, landowner's or farmer's attitude to the activity, the views of competing users, such as conservationists and recreationists, or the views of one set of recreational users about another. (1992, p. 7)

However, the discourse on values is far from neutral. Values themselves have little credibility without the means of legitimation. It may suit certain groups or classes to construct relative positions in terms of values, but the relativity is more associated with the force of legitimation, the power to substantiate value claims, than it is with values *per se.* It is clear that the dominant values associated with access to the countryside have little to do with notions of equity, need or citizen rights and everything to do with property, underwritten by the power of a legal system in which the market is presupposed (Bergeron, 1993). However, to represent this, in itself, as evidence of class or spatial oppression is, perhaps, to misinterpret the duplicitous role (whether conscious or otherwise) of the non-landed. For in legitimating the power of rural property the wider citizenry is also engaged in the hopeful process of legitimating the power of its own property-based rights and aspirations, while apparently and simultaneously denying this legitimation through its claimed hostility to paying farmers for access (Clark *et al.*, 1994).

Any representation of the access 'problem' as one of rights is ultimately, therefore, an obfuscation of what is more fundamentally a means of alienation and control. This is based on the deceptive notions of civil, or social, rights promulgated by the dominant ideological forces associated with landed property. This dominance has achieved the acquiescence of the 'non-landed' in the deception that what attaches to 'landed' property is necessarily replicated in the 'non-landed'. At some level, therefore, it appears that there is a general acquiescence in the duplicity that access claims have been materially substantiated, when in reality all that has happened has been a redistribution of resources within the dominant group, ensuring the maintenance of the property-based power of a numerically small class fraction.

Thus the deception goes much deeper than mere resource allocation, into the very legitimation of property itself, particularly in attempting constantly to overcome the disparity between the message of property-based capitalism and the reality for most people (see Fudge and Glasbeek, 1992). As such, the benevolent and 'voluntary' extension of access has been more about coercion and control than it has about the rights of people. For in benevolence, as indeed in all patronage, there is the juxtaposition of the positive act with the malice of indebtedness (Hay, 1975). Rather than 'freedom to roam' or some similar evocation, therefore, what the recent access initiatives have promoted is the reinvention of a sanitized countryside in which recreation is allowed, or actually encouraged, and in which people's respect for the countryside is 'tutored'. This is a corollary of the 'honey pottism' of the 1960s and 1970s where relatively insignificant areas of country-side were 'sacrificed' to the visitor as a diversion from more 'important' or valuable pieces of land, in visual, ecological and tenurial terms. Now the diversion is not from other land, but from wider and more deeply philosophical issues about the relationship between public policy and certain types of private property; between the 'rights' enshrined in law and the delegitimized notion of 'public' values.

By effectively separating the politics of the access debate from the economic implications of its outcome, many issues remain unanswered, not least the potential popularity of the schemes, the distribution and longevity of any rights created and the degree to which the 'staged irrelevance' of the schemes has deflected claims for wider freedom to roam. What has become patently clear, however, is that the annexation by the market of access 'rights', together with the draconian criminal-ization of trespass, is yet another stage in the reconstruction of civil society away from fixed social divisions and the increasingly spurious ontological priority of existing class relations.

As such, it is clear that whatever may have been achieved in the social democratic post-World War II era, it was not the reconstruction of the state away from its roots in the protection of the 'naturalness' of property. Indeed, just as surely as the state/property alliance of the eighteenth century ensured its authority through the threat of the death penalty for trivial crimes against property (Hay, 1975), the state has continued to sanction the deification of property through the provisions of the Criminal Justice and Public Order legislation. The current state of the 'access debate' indicates, therefore, the continuing and evolutionary hegemony of the state/property partnership, with its annexation of the hedonism of 1980s consumer culture as a further legitimation of its social and political approbation. Since property is the 'ultimate' commodity, this process must lead eventually to the una-bridged commodification of citizenship, thereby completing a cultural regression to the wealth-related and propertied elitism of eighteenth century England, as described by Hay:

> ... wealth does not exist outside a social context, theft is given definition only within a set of social relations, and the connections between prop-erty, power and authority are close and crucial. The criminal law was critically important in maintaining bonds of obedience and deference, in legitimizing the status quo, in constantly recreating the structure of authority which arose from property and in turn protected its interests. (1975, p. 25)

The juxtaposition in late twentieth-century England is, thus, not so much rights versus values, or even partnership versus privatization, as it is legitimation versus criminalization. Regardless of the empirical construction and regulation of public rights over private land, it is clear that the current and future 'citizen' project is not so much about property itself as it is about the binary division between the ruling elite and the evermore deviant 'other'.

4

Is the Right to Roam Attainable? An Aspiration or a Pragmatic Way Forward?

DEBORAH PEARLMAN AND J.J. PEARLMAN

Introduction

As the Old Testament demonstrates, the concept of wilderness has been recognized by people for many thousands of years. At first it was seen as a wild and foreboding place. But with the rise of the Romantic Movement in the eighteenth century, when people were beginning to react against order and neatness, open space and wilderness became an important feature for the opening of minds. Art and literature created 'wilderness' as a place of freedom, godliness and true nature. The movement effectively turned wilderness from a concept that was feared to something that was revered. This is well portrayed by Estwick Evans in 1818, 'How great are the advantages of solitude! – 'How sublime is the silence of nature's ever active energies! There is something in the very name of wilderness, which charms the ear, and soothes the spirit of man. There is religion in it.' (quoted in Nash, 1982) The ideas of spiritual regeneration and escapism for the bourgeoisie and new middle class were inspired by the movement (Pepper, 1984). At the same time the industrial working classes were escaping to the countryside to 'recapture the humanity which they had lost in the factories and mines of the industrial revolution' (Hill, 1980). So the concept of a need to escape the urban culture is not new.

Why then do people want a right to roam? The qualities of moorland as discussed by Shoard (quoted in Pepper, 1984) show what people can gain from such an outdoor experience: '*Wildness*', the antithesis of domestication, and '*naturalness*', an apparent absence of human handiwork ... there is height, perhaps fulfilling people's needs for aloofness, and the *freedom* to wander at will, both satisfying the desire for *solitude* and *individuality*. And there is the much praised quality of *simplicity*, in the homogeneity of form. The openness and grand vistas which are afforded, in which the sky dominates, facilitate *communion with the creator*, providing 'almost a religious experience'. C.E.M Joad (1945) had similar feelings about the need to wander at will: 'a man walks that he may be impregnated by nature, to be a calmer and quieter person, with a replenished fund of energy'.

A proportion of today's walkers still feels that there is a great attraction in taking one's own line over challenging country. There is also the argument that the idea of being able to walk across open country in an unrestricted way adds 'a valued dimension of liberty to lives that are inevitably lived under many constraints' (Kirk, 1990). The Ramblers' Association emphasize this view in their publications by stating that walkers who navigate over 'wild, uncultivated land need freedom to explore summits, valleys, waterfalls and crags' (Ramblers' Association, 1993a). Indeed it is the combination of many of these factors that may explain the dispute about our existing access laws and their deficiencies. But despite its long history the true need of escape, namely a right to roam in open country, has never been properly fulfilled.

The differing philosophies which come into conflict are well encapsulated by Holt (1990) where she states 'the idea that land should be walked over freely where there is no footpath, by people who neither own it nor have permission of the owner, has frequently been dismissed as ridiculous or subversive'.

This chapter sets out to examine why the present situation concerning the right to roam has come about, what exists at present in terms of access, what various organizations feel about the right to roam and how the Ramblers' Association are perhaps putting forward some workable solutions.

The Right to Roam – An Historical Overview

A certain ambiguity is often attached to the word 'access' when it is used in the context of rambling. Footpaths and bridleways are means of access to the countryside, but the word is also used in a very specific sense, to indicate a right to wander freely over uncultivated land where there is no footpath. (Holt, 1990)

The Director of the Ramblers' Association, Alan Mattingly, said 'Freedom, we are told, is the bedrock of Western democracy. Freedom of speech, freedom of belief and freedom of movement are all seen as fundamental human rights. Yet in Britain freedom of movement is often strictly constrained. Or, at least, it is if the freedom you seek is that of roaming on foot over moors, mountain and heaths of your native land' (Ramblers' Association, 1993a).

It has been said that 'English Law cares more for property than person'. To the lawyer the law of trespass to land is considered to be any unjustifiable intrusion by any person upon land in the possession of another. It is one of the few civil wrongs that is absolute, namely, there is no defence. An early commentator stated:

> Every unwarrantable entry on another's soil the law entitles a trespass by breaking his close; the words of the writ of trespass commanding the defendant to show cause *quare clausum querentis fregit*. For every man's land is in the eye of the law enclosed and set apart from his neighbour's; and that either by a visible and material fence, as one field is divided from another by a hedge; or by an ideal invisible boundary, existing only in the contemplation of the law, as when one man's land adjoins to another's in the same field. (Blackstone's Commentaries, 1809, p. 209)

It is said that the slightest crossing of the boundary is sufficient and, in the case of *Ellis v. Loftus Iron Company* (1874) L.R.10.C.P., the then Chief Justice (Coleridge) said: 'If the defendant places a part of his foot on the plaintiff's land unlawfully, it is in law as much a trespass as if he had walked half a mile on it.'

With that extreme protection for the landowner or occupier it is not surprising that well known phrases such as 'What I have I hold' or 'An Englishman's home is his castle' are not just part of English law but part of the English culture and the mores of society. It is worthy of note that more often than not it is the culture and values of those in possession that is enshrined into law.

Each legal system develops from a variety of sources. The very culture, history and even the topography of the land, which eventually becomes a state, affect the relationships between people or the relationships between persons and the state. In fact that is 'the legal system'. Thus it is unsurprising that 'the concept of public access runs counter to the deeply ingrained English obsession with private property' (Holt, 1990) and 'countryside recreation in modern society is seen to be a cultural legacy which enshrines many of the attitudes and values of society in the past as well as reflecting the continuing influence of proprietorial rights' (Harrison, 1991). However, despite these factors, there does appear to be an interesting dichotomy between the law and actual practice. Whilst the landowning values are instilled into the British psyche, there has nevertheless in the past been a tradition of *de facto* access over much open country, some of which does continue today. To demonstrate one can take two extreme, and opposite, examples. On the one hand the empty spaces of Sweden may give rise to a right of *allemansträtten*. On the other hand the fiercely possessive and protective ways of Scottish Lords may have led to massive dispossession and have produced a legal system of which *allemansträtten* is the very antithesis (see Chapter 9).

In medieval England the great wastelands of the manors may have been areas where there was a right to roam, but on the other hand the average member of the population had little recreational time to roam. In any event, such wastes were the prime object of the enclosure movement. Land over which one could roam became less and less. Actual rights for the recreational use of land by the 'public' have, through time, been limited to the use of village greens. No other prescribed rights for recreation existed.

The philosophy of the enclosure movement was truly the acquisition of land. The excuse that was given was that it was to increase the productivity and quality of the land. In any event the average citizen always lost out. It is therefore not surprising that there is not and never has been a right to roam in English law. In fact the only way in which it is ever described is in Latin, namely a *jus spatiandi*.[1] Save for an unusual approach to it in a recent case of *R v. Doncaster Metropolitan Borough Council ex parte Braim* [1987] JPL 35,[2] a *jus spatiandi* does not exist in English law. Even the right of access to urban commons, created by Section 193 Law of Property Act 1925, is a specific creature of statute and not of the common law of England.

Whatever rights were enjoyed by the populace in the seventeenth and eighteenth centuries, so often described by John Clare (for example in his poem *Enclosure* he states 'Just as the even-bell rang, we set out/To wander the fields and the meadows about'), there is little doubt that what was lost was not forgotten. By the early nineteenth century there was a developing movement seeking to obtain rights in the countryside. There are well-recorded incidents of groups of people seeking to protect public rights of way and other rights. They threw down fences (e.g. on Berkhamstead Common, Hertfordshire) and later fought to protect commons and other open areas (which eventually gave rise to the birth of the Commons Open Spaces and Footpath Preservation Society in 1865 – now the Open Spaces Society). In the face of the general English attitude to possession of land, it is not surprising that the movement towards having a right to roam over open land was slow to develop.

Poets and artists may have appreciated the beauty and the benefits of mountains and open country; meanwhile the industrial working classes were becoming more restricted in their means of reaching a healthy place to walk in, either because the sprawling towns were being built on open spaces or the open spaces were closed off by landowners. Therefore many trespassed. However, those who owned the land felt that they owned it exclusively. This inevitably led to conflict.

The first attempt to change the law became one of the longest legislative stories and ended up in virtual defeat. A Liberal MP, James Bryce, first introduced his Access to Mountains (Scotland) Bill into the House of Commons in 1884. Clause 2 stated that no owner of uncultivated mountain or moorland should be entitled to exclude any person from walking on such lands for the purpose of recreation or scientific or artistic study (Stephenson, 1989). Of course at that time there was no Labour Party, merely the Liberals and Tories, and the Bill was lost. Bryce and his successors attempted on ten separate occasions in the intervening fifty years to introduce such a Bill, without success. As the century progressed many social changes occurred, but it was not until 1939 that the Access to Mountain Act actually came on to the statute book. There are two ways in which a determined anti-legislator or politician can frustrate public aspirations: one is by clear defeat, the other is by emasculation. The Access to Mountains Bill was truly emasculated. When the Act came on to the statute book, it meant and did very little. According to Joad (1945):

> The Act places an intolerable burden upon applicants. Its approach to the problem is piecemeal. (Scotland, for example, where the demand for access first arose, is not included in it.) It is overloaded with petty restrictions. It involves applicants in considerable expense; the expense of the inquiry, the expense of printing notices and sending them to the police, the expense of providing and erecting notice boards, expenses which ramblers, who are usually poor people, cannot afford; and it entails considerable acquaintance with legal forms and procedures on the part of those proposing to make application, involving and including the giving of evidence before a public enquiry. It is significant that though the Act has been on the Statute Book for six years, no application for access has up to the time of writing been made, and the cumbrous machinery of the Act has not, therefore, yet been brought into operation.

In spite of arduous efforts and prolonged negotiations, the public has not, in fact, secured access to a single square inch of uncultivated land.

Perhaps the Act only came on to the statute book because of the mass trespasses which took place, particularly in Derbyshire, in 1932. It is perhaps interesting to note that during this time 'the ramblers were prone to perceive trespass as a reclamation of their rights, rather than an infringement of the rights of the landowners' (Holt, 1990). This period of history is well documented by Stephenson (1989), Hill (1980) and Rothman (1982).

World War II, the defeat of the Churchill government and the election of the Attlee Labour government meant that the aspirations of the many were for the first time attainable. The election may have been won on the promise that every house would have a refrigerator but Hobhouse (1947a, 1947b) and Dower (1945) with their major reports had already set the foundation for legislation relating to many aspects of the countryside and access. Hobhouse, in particular, examined almost every relevant aspect of the problem of access to land. He recognized the conflicting interests in land, and the claim that the value of land might be diminished. He therefore recommended that in place of the Access to Mountains Act there should be a simple and comprehensive machinery for obtaining access to uncultivated land. 'Access Land' was to include all uncultivated land, whether mountain, moor, heath, down, cliff, beach or shore. The designation should be made after enquiry by the planning authority, who should then have power to designate suitable stretches of inland water. Clearly opposing forces were at play because the Act did not come on to the statute book in exactly the manner expected by Hobhouse. Both Cherry (1975) and Holt (1990) examine the manner in which the government quietly gave too much leeway to landowners.

What the National Parks and Access to the Countryside Act 1949 does is to provide that there are certain circumstances in which entry upon access land is no longer a trespass, although it can become a trespass again if various provisions set out in the Second Schedule to the Act are not complied with. Each local authority was to decide upon areas to which access should be allowed and if it concluded that there were none, protesters could call upon the government to convene a public inquiry. (The only known public inquiry was one called into the dispute about the lack of access to the Devonshire Estate at Bolton Abbey, Wharfedale, in the then West Riding of Yorkshire 1959).

Implementation of the National Parks and Access to the Countryside Act 1949

It is easy, in a case of confrontation, to assume that there are two diametrically opposed positions; that on the one hand there are those who want to have access and cannot have it, and on the other hand those who hold land and do not want anyone to enter on to it. It may appear to be absolutely black and white but in truth there is a great deal of grey in between. Large areas of land have traditionally been the subject of 'informal access', a phrase developed to describe lands over which there is *de facto* access compared with land over which there is legal or *de jure* access. When there was sufficient *de facto* access, there seemed to be no need to interfere by employing the provisions of the National Parks and Access to the Countryside Act 1949, which deals with access agreements and orders.

In fact, as will be mentioned later, there is an area of land which is subject to another form of access and which, whilst not a *jus spatiandi*, is equivalent to it (i.e. common land falling within urban areas). There is the oddity in that a great deal of the Lake District fell country lies within a former Urban District Council, namely Windermere Urban District Council, and thus the provisions of Section 193 Law of Property Act 1925 apply. As a result, members of the public have rights of access for air and exercise. It is only where a landowner was intransigent that the public, through the campaigning organizations (particularly the Ramblers' Association), needed to fight for access. These were the high profile cases, as in the Peak District and the Yorkshire Dales. Nevertheless there were and are low profile cases. Perhaps looking back, the Forest of Bowland is the most serious case of an area in England which is still effectively closed to the public, although many areas in Wales are equally devoid of access. Scotland, having a different legal system and subject to different policies, is a distinct and larger issue.

Why can one say more than forty years after the Act that areas 'are devoid of access'? According to Bonyhady (1987):

> For a variety of reasons – including the lack of interest of planning authorities, costs, the opposition of the landowners and the extent of *de facto* access – only about 100,000 acres or just 0.3% of the total area of England and Wales is covered by access arrangements. About half of the access land is in the Peak District where the Peak Park Joint Planning Board has made an exceptional effort to overcome the access problems which in the 1930s resulted in the 'mass trespasses' in protest at the exclusion of the members of the public from such areas as Kinder Scout and Bleaklow. Several Planning Authorities failed to make any access

arrangements whatsoever. Almost no agreements had been made in relation to woodlands and waterways.

Prendergast (1993) shows that 239 Access Agreements have been made under the 1949 Act. Half of this access land was designated by National Park Authorities.

It is also interesting to assess the implementation of Part V of the National Parks and Access to the Countryside Act 1949, in relation to SS 59–63 (i.e. the requirement that local planning authorities review and map 'open country' in their areas). Evidence shows that the requirement was widely neglected (Kempe, 1992). Little action was taken to extend access under the requirement. The post-war burden was felt heavily by local planning authorities (e.g. the definitive rights of way mapping exercise), and the wording of the Act almost made it an option as whether or not to undertake the exercise.

Although a detailed examination of the relevant provisions of the National Parks and Access to the Countryside Act 1949 shows that agreements could still be made, the fact that no agreements or orders are being made demonstrates that either the motivation has gone or it is simply out of fashion for a local authority to think in terms of access agreements or orders. (A recent example is access to Aysgarth Upper Falls where the Yorkshire Dales National Park, after spitting fire and brimstone in 1991, had by 1993–4 become suspiciously quiet). One must conclude that as at 1994 there has been very little progress in terms of gaining access. Whilst one cannot say that the 1949 Act has been totally emasculated, perhaps one must say that its aspirations have been denied. Whether or not local authorities believe that they have been pragmatic, i.e. there is *de facto* access and therefore they need not fight for anything else, or whether they have been dominated by farming and landowning majorities of members, is a matter for further enquiry.

Other Forms of Access to Open Country

This overview would not be complete without reference to other statutory and non-statutory provisions for access. Access by agreement is allowed by other legislation e.g. Section 193 Law of Property Act 1925, Wildlife and Countryside Act 1981 (e.g. management agreements under Section 39) and the Countryside Act 1968 (e.g. country parks). The Forestry Commission operate a policy of allowing *de facto* access to their forests. Even though the government has recently withdrawn the proposal to privatize the Forestry Commission, access has been shown to be at risk when the Commission sells land (Ramblers' Association, 1993e). Other *de jure* access has been created by various local Acts of Parliament (allowing varying degrees of access with conditions and restrictions), such as the 1878 Manchester Corporation Water Works Act, which stated that 'access should not be interfered with' around Thirlmere. The 1892 Birmingham Corporation Water Works Act gave a right of access to 70 square miles of the Elan Valley, mid Wales. Also, any common land owned by the National Trust has in theory a right of access for the public (Section 29 National Trust Act 1907, which is subject to (and claimed confused by) Section 21 National Trust Act 1971). However in practice the concept is often problematic.

In this section, three particular forms of access to open country are examined: access to common land, access via the Countryside Steward- ship Scheme and access via Inheritance Tax exemption. Although all three cases appear to extend access, there are also various issues with each form of access.

Common Land

Section 193 Law of Property Act 1925 confers on members of the public rights of access for air and exercise to certain lands. These are defined as:

(a) 'Land which was Metropolitan Common within the meaning of the Metropolitan Commons Act, 1866 to 1898, or manorial waste, or a common which is wholly or partly situate within a borough or urban district'. There are problems of interpretation with this definition, but the references to borough and urban district are now usually con- sidered in the light of local government reorganization to be to land which before 1st April 1974 was a borough or urban district.

(b) 'In addition the right can be given by the Lord of the Manor or any other person entitled to the soil of any land by entering into a revocable or irrevocable deed'. Access by the public to this land is subject to restrictions set out in the section and by local bylaws. It should be noted that areas of land covered by section 193 of the Law of Property Act 1925 are not indicated on Ordnance Survey maps and are therefore not necessarily known by the general public.

It is because of this law that areas such as Berkhamstead Common in Hertfordshire and part of the Lake District have an equivalent of a 'right to roam'. Otherwise in terms of common land it is estimated that the public have *de facto* access to only one fifth, and it is submitted that it is diminishing. Some other areas of common land are covered by local Acts of Parliament, which allow access (often for local people): for example, the 1871 New Forest Act gave a 'privilege of access'.

The Common Land Forum (Countryside Commission, 1986) recommended that a public right of access should be granted over all common land in association with a management scheme. Despite election promises the present government has refused to implement the report.

Countryside Stewardship

A worthy scheme with an admirable principle relating to access is the Countryside Stewardship Scheme. This was initiated by the Countryside Commission in 1991 and combines the principles of habitat conservation and enhancement, recreation and access. The scheme can apply to various landscape types: chalk and limestone grassland, lowland heath, waterside landscapes, coastland, uplands, old meadows and pastures, and historic landscapes (Countryside Commission, 1991b). (It is perhaps no coincidence that many of those listed are also defined as open countryside in the 1949 and 1968 Acts.) As part of the scheme, landowners are encouraged (via a hectarage payment) to allow access to the land (at no charge to the public) if no such right already legally exists (for example in the form of rights of way). Any access created under the scheme is of a permissive nature and is not embodied in any permanent legal form.

A major issue surrounding access under the scheme is the possibility that when the Stewardship arrangements end (the present schemes should last for ten years), the access to the land could be withdrawn. This relates most pertinently to areas which, before they entered into the Stewardship scheme, allowed *de facto* access. The scheme has 'replaced' this tolerated access with permissive access. The Ramblers' Association has found that one-fifth of schemes that have made provisions for access (one-third of all Stewardship schemes) replaced *de facto* access (Ramblers' Association, 1993c). What will be the situation once the scheme ends? Will access be curtailed as the landowner is presently being paid for allowing what in the past he tolerated anyway? An example of such a situation is on the moor above Malham Cove in the Yorkshire Dales National Park. Thus, one must ask what good or benefit to the public can this form of access give. The money for Stewardship is coming from the public purse to pay landowners to allow something that was in some cases already allowed. It could be argued that the access purchased is actually of little public benefit and represents poor value for money; indeed, the majority of access land under the scheme appears to be unrelated to the needs of walkers (Ramblers' Association 1993d). If the worst-case scenario occurs, many scarce areas of open country could eventually be lost to the public.

Inheritance Tax Act 1984

Sections 30 and 31 Inheritance Tax Act 1984 provide that a transfer of value will be exempt from Inheritance Tax to the extent that the value transferred is attributable to property that falls within certain descriptions. In addition to certain artefacts this includes 'any land which in the opinion of the Treasury is of outstanding scenic or historic or scientific interest.'

Essentially a person can delay and (in practical terms) virtually avoid the payment of Inheritance Tax. There is a relevant condition to this opportunity, in that the person must undertake to take such steps as are agreed between the Treasury and the person giving the undertaking for the maintenance of the land and the preservation of its character and *for securing reasonable access to the public* (our emphasis). There have been two major problems: The first is that whilst one Government minister specifically said: 'Moreover, the effect of the legislation is to get the public's right to have this access established on a firm legal basis rather than to have it dependent on the owners' personal whim as previously' (letter from Mr Norman Lamont – then Financial Secretary to the Treasury – to Dr David Clarke M.P., 28 August 1987). This seems to imply (if not expressly state) that any access should be at least on the basis of formal public rights of way or, possibly, an irrevocable access agreement. However that interpretation does not accord with subsequent Government policy. It would seem from examples known that one permissive footpath over an estate of 30,000 acres will be sufficient for the Government to allow conditional exemption from Inheritance Tax, which could amount to as much as £12million. The second problem is that although there had been up to 350 exemptions granted since 1976, so called 'fiscal confidentiality' has prevented the public from being given information about the location or nature of this access (Pearlman, 1992).

It is only recently, since the Countryside Commission started to publish details of access available under stewardship arrangements, that mixed in amongst them are found the new cases where access is due to conditional exemption. Cases granted before 1990 might never be known to the public. The oddity is that by virtue of changes in taxation, it is unlikely that many landowners will need the conditional exemption because agricultural land will probably not attract Inheritance Tax since 1992.

The Desire for Further Access – Views of the Representative Groups

It is now recognized that walking in the countryside is one of the most popular pastimes of the British public. Statistics from the Countryside Commission and the OPCS (Office of Population Censuses and Surveys) General Household Survey support this. For example, 376 million visits were made to the countryside for walking or rambling in 1993 (Countryside Recreation Network, 1994). Many popular areas can be congested with walkers in the summer months and footpath erosion is a major problem. It is also recognized that walking is becoming even more popular. The data collected do not in any way detail what further access to the countryside is desired or required; in fact the opinions of the general public are not known. However, there are various access-related organizations that are campaigning for further access, who could claim that they represent the views of a reasonable section of the public who walk in the countryside. The following section considers their views.

Many Non-Governmental Organizations are involved in access-related issues and campaigns. Some campaign actively for a right to roam, some seek to discourage it. These two groups fall along classic lines in countryside-related matters – the access/recreation lobby and the landowner/farmer lobby. At various times in the past these two groups have been in serious conflict over the issue of access to open countryside (Stephenson, 1989 and Hill, 1980). The power base of the landowning group has had a significant influence in ensuring that a right to roam, as envisaged by the access lobby, has never come into being. However, the most active group campaigning for a right to roam, the Ramblers' Association (1993), after recently clarifying its objectives on this matter, is currently putting forward a well-balanced and realistic argument for a right to roam. Many (including the Country Landowners' Association (CLA) and National Farmers Union (NFU)) have argued against the right to roam, and in the case of the Moorland Association against a right of access to common land, because they see it as an infringement of private property rights. The latter is regarded by them as a central tenet of our society and is clearly linked to the law of trespass. Others, such as the Royal Society for the Protection of Birds (RSPB), have argued against a right to roam in terms of harm to wildlife. The Ramblers' Association commissioned research to investigate the effect of countryside access and disturbance to birds (Sidaway, 1990; Watson, 1991), which has suggested that recreational disturbance is only a perceived problem in the minds of the conservationists. Some damage has occurred (and will no doubt continue) but is of a localized nature. There is also little evidence that access causes disturbance to game birds as feared by those who have commercial interests in moorlands. 'These problems are relatively insignificant when compared to the major ecological problems. ... caused as result of acid rain, over grazing and fires' (Sidaway, 1990). Therefore it is vital for groups involved in the struggle for and against extending access to put all issues in perspective and attempt to take a pragmatic, flexible and realistic view.

The Ramblers' Association (RA)

The RA has campaigned tirelessly for a right to roam. 'Since its formation in 1935 the RA has believed that people who walk on moors, mountains, heaths and downs, solely for the enjoyment of fresh air, exercise and the beauty of the countryside, should not be treated as trespassers' (RA, 1993a). Indeed the RA's constitution states that it will 'work for and assist in: ... (b) (iii) The provision and preservation of public access to open country' (RA Constitution).

However, its campaigns for a right to roam involving 'direct action' have set the tone of the conflict. Despite this, public support for the recent Forbidden Britain campaigns has created national debate on the

Figure 4.1 Cartoon by Jim Watson

subject and allowed the RA to make clear to all, especially the land-owning lobby, its requirements in terms of access and what it means by the term. It has worked hard to allay the fears of the landowning lobby by arguing that the access it requires is controllable, not damaging, not completely unfettered and should be in balance with economic uses of land such as hill farming and game management. The RA has also long been concerned that walkers' freedom to roam should be in harmony with wildlife conservation, thereby working towards proposals that would be in tune with the objectives of conservation groups such as the RSPB.

It could be said that the RA is pressing for a right to roam as a matter of moral principle – it is being fuelled by an historic and romantic desire to achieve past objectives. However there has been a very positive and practical response from RA members to *Harmony in the Hills*, a consultation document relating to the right to roam. Increasing membership and high renewal rates show a large commitment to the RA and thus implicitly to the principle of right to roam. The RA has also detected a lessening of landowner opposition, which has appeared in the form of proposing alternatives rather than outright opposition.

The RA's latest policy document, *Harmony in the Hills*, contains 'reasonable and well considered proposals' (RA, 1993b). It is perhaps the most pragmatic solution yet proposed, taking a realistic view of what has to done to achieve a right to roam. Indeed it could be described as a calculated compromise.

Six 'Steps to Harmony' are proposed:

1 Behaviour

Walkers could be treated as trespassers and may be fined if they cause damage, destroy or cut a plant, fail to shut gates.

2 Suspension of Access

Access to open country could be suspended for various reasons e.g. grouse shooting, fire risk, lambing, restoring vegetation, etc.

3 The Precautionary Principle

Access could be suspended if a conservation agency has grounds for believing that access might be harmful to wildlife. This could last for three years.

4 Wardens

A local authority could appoint wardens to advise people, to explain any restrictions and foster respect for the land and co-operation between walkers and other interests.

5 Compensation

Although the RA feel that any land covered by access would not be significantly reduced in value, they do state that if the owner or other person who has an interest in the land can show that they had suffered a material loss, then they should be paid compensation (the cost to be met by the Exchequer) representing good value.

6 Guardians of the Environment

This proposal relates to the wider situation of the hill farmer and calls for reform of the hill farming subsidy system.

Harmony in the Hills really does appear to represent 'responsible access', the aim being to allow access, hill farming and wildlife conservation to co-exist without any serious conflict. The RA feels that to attain its major long-term objective of a right to roam being enshrined in legislation, it must have proposals that do not unduly affect the interests of the landowning and conservation lobbies. The compensation issue and the precautionary principle show a definite development in this respect.

Harmony in the Hills has laid the foundations for an Access Bill, which is currently being prepared by a team of experts. Its preamble will probably read 'An Act to amend the law of trespass, so as to enable members of the public to resort on foot to open country and certain other land in England and Wales for their recreation: and connected purposes' (RA, 1992a). There is currently some debate as to whether the Bill should be in a 'word' or 'map' format. The RA realize that for any Bill to get through Parliament it requires the support of the party in power. Therefore if a Labour or Liberal Democrat administration is returned at the next election there is thought to be a real possibility that an Access Bill could be launched. If a Conservative administration is returned, the chances for legislation are, to say the least, minimal. The Conservative government's failure to fulfil its election promise of enacting common land legislation and its recent creation of a criminal offence of aggravated trespass show a lack of sympathy or under-standing of the aspirations of the access lobby.

Various other groups are also in some way or another actively seeking a right to roam over open country.

The Views of the Supporting Groups

The British Mountaineering Council (BMC) have a policy that there should be 'a right of access on foot to Open Country' (BMC, 1991). Also, the BMC's Access and Conservation policies state: 'The BMC will campaign for more effective access legislation, principally for legislation which grants a right of access on foot to open country' (BMC, 1992).

The Council for National Parks (CNP), in their policy document *A Vision for National Parks* (1990), state: 'there should be a right of free access on foot to all open countryside in National Parks and indeed elsewhere' (CNP, 1990).

The Youth Hostels Association (YHA) has views that often overlap with those of the RA, especially on rights of way. However, with the right to roam they are slightly divergent. They would favour, in principle, access to uncultivated mountain and moorland; however, the YHA feel that as a landowning organization, private property rights must be protected. It is on this point that they differ from the RA. They also do not believe in high-profile, direct action campaigns to secure access. The YHA has not as yet surveyed its members to see whether the policy can be backed by member demand. The YHA also state that securing access is only one small area in which the associations works (Kinsbury, 1994).

The Open Spaces Society (OSS) has similar views to the RA and endorses their policy objectives. It supports the report of the Common Land Forum 1986, which would give a right of access to common land. The OSS also wishes to encourage all county councils to use their powers to make access agreements or orders over open country as defined in the Acts of 1949 and 1968 (OSS, undated).

It is also interesting to note that both the Labour and the Liberal Democrat parties stated in their election manifestos (1992) that a right to roam would be legislated for if they achieved office.

The Views of the Ambivalent Organizations

The Royal Society for the Protection of Birds (RSPB) considers that further public access to the countryside is desirable. 'People must be allowed to appreciate wildlife in its rightful setting and a measured expansion of access is desirable and essential to achieve this' (RSPB, 1990). The RSPB do have concerns over 'recreational disturbance' to birds on all types of open country (especially upland and coastal) and regard restrictions on access at certain times as essential.

The Council for the Protection of Rural England (CPRE) believes that the public should have better access to the countryside but do not necessarily feel that a right to roam is a way to provide this. They feel their 'softer' approach to the access issue reflects the views of the members.

Counter Views

The Country Landowners Association (CLA) (when responding to *Harmony in the Hills*) categorically stated that its own policy *Recreation and Access in the Countryside: A Better Way Forward* (1991) was a better alternative. In this document the CLA states that an unqualified right to roam should be resisted by the Government (note that the RA has never called for an unqualified right to roam – they have always conceded acceptable byelaws or restrictions to regulate people's behaviour). The CLA believes that when a need for access is genuine, existing powers of local authorities should be used to negotiate voluntary agreements to secure managed access.

The National Farmers Union (NFU) believes that a right to roam should not exist as it would conflict with the notion that recreational activities should be pursued without risk or injury to crops and live-stock. No change of their view on right to roam is expected (Cushing, 1994).

The Way Forward?

It is undeniable that the campaign for access has excited the public interest. No statistics exist to show how many members of the public actually want to walk in a manner that can be described as 'roaming freely over open countryside', in part because the desire to have free access is an aspiration that some people will not seek to attain. Perhaps their actual feeling is that they do not wish to suffer the constraint of always believing that they may be transgressing the law if they move from the thin line of a public right of way. In view of the support which the Ramblers' Association has attracted both amongst its members and the media, it is a reasonable assumption that theirs is a cause that has public support. However, it will not be anything more than a pure policy objective unless three particular angles are constantly controlled and encouraged.

The first is that the campaign and the activity must always be directed to some particular location, estate or problem so that the public recognizes that there are sufficient issues, of a great enough magnitude, to justify the acceptance of the policy. They must feel that the future way of enjoying the countryside will not cause them more problems than they have suffered in the past. The second is that all proposals generate counter-proposals. A small number of owners of grouse moors (said to be 130 in total) formed The Moorland Association, which effectively caused the Government to renege upon its promise to carry the Common Land Forum (Countryside Commission, 1986) recommendations into law. One can assume that there will be similar and perhaps more forceful attempts by landowners to frustrate the access policies of the amenity organizations. Also, some of the amenity organizations may feel that some parts of the campaign run counter to their existing objectives; as has been seen above, the RSPB and CPRE have some reservations about general access policy. However, as they learn more about the detailed proposals of the Ramblers' Association, it is quite possible that opposition from such quarters will not develop.

Finally although this is not a campaign for a change in the law (it is really about a change in public perception), a change in the law is a necessary part of the attainment of the objective. Therefore there must be party political support from a party that will eventually form a government in the House of Commons, and there must be enough support to carry the matter through the House of Lords. As has already been noted, the Labour and Liberal Democrat parties appear to be good allies in such a cause. If however the Conservatives remain in power, the prospect for legislation is minimal.

It is understood that the policy is still in a dynamic state; indeed, one of the writers of this chapter is a member of a group of ramblers with specific expertise and experience who are finalizing the drafting of a Bill, which, it is hoped, will be adopted by a government in power. Several points are being addressed.

It is proposed by the Ramblers' Association that the right of access will be to differing types of land and will be somewhat wider than the existing descriptions in the National Parks and Access to the Countryside Act 1949 and the Countryside Act 1968. The exact wording is likely to incorporate the classes now described in the two existing Acts and may cause a slight widening of those classes. In addition, in light of the experience (or lack of experience) of implementing the National Parks and Access to the Countryside Act 1949, consideration will be given to a completely separate and different type of legislative provision. Although Part V of the Act may have partially failed, it has set a precedent for another scheme (i.e. Section 43 of the Wildlife and Countryside Act 1981). The established principle behind both the Acts can be used as a way forward for new legislation. Section 43 of the Wildlife and Countryside Act 1981 (as amended) required that each county planning authority whose area comprises the whole or any part of a National Park should have prepared a map of the Park or the part thereof showing any area which originally was described as being moor or heath but now is an area of whose natural beauty it is important to conserve. It is known that the judgement supplied by those planning authorities in compiling the maps became quite subjective. Indeed, the wording of the legislation attracted such an approach. There will be differences of opinion (probably between landowners and users) as to whether or not land falls within the proposed description of access land. Therefore in any new legislation there must be a mechanism for dealing speedily with disputes of this nature and without detriment to either party.

The concept that changes trespass to legitimate access is dependent on the manner in which the law is changed. The scheme of the National Parks and Access to the Countryside Act 1949 seems to have been satisfactory and is a good basis for future legislation and may well be carried in full to the new Bill.

Finally, the most vexed question will be that of compensation. One complaint made by landowners, when they believed that the Common Land Forum report was imminently to be given statutory authority, was that they were being deprived of their full rights as landowners (because they would be obliged to allow people to have access) and yet they were not to be compensated for it. On the other hand, there have been claims for compensation upon the making of a Highway Creation Order where the amounts awarded have been astronomical. Claims of this nature do not help the landowners' cause. In due course a basis for a compensation provision in any proposed Bill is likely to be promulgated.

Conclusion

It can be seen that the right to roam, a concept that is not even defined in English law, has had a long and rather dramatic history that has brought about various levels of conflict. There is no statistical or factual evidence to prove the level of public demand but the situation captured by the media interest argues strongly in favour of recognized need.

One final question has to be proposed. Are we actually working towards a position where all the parties involved can lay their cards on the table and deal a broker's compromise? The Rambler's Association is ready to do this; can those in opposition finally accept that there is a workable way forward and thus fulfil a need, as yet unsatisfied, to the population of England and Wales? The whole issue may depend not only on the flexibility and open mindedness of the landowning lobby, but perhaps as importantly on the vagaries of English politics. Unfortunately neither is predictable nor dependable. However, with a great deal of persuasion and active public relations on behalf of the access organizations, they may finally be able to persuade everyone of the benefits and value of a right to roam in open country.

Notes

1. *jus spatiandi* – namely 'wandering at large'. *Gayle on Easements* (1972), p. 28.
2. This case was decided by Mr Justice McCullough upon its own peculiar facts, that Doncaster MBC were found to be holding the land for the public on terms that the public could use it.

5

Countryside Stewardship and the Consumer–Citizen

GAVIN PARKER

Introduction

The disorganization of capitalism, or the move towards 'flexible special-isation' or post-Fordism (Marsden *et al.*, 1993; Lash & Urry, 1987; Roche, 1992) is said to represent an economic face of a post-modern society. Post-Fordism and post-modernism have been linked to shifts in production and consumption at the global level. This is not the place to set out a fuller description of modern/post-modern societies and economies, which has been extensively attempted elsewhere (Berman, 1983; Featherstone, 1991; Bauman, 1992; Harvey, 1989). It is enough, however, to acknowledge these processes as a context to this chapter.

It is widely accepted that national economies are undergoing change in terms of production and of consumption associated with the mobility of capital, the rapidly increasing use of technology and the develop-ment of fragmented class structure, political allegiance, interest groups and cultural configurations (see Chapter 11; Marsden *et al.*, 1993; Squires, 1993; Hall and Jacques, 1989). Many changes may not appear significant when abstracted from others taking place in other areas of public policy or when observed as historically static. It is when linkages with other policies are made that conclusions, as to the intention and the outcome of policies, can be made in terms of possible future implications.

The political constraints on government, especially from the land-owning and agricultural lobbies, mean that policy formulation balances wider economic considerations with domestic political considerations. Therefore, policy in this area tends to appear anachronistic with disparities in national policy; this was acknowledged by Cloke and

Goodwin (1992, p. 321), who noted that a 'fragmented coherence reflecting different forms of commodification in rural areas' was a reality, but warned of premature acceptance of an epochal shift or 'an extensive shift in rural society from Fordism to its successor' (p. 324). In terms of agriculture this perhaps reflects the mixed nature of the economy in this country, with state regulation and subsidization of the agricultural industry still prevailing. It seems that regulation holds agricultural land use in socio-economic stasis. In relating this chapter to wider research concerning rural restructuring it is useful to consider Marsden *et al.* (1993, p. 4) who, in *Constructing the Countryside*, recently set out three broad questions to be addressed in rural studies. They were:

> How are international processes of economic and social restructuring being expressed and mediated within one nation state? How is the state 'regulating' rural change and to what extent does the late 20th century represent a break with the past? How can conceptual advances in mainstream social theory be applied to the rural arena and, conversely, how can locally based social action be effectively incorporated into our understanding of uneven development?

This agenda for rural research is challenging and welcome. The particular aspect considered here is that of access to agricultural enclosed land. This chapter seeks to signal the links between changes in rural regulation, the role of the land as site of production and the land as site of consumption, and the significance of those changes for citizenship construction. The consideration of national constructions of citizenship rights and property rights within the economic transitions outlined above are analysed, within this wider context, using a political economy approach (Cloke, 1989; Marsden *et al.*, 1993). The contexts within which property rights and citizens' rights have been framed over space and time are important factors in understanding the arguments over specific rural issues. In short, it is necessary to situate the discussion of a specific land-use issue within the wider context of socio-economic change and in terms of the effects on rights distributions. Those wider and more theoretical notions are then evaluated against a particular policy, Countryside Stewardship. The implications of Part V of the 1994 Criminal Justice and Public Order Act are also mentioned in terms of its effect on rights distributions.

Rural Land Use and Rights Transfers

The analysis of systems of rights, in this case when focusing on countryside access in terms of citizenship, requires an understanding of the historical circumstances under which putative rights over land have evolved. The historical context provides commentary on the development of a dominant culture and citizenship/private property right relationships. This chapter addresses the transfers of rights in relation to access to the land; therefore, the 'rationalization' of the land and its use during the eighteenth and nineteenth centuries is important. Transfers of rights over land were taking place rapidly whilst other civil and political rights were being transferred in other spheres of social life (Marshall and Bottomore, 1992; Held, 1989). The story of the enclosures and the effect on rural society (and in terms of countryside access) is an area that has been extensively documented and discussed (Chambers and Mingay, 1966; Shoard, 1987; Thompson, 1993; Donnelly, 1986). The historical development of countryside access is well documented, as is the social history of rural England during the enclosures and the agricultural 'revolution'. The system of access provision has historically rested on a mixture of legal/common rights, individual benevolence, state tolerance of simple trespass and latterly the development of policy such as Access Agreements, Country Parks and now Access Payment schemes. For accounts of this process, see, for example, Shoard, 1987; Malcolmson, 1973; Thompson, 1993; Cherry, 1975; Blunden and Curry, 1990; Bonyhady, 1987). The transfer of common/ customary rights to and from legal rights status, and rights held individually as civil rights, is important. All those transfers over time can be viewed as transfers of citizenship rights, to and from one social group to another, leading to contemporary rights distributions. The introduction of Access Payment schemes (particularly the Countryside Stewardship scheme) are discussed here in relation to the inferences that can be drawn for citizenship and rights transfers, or the hegemonization of status and power maintained from holding certain exclusive rights.

Some change in land use in terms of levels, types and modes of production is becoming accepted by farmers, landowners, politicians and the public. The terms of the changes are, however, subject to extended debate. There is concern that some informal rights and activities may be lost during the process of restructuring in the countryside (Cloke and Goodwin, 1992; Lowe, Clark and Cox, 1991). The agricultural industry is gradually moving away from its productivist role, attempting to exploit alternative land uses, or engage in multiple land usage in order to sustain incomes from the land; a general policy formally framed within the 1986 Agriculture Act (Countryside Commission, 1993; 1987; Cloke and McLaughlin, 1989; Ilbery, 1992). The changes in production and consumption outlined above hold many potential implications for existing rights in the countryside and for the construction of citizenship now and in the future. A Marshallian concept of citizenship is employed in evaluating rights distributions in relation to countryside access. Marshall's understanding of citizenship is where each citizen is the full member of a community, a status which bestows upon individuals equal rights and duties, liberties and constraints, powers and responsibilities (Marshall and Bottomore, 1992, p. 18). The terms upon which old and new rural land uses are produced, consumed and regulated could bring far-reaching changes in rural society. Here, the regulation of those land uses are of concern; it is the mode of regulation that enforces particular conceptions of citizenship through the demarcation of deviancy and orthodoxy with respect to the exercise of rights claims. This process of demarcation is highly political, and the definition and extent of those 'rights and duties, liberties and constraints, powers and responsibilities' will be subject to dispute. In the case of countryside access the provisions of law, the characteristics of access's institutionalization and the legitimation of the consumption of countryside goods via the state, the market or as of 'natural right' are identifiable as the main issues that are still contested.

In this examination of countryside access, the changing role of agricultural land, as a site of production towards enclosed agricultural land as a site of consumption, is examined as a location where rights are being 'traded'. It is the means by which this change is mediated and regulated that is of interest here. The shift in emphasis from production towards consumption of countryside goods, and the way in which that consumption is formalized, has political repercussions, with potential to increase tension between landowners and the public. As Marsden *et al.* point out (1993, p. 21):

> In agrarian political economy ... emphasis has been on an understanding of the dynamics of production processes, with limited attention paid to social rigidities or changes in consumption practices ... In the context of rural areas, it is particularly pertinent to consider the interrelations between production and consumption, given the increasing role of such areas as consumption spaces.

It is clear that any rights distribution is a contingent distribution and therefore the legitimacy of rights may be temporary, if not continually contested. Some rights at particular points in time are viewed as unassailable; for instance, the right to own property in civil terms, the right to vote in political terms and the right to an education in social terms. Various critiques of citizenship theory have outlined the dynamic nature of rights and the processes by which rights are won, lost, maintained and reinforced (Held, 1989; Heater, 1990). There is interdependency between different sets of rights, their construction and the political impacts of those constructions. The tensions expounded within debates over rights distributions in the context of countryside access are between property rights as legal and civil rights and between differing property rights claims which are not integrated within putative property rights constructions. Both, in this context, can be claimed as citizenship rights. The construction of production and consumption rights and their meanings are substantially formed by the processes taking place in the social world (Mouffe, 1993; Clark, *et al.*, 1994). The effects of specific policy and economic restructuring on production/consumption rights, specifically in terms of the interface of property rights and citizenship rights in relation to countryside access (Fudge and Glasbeek, 1992; Ravenscroft, 1993), are such that claims to vary existing rights distributions are likely to develop, given the economic position of agriculture and the need for alternative land uses and incomes from the land.

It is asserted here that whilst it may be true that social and economic changes are occurring globally, other agendas are being pursued which complicate post-Fordist and post-modern trends, not least of which are political agendas set by actors holding particular notions of citizenship as desirable. Smith (1989, p. 148) refers to this briefly:

> The late twentieth century *may* be characterized by the reorganization of capital and transmutation of social meaning, but these processes are entwined in a politically inspired restructuring of human rights.

Current policy efforts are linked yet constrained by reform of the Common Agricultural Policy and notwithstanding, the influence of the land lobby remains strong over central government. The common labelling of recent Conservative Party administrations as 'neo-Liberal' comes about in recognition of the emphasis placed on a 'free' market economy and a minimal state within government policy over the last fifteen years. Cox (1984) emphasizes that policies to return land and property markets to a free market have failed in the past as have efforts to nationalize land. The power of constraint, or Denman's 'positive power' of property ownership held by landowners (Denman, 1978), constrains the power of policy initiation held by the state, which in turn renders radical progression along the route towards free markets or land nationalization unlikely. In the case of contemporary policy initiatives for agricultural land use, there is an underlying shift to address land use to market demands, which public access provision to the countryside is sensitive towards because of its fragility in legal and economic terms.

Clearcut situations with clear alternatives and with all parties clear of their rights and responsibilities may be the ultimate aim of certain shades of administration. It *could* be argued that the establishment of black and white scenarios is a utilitarian and in some ways a welcome thing *per se* – if only in the sense that citizenship rights and responsibilities may become more easily comprehensible. The terms of such 'rationalizing', perhaps totalizing, outcomes involving most commonly the expansion of market-oriented systems of allocation, in land use terms, is manifested in the commodification of countryside goods. Who will benefit or disbenefit? How will those outcomes be legitimated? If the aim of government in this instance is to pursue this rationalizing process over agricultural land use against a tide of fragmenting capitalism in other spheres, have these policies been adequately theorized by government in an attempt to follow through the effects that such rerationalizing/restructuring policy could have in terms of the construction of citizenship?

Market rights offer a particular definition of entitlements (Fudge and Glasbeek, 1992; Lowe, Clark and Cox, 1991). Notionally the market serves the interests of the landed and the consumer, ensuring that rights in respect to countryside access become consumer rights. The main issue seems to be the construction of citizenship itself and how the market plays an important role in sustaining certain conception of citizenship whilst emaciating others. The access issue is but one issue abstracted from a clutch of land-use issues currently identifiable for scrutiny by academics and politicians. Perhaps to some it is not the most important of those issues; however, the subject exhibits features of a struggle for power, for rights couched in terms of freedom and equality and the role of the state, the market and the citizen. The crux of this struggle comes where rights interface, conflict and overlap, or, where one rights' claim disallows other rights' claims. It is claims over land use that seem symbolically resonant in debates over countryside access (Shoard, 1987; Thompson, 1993). Countryside issues can arouse deeply held views, beliefs and individual conceptions of optimal citizenship. The political tensions within differing constructions of citizenship are examined below.

Citizenship and Countryside Access

Once a right is priced it enters the realms and the language of the market place. The 'right' becomes a commodity to be traded, exchanged, bought, sold or leased, rather than (in the case of countryside access), something that has always existed, happily or unhappily, within an uncertain grey area. This has allowed non-market-based claims derived from natural justice, equity, social need or benevolence to be exercised.

As Lowe, Clark and Cox anticipate (1991, p. 8):

> One of the problems of a transition from a paternalistic, welfare tradition to a market oriented one is that many informal public benefits may be lost in the process ... The risk is that the new private owners will look either to terminate such access or to raise revenue from it. With such proposals on the agenda, there is a pressing need to consider turning certain customary freedoms into rights to moderate the scope of private market power.

It is claimed that particular constructions of citizenship could conceivably address the traditional tensions between individuality and collectivism or freedom and equality: as Bauman posits, the ethical paradox – how to balance the opposing positions (Bauman, 1992). The aim of all constructions of citizenship rights is to protect the individual against the state, minorities against discrimination and for the collective to prosper. The difference in varying conceptions of citizenship lie in the political 'world views' associated with certain rights constructions. Smith (1989, p. 148) claims that 'citizenship theory provides a vision for the transformation of society which rests neither on the overthrow of the state nor on the sanctity of the market'. The progressive transformation that Smith envisages is based on a democratic development of the constitution of citizenship rights and responsibilities. It is interesting to analyse the development of citizenship theory and the differing conceptions of citizenship portrayed as optimal. Citizenship theory in the past has been concerned with the types of rights of citizenship and what those rights consisted of, how they were won, legitimated and defended.

T.H. Marshall's seminal work *Citizenship and Social Class*, first published in 1950, sets out the argument that various types of rights namely civil, political and social rights, have developed over time, in an evolutionary manner (Marshall and Bottomore, 1992). This argument has been criticized by contemporary writers. It is clear that many rights only came about through political lobbying; it is not at all clear that the rights gained were a 'natural' development within society. Giddens (1985), for example, argues that these rights were fought for via class conflict, and Held (1989) underlines the idea that these rights require continual defence. Some rights become firmly embedded in the culture of society whilst others are defended less vigorously, presumably because those rights are either less important in the scheme of people's lives, important only to minorities, the relatively powerless or the rights become obsolescent. In many instances the citizens' rights that benefit power holders are those rights that become most firmly entrenched politically and socially, as well as rights that hold support from large majorities of the population. The identification of the development of these rights is still important and the monitoring of the efficacy and universality of such rights, for all individuals, may be possible to undertake within a structured relationship with the state. In most cases citizenship envelopes will shift towards one political pole or another without presenting a marked movement towards one conception of citizenship or another. Particular rights and their classification are only justified and legitimated under particular conceptions of citizenship or outcomes associated with political projects. Therefore the types of movement along a rights continuum from Liberal to Communitarian (see below) will be dependent on a number of contingent factors, which will have bearing on a particular right's legitimation and justification. These factors include, for example, economic impact, crime levels, levels of environmental degradation and, crucially, the effect on existing rights. If the alternative conceptions of citizenship that are considered below were in currency, differing constructions of rights could be legitimated.

More recent work concerning citizenship theory follows the tradition of the analyses by Marshall, Parsons, Giddens and Held. Rather than charting the development of rights and investigating typologies of rights, it is the constructions or packages of citizenship and the legitimation of those constructions or packages that are analysed here. The Liberal or 'individualist' citizenship and Communitarian or 'pluralist' citizenship are applied to compare countryside policy (Mouffe, 1993; Van Gunsteren, 1994). These notional citizenships can be characterized as points along a simple political continuum from individual liberty to social equality. The Liberal construction and the Communitarian construction of citizenship rights provide appropriately contrasting positions for analysis in the context of countryside access rights. The Liberal construction emphasizes the individualism of the citizen, 'the citizen as rational being, the calculating bearer of rights and privileges' (Van Gunsteren, 1994, p. 39). This Liberal citizenship is theoretically calculated to result in the maximum benefit for the individual. The limits or failings of this conception lie predominantly where the liberty of the individual compromises the liberty of another individual (see J.S. Mill's *On Liberty* for a classical analysis of liberty). The individualist notion of citizenship has recourse to philanthropy and the benevolence that has characterized much countryside access provision in the past, notionally to achieve 'social' objectives. The Liberal version of citizenship leaves philanthropy and altruism as the remedies for disparities in conditions and access to opportunities – not just in spatial terms (Gyford, 1991; Dahrendorf, 1979). Citizenship construction in terms of countryside access has in the past exhibited Liberal characteristics. Rights of access gained since the 1949 National Parks and Access to the Countryside Act and in subsequent legislation or policy have partially ameliorated a distribution of rights, which has favoured landowners.

Whilst a relative equilibrium may have existed under the 'benevolent' landowner (Newby *et al.*, 1978), the development of market-oriented mechanisms over countryside goods removes the logic of philanthropic *de facto* access provision over land which could provide income. It is commodification and monetization which prepare the way for countryside access to become a market commodity. This would effectively create a multi-tiered system of access dependent on the ability to pay. The Countryside Stewardship scheme sets precedents by unpacking costs for various countryside access elements and places money values on them (Countryside Commission, 1994b). Charging for access provision has to become politically acceptable and therefore needs to provide legitimation for extracting revenue from an activity previously unpriced under another means of transfer. Is it necessary for the community or enough of the community (perhaps in terms of power holders or in terms of a simple majority) to accept such change? This point leads to another set of issues concerning the rights to resist or protest against changes in other rights, which cannot be fully addressed here. It is worth noting, however, that the provisions of the Criminal Justice and Public Order Act 1994 may have serious consequences for certain rights, in particular those that could be characterized as 'jostle rights', that is to say, rights that are necessary for the movement along any rights continuums to take place or rights that enable protest over rights transfers to take place. When charting this against a Marshallian typology of rights, we can see that alterations in these particular 'civil' rights have knock-on effects over 'political' and 'social' rights and the defence of those rights. The concept of citizen-ship is a relatively amorphous one; as acknowledged above, rights are contingent in nature. This mutability is one of the strengths of citizenship rights within a democracy. In order that such contingent rights are not hegemonized, it is important that such 'jostle rights' remain as an integral part of any construction of citizenship.

It is the Communitarian notion of citizenship that has recently been associated with a New Left vision for the UK (Phillips, 1994). This Communitarian view (Van Gunsteren, 1994; Mouffe, 1993), or the social/political model of citizenship (Gyford, 1991), emphasizes the role of community membership and sees the individual as being derived from that Communitarian citizenship. The community lives within a code in this instance; whilst this code will necessarily be amended over time, it theoretically provides the framework for re-producing 'successful' or 'acceptable' citizens. The model is dependent on the conscious creation (and recreation) of a community. In contemporary society this may be a contradictory position. Heater (1990; p. 285) realizes that citizenship as an ideal is 'in danger of being torn asunder ... As more and more diverse interests identify particular elements for their doctrinal and practical needs ... under the strain of these centrifugal forces, citizenship as a total ideal may be threatened with disintegration'. The construction of Communitarian citizenship is also rendered problematic by the diverse nature of a culturally frag-mented society. If it is accepted that a common basis for citizenship could be acceptable for all, with diverse opinions and views integrated, this would be a fundamental reconstructive step. Rights claims could be negotiated in addition to a common code resulting in a society tenta-tively labelled as 'Liberal socialist' (Mouffe, 1993, p. 84) or in Van Gunsteren's view a 'neo-republican' society (1994, p. 46).

There is a multiplicity of combinations of rights and responsibilities that could be legitimated at any particular time or in any particular place. It is land, capital and the power accruing to the holders of these assets that impact on the effectiveness of rights systems. It is striking that several contradictions are found in political policy stances. The present government's 'back to basics' idea seems *prima facie* to return to a Communitarian 'code' developed within 'civil' society. This highlights another possible contradiction in present political policies impacting directly or indirectly on land use. Typologies of citizenship rights when applied to the full range of British rights show tensions between the categories of rights and between the groups who hold those rights. It is obvious that the mantle of citizen is notionally shared; the same ability to exercise or enjoy rights is not equally shared. When placed alongside the Marshallian definition of citizenship, it is clear that there is not equality in terms of rights and duties, liberties and constraints and powers and responsibilities. The fragmentation of contemporary culture means that any construction of citizenship would have difficulty in satiating all citizen rights claims. The Liberal construction of citizenship is one which attempts narrowly to define acceptable, proper or good citizens' behaviour (Ravenscroft, 1993). This Liberal construction of citizenship is augmented by the 1994 Criminal Justice and Public Order Act, Part V (and has at least one antecedent in the 1986 Public Order Act), in which 'deviant' citizens such as roads protesters, hunt saboteurs, ravers or travellers are penalized because of actions that transgress the code of responsibilities, duties or constraints prescribed by the state. In relation to countryside access, the Act cannot distinguish between individuals; thus anyone using the countryside may be construed as transgressing certain sections of this law.

The Consumer–Citizen

It is the development of access rights as private property rights, with prices attached to those private rights, that signify the move away from citizens' rights of access to consumer rights of access. The consideration of citizenship and the relationship between citizens and the market is important. Where the market interfaces with citizenship and where tensions may arise in terms of access provision is of importance within this essay. The main point to consider is the difference between the consumer and the citizen – a change in emphasis that a monetized access system may herald. This shift from citizen to consumer, or to the Liberal individual citizen, is a crucial difference noted by many writers (Gyford, 1991; Ravenscroft, 1993; and Lowe, Clark and Cox, 1991, p. 4):

> Mensuration of consumer preferences cannot denote the social value of something. The consumer reacts to the market mechanism, and the citizen exercises rights through the political system. To confuse the two is to make a category mistake.

This conception of citizenship seems similar to one envisaged by the present government, particularly in terms of the Liberal notion of property rights and the neo-Liberal political philosophy of the present and immediate past administrations. To quote from Ravenscroft (1993, p. 33):

> This divisive construction of a new citizenship, with material wealth and freedom available to the 'good' citizen at the expense of the deprivation, rejection and suppression of the 'deviant' citizen is at the centre of a new political order where choice has been replaced by means and where the classless paradigm envisaged by John Major will be a classlessness of constructed omission.

The notion that a consumer is not a citizen or vice versa is a substantive point in this discussion. The above quotations illustrate the notion that in some way the consumer cannot act as a citizen within a political context but, paradoxically, this consumer–citizen is a construction defined politically. It is acknowledged that the roles of consumer and of citizen are not mutually exclusive. The construction and applicability of notions of citizenship or consumer are at issue; where, when, and why individuals are called upon to act as consumers or citizens in particular situations and how those roles in particular situations are justified or legitimated are necessary questions. Citizenship construction is a role that government undertakes, either as an acknowledged part of political policy or, more obliquely, as a result of policy that unwittingly helps construct citizenship. As Van Gunsteren acknowledges (1994, p. 46):

> Individuals are not naturally given, but socially formed. The republic does not simply leave the 'reproduction' of citizens to existing communities, but verifies whether the social formation enjoined by those communities allows for admission to citizenship. Where this is not the case or where the people lack the formative support of the community, the government interferes. The task of reproducing citizens is implied in every government action. Every government action can and may be examined in terms of its effect on [the reproduction of] citizenship, just as we now judge nearly all government action in terms of its effect on the financial deficit.

Under the Liberal conception of citizenship, the market mechanism is the predominant method of procurement of a citizen right. In order to exercise a notional right, a contract of exchange needs to be entered into by all parties. The medium of exchange in this construction is normally money and the 'good' being exchanged – access – can then be expressed, as a property right, a consumer right and a citizen right. A property right is a citizenship right under the present structure of citizenship. Under this structure private property rights are defended against other citizen right claims. This, as Lowe, Clark and Cox (1991) point out, renders exchange of rights through the political system problematic. Once entrenched, markets and 'values' are installed as the legitimate mode of regulation and transaction. Policies which operate according to market criteria have social ramifications for the community (of which the construction of citizenship is putatively there to protect), as Van Gunsteren points out, 'a community that is merely expedient is not a community' (1994, p. 41); the implication is that 'community' is a complex and often intangible construct exhibiting features such as altruism, compassion, helpfulness and identification with place. By inference here the composite phrase would be: 'a citizenship that is merely expedient is not a citizenship'. Expediency is one of the key words of the free market. The issue of the effects of markets on citizenship and community therefore concerns the expediency of the market and the 'value' of 'community' at local, national and even international levels of construction (for example, the role of the European Union in constructing a European citizenship). The notion of citizenship and of community is one that is built on complex and sometimes fragile social, economic and historical foundations. The market has rationalized these relationship, and 'value' in this sense is based on the willingness to pay for goods and services. How community is valued, and by association, how various conceptions of citizenship are valued, is a notion that has been subject to some scrutiny. For example, Sagoff (1988) distinguishes a logical difference in consumer and citizen preferences. When an individual lodges a preference as a consumer, the community-regarding values that the individual may hold are set aside in order to ensure that the individual's personal interests are pursued. Community-regarding values are put aside in this situation even though the individual is part of the community. Sagoff suggests that those values should be reflected in social regulation, rather than through individual preferences that are commonly valued through the market. Presently, the Countryside Stewardship scheme is a form of such social regulation. It should be recognized that the role of private property rights and the shadow pricing of access significantly blurs the interests that are notionally and actually served by such a policy.

Countryside Stewardship as Access Payment Scheme

The investigation of new policies designed *prima facie* to extend countryside access, known collectively as Access Payment Schemes, is where this chapter relates to policy and practice in countryside planning. These schemes, policies or programmes are those which involve landowners being paid grants in order to provide access land (in addition to other environmental benefits such as conservation of landscape features and habitats, or farming in more environmentally sensitive ways). They include Environmentally Sensitive Areas, the Countryside Premium Scheme, the Farm Woodland Scheme and the Countryside Stewardship Scheme (Countryside Commission, 1993a, 1994a).

Unsurprisingly, the Agriculture Act of 1986 was tentative in its development of Liberal policy in the countryside. Corporatism has been a feature in the agricultural industry since state involvement in agriculture. It was the Agriculture Act that formally introduced the policies designed to encourage alternative land use (other than agriculture) in the countryside, ostensibly to steer land use around to address market demands and thus reduce outputs of food and fibre. These policies were designed to encourage diversification, satiate claims from the environmental lobby and 'improve' levels of public access to land. Recreation in the countryside was an obvious target activity for policies encouraging diversification/extensification in agricultural land use.

The Countryside Stewardship Scheme (CSS) provides an example of new 'regulation of rural change' and of 'the increasing role of such areas as consumption spaces' (Countryside Commission, 1994b, 1993a). It is used to exemplify the notions of citizenship constructions and rights transfer noted above. As part of the scheme, one-fifth of the land under the CSS has been opened for access; 2100 access agreements were made in 1991 and 1300 in 1992, with the Countryside Commission apparently filling their targets for scheme entrants in 1993. It is clear that, year on year, a substantial acreage has been brought into the CSS, although confirmation of the area under access agreement is problematic at present. Reports estimate that 30,000 acres and 350 miles of linear routes had been designated by October 1993 (Pond, 1993). The scheme is set to expand, with the Ministry of Agriculture, Fisheries and Food taking over its administration from the Countryside Commission in 1996. One of the possible effects of paying for access in this way is to polarize rights of access on the ground. It has been suggested (Pond, 1993) that areas of land now under the Access Payment schemes had already been used for *de facto* access prior to their designation as access areas under those schemes. An example in practice of a problem arising from the introduction of payment schemes would be where a landowner had historically allowed *de facto* access on his or her land. If the land is accepted as land to be operated as designated access land under one of the payment schemes, the landowner is paid for previously free access and the areas of land not covered under the payment schemes would not be available for public access. This results in a net loss of public access and an increase in public expenditure. Importantly, the institutionalization of access in this scenario results in rights becoming formalized, with access becoming delineated. Once rights are rationalized in this way with pricing attached, access as a right becomes more firmly entrenched as a private property right. This is clearly one area where further research needs to be conducted in order to investigate the impact of payment scheme access land on *de facto* access land.

In the past, access policy has lacked effective strategic planning (Nuffield Commission, 1986). Much planning for recreation has been constrained by land availability and finance. Amongst the concerns with Access Payment schemes is a view that they continue the trend that state-funded access land may not be located in places of need, for instance near settlements; secondly, that the actual motivation for their development is linked with other potentially conflicting objectives such as agricultural support. Some new policy initiatives (such as Community Forests and Pocket Parks) aim to redress this locational deficit, but their success is not yet known. The issues of accessibility, accountability and futurity are not far removed from the issue of the provision of access and the distribution of rights and are therefore important in the context of policy planning and implementation. Whilst looking at the impact that these payment schemes have in any practical sense, through enhancing the quantity of countryside access available, other questions need to be asked: *where* is the new access? *what* was the status of the land before the scheme? *how* much does it cost? Only after adequately analysing the answers to those questions will we know if the schemes are justifiable transfers of rights and will we be able to analyse the means by which these types of policies are legitimated. Crucially, the effect on rights and rights claims is the issue of concern; the entrenchment of one particular conception of citizenship in respect of access to land would be a development requiring explicit justification.

Legislation and policy initiatives involving countryside access have left a system of access provision that is piecemeal and largely incomprehensible to the public (Blunden and Curry, 1990). The means of access provision varies, as does the associated exercise of power from the state, individuals and interests groups. Over time access provision has been delivered within a grey area of multi-layered policy and it rests, to a large extent, on the benevolence of individual rights holders. This situation lacks clarity and distorts the effectiveness of access policy and the meaningful measurement of demand for access. This situation does not equate to models of Liberal or Communitarian citizenship. The present access situation is relatively fluid, allowing a variety of rights claims to be expressed and variously accepted as legitimate. This allows for movement, in either direction, towards Communitarian citizenship and Liberal citizenship constructions. The Liberal construction of citizenship necessitates the assimilation of the citizen, where assimilation involves the citizen being submerged into the society at the expense of their own individual characteristics or views. The Communitarian construction *prima facie* integrates the citizen, where this integration involves more tolerance of difference. Paradoxically, the rhetoric of the Conservative Party stresses the role and importance of the individual while allowing restricted individuality. New access policies seem to represent a move towards Liberal capitalist rationalization – a further 'enclosure' of enclosed land in terms of rights – and the narrowing but possible clarification of acceptable and unacceptable, of what is 'right' and 'wrong'. This fits into the construction of Liberal citizenship, which in the instance of access as commodity would hegemonize access rights to those presently holding land as unassailable (and priced) private property rights. This avenue, if followed, leads to black and white outcomes where relatively clearcut rights are eminent. Somewhere along the continuum (the grey scale in this metaphor), property rights and access rights have been transferred, claimed, won and lost. Neo-Liberal philosophy is reliant on the market to clarify demand, to provide black and white scenarios as developed under the *laissez-faire* conception of political economy of the eighteenth and nineteenth centuries.

Conclusion

The policies presently being introduced in countryside planning, which have been developed to encourage alternative land use in the countryside, provide evidence of a shift towards shadow pricing policies for agriculture, whilst maintaining the welfare of landowners and farmers, through state subsidized policy. Payment schemes may represent the first of two complementary thrusts of policy in terms of a construction of Liberal citizenship. The Access Payment Schemes have the effect of preparing monetized values for countryside access, thus enabling individual preferences to be made via the market, and coinciding with a Liberal citizenship. The second policy thrust is Section V of the Criminal Justice and Public Order Act 1994, which restricts freedom of movement and criminalizes trespass. Contemporary discussions of rights are especially pertinent with the political furore caused by the

Criminal Justice and Public Order Act. This legislation represents an attempt to further hegemonize rights distributions. The Act effectively helps stabilize a new Liberal construction of citizenship. It reinforces and extends protection of private property rights against those express-ing community-regarding values and asserting rights claims, which may be legitimated under a differing construction of citizenship. It remains to be seen how the Act will be implemented (by the police and the courts) and how rights – not only in terms of access – will be affected. The Act provides powers to the police and landowners to arrest people exercising *de facto* rights or those who transgress the construction of citizenship envisaged by John Major.

There are four phenomena identified in this chapter, which, when viewed together, indicate a significant movement towards a particular political project: namely, the delineation of rights into a 'rationalized' public/private dichotomy, the construction of Liberal 'consumer–citizens', the development of market-oriented access payment schemes, and the Criminal Justice and Public Order Act 1994. These develop-ments represent a process, whether intentional or unwitting, in con-structing citizens and scenarios that emphasize the individual, the market, the sanctity of liberal notions of private property rights and the curtailment of rights of protest that would conflict with those Liberal constructions. The impact of these constructions of rights and responsi-bilities in the future is debatable. It is clear that research into the initial impacts of schemes such as the Countryside Stewardship Scheme is required, especially in relation to long-term and widely focused issues of rights relationships and citizenship in the countryside.

In the context of party politics, the Labour and Conservative parties are as far apart as ever in policy and theoretical terms over countryside access and its regulation. This highlights the intensely political nature of countryside access, touching on the interface between individual rights and community interests and between the dual, yet sometimes conflicting status of the land as both site of consumption and of production and its status as economic and social good. In 1884, James Bryce introduced his first Bill for a 'right to roam' over mountain moor and heath (Blunden and Curry, 1990). The Labour Party, if elected, plan to table a John Smith Memorial Bill aimed at introducing the same measure that Bryce attempted (Planning Week, 1994).

Part II

Culture

6

'Bradford-on-Avon but Shell on the Road': The Heyday of Motor Touring through Britain's Countryside

BARBARA ROSCOE

The title of this chapter was taken from an advertisement originally used by Shell-Mex and BP Ltd in the 1930s, although it was also used in the 1950s.[1] The chapter itself concentrates on the period between 1950 and 1970, when motor-touring advertising was reaching a peak. However, because Edward Bawden's drawing seemed to encapsulate so clearly the (continuing) way in which oil companies were appropriating representations of Britain and its landscapes to market their products, I was unable to resist using it as a shorthand example of the genre. In this advertisement, one of a series in a similar vein, shire horses are humorously used to furnish Shell's modern transport products with a traditional pedigree. Such horses, apart from their image as reliable and tireless workers, are a common symbol from the period of Victorian high agriculture and, as such, embody a quintessential part of England's heritage, as imagined in the twentieth century. At the same time, the trademark of Shell is balanced, and thus linked, with an English place name. These two advertising constructs recur with increasing complexity throughout the middle years of this century.

The 1950s and 1960s were the first decades of mass motor touring in Britain. This was primarily encouraged by the growth in hire purchase and the fall in the real price of cars. Motor cars had ceased to be an upper-class luxury and were becoming instead an affordable commodity. Car ownership increased from just under four million in 1956 to approximately eleven and a quarter million by 1969 (Plowden, 1971). Book sponsorship, and other advertising by the major petroleum companies in these decades, sought to exploit the economic boom. The 1960s provided a further reason for the development of motor touring: the construction of a British motorway network. By 1960, 125 miles of motorway had been completed in Britain, principally comprising the M1 from London to Coventry. A further 180 miles were projected for completion in 1961, and development continued throughout the decade. It is worth remembering that, before the opening of that first stretch of the M1, it took a heavy goods vehicle an average of seven hours to complete the journey between London and Birmingham. As the motorway network progressed, it became increasingly easy for motorists to access formerly remote areas of Britain within a relatively short space of time (Shell-Mex and BP Ltd, 1961, pp. 3–5).

By the mid-1960s, motor touring and the British countryside had become inextricably linked in the minds of most people. Earlier tourists were attracted to venture into the rural landscapes of Britain by railway posters and the advertising of charabanc trips by coach companies, but since the 1960s the motor car has dominated the accessing the countryside. According to the results of the recently published survey of United Kingdom Day Visits by the Countryside Commission, half of all visits to the countryside in the summer of 1993 were made by car, amounting to some 295 million (Countryside Commission, 1994c, p. 1).

Coinciding with this growth in motor touring was a distinct flourishing of natural history and countryside-based advertising (in the form of posters, books and television programmes) sponsored by oil companies. The reasons for this are obvious, and were well understood by the marketing teams in these companies. If motorists could be shown attractive representations of the countryside and its natural history, then they were likely to wish to observe them at first hand. The more they were encouraged to tour in this fashion, naturally the greater the volume of petrol sold (Shell-Mex and BP Ltd, 1964a). Of the companies involved in this publishing and advertising expansion, one of the foremost was the joint Shell-Mex and BP marketing company, set up in 1932 and active until 1975, when cut-price petrol wars forced a parting of the ways between the two companies. Another was National Benzole, which, although taken over by Shell-Mex in 1957, retained a separate trading identity and produced its own distinctive 'National Heritage' volumes. BP also published a separate list of paperback touring guides in the 1960s.

In conjunction with advertising their products, Shell-Mex/BP Ltd also sponsored the arts, commissioning painters such as John Nash, Rowland Hilder and S.R. Badmin to produce images of British scenery and natural history. Figure 6.1 shows Stanley Badmin's[2] representation of Derbyshire, one of the 'Shell counties' series of paintings. In it two of the county's well-known sons are commemorated: Charles Cotton, who wrote the poem *The Wonders of the Peake*, and Izaak Walton, to whose book *The Compleat Angler*, Cotton contributed the second part. Both literary allusions refer back to a seventeenth-century tradition of rural recreation. The books are set against a landscape that combines Haddon Hall, traditional limestone walling and grouse moors with a suggestion of smoky Sheffield in the distance. The foreground is framed by the mouth of a cave and displays, among other things, a Derby porcelain shepherdess, some lead ore and a Bakewell tart, resonant of nineteenth-century interpretations of industrial images of Derbyshire painted by Joseph Wright (Daniels, 1993, pp. 43–79). The 'counties paintings', commissioned between 1958 and 1963, were originally used in advertising wall charts, which Shell also sent to all schools throughout the UK.

Jack Beddington, Publicity Manager for Shell-Mex/BP Ltd, saw the company's role not only as an educator of the British public about its local landscape and history, but also as a channel through which the public could become familiar with modern movements in art and design. As a commercial patron, Beddington believed that Shell's

Figure 6.1 'Shell Counties' painting of Derbyshire by Stanley Roy Badmin (© Shell-Mex and BP Co Ltd)

position was in the very forefront of mass reproduction of modern art. Gone was the day of the grand private patron, he believed; it was to be replaced by 'collective patronage', where control had passed 'from the independent individual to the State or semi-public corporation' (Beddington, 1938, pp. 82–7). The main differences as Beddington saw them were, firstly, that 'commercial' or 'collective patronage' meant that art and design were reaching a mass market, and, secondly, that what was being produced as art was dictated by the aesthetics and needs of a commercial organization.

'Art in Advertising' exhibitions, which included the 'counties paintings' and natural history subjects that had been used in various corporate publications, were sponsored by Shell and held at art galleries throughout the country during the 1960s. Featured artists were requested to carry out the opening ceremonies. In March 1964, Rowland Hilder opened one such exhibition at Worthing Art Gallery. The catalogue for this exhibition provides an insight into Shell's advertising philosophy: in it Robert Byron (one of Shell's authors) states:

> A natural extension of this policy of responsible publicity is to bring the scenic beauties of England and Scotland to people's notice by means of posters. This can be done in two ways: either by depicting in as matter-of-fact terms as possible the hackneyed incidents and localities which holiday makers are traditionally supposed to enjoy; or by presupposing sufficient pleasure in beauty on the part of the public to present it with pictures in which the artist conveys to his audience not merely the physical joys of paddling or sunbathing, but something of the spirit of the landscape . . . If this will sell petrol, it is this which, at the same time, none but the true artist can achieve. Advertising can thus be brought to improve, rather than obstruct, the public taste. (Shell-Mex and BP Ltd, 1964a; Byron, 1964)

It is clear that Shell believed it had a didactic role in relation to the nation's aesthetic values, and a somewhat more sophisticated advertising approach than the more demotic forms of publicity. At the same time, it was not only forging strong links between the beauties of nature and their appreciation by way of motor touring, but also fostering a particular vision of Britain. Churches and stately homes often featured in these paintings, although factory skylines and uncultivated landscapes were not ignored. The combination of local architecture, cultural and natural history and cultivated landscape were common elements in most of the 'county paintings'. These generally placed cultural artefacts and examples of local flora and fauna in the foreground, and amalgamated what the artist and sponsors considered were representative local landscape features in the background. I believe we owe some of today's acceptance of what constitutes a desirable 'landscape' through which to motor or to visit, to the strong images presented by Shell at this time. Images of the landscape, particularly rural ones, continue to be potent selling agents and have also become closely affiliated to definitions of British regional and national identity (Daniels, 1993; Matless, 1990).

The 'counties paintings' were accompanied by a map and text when used on advertising wall charts. These aimed to provide a 'key to the countryside'. An example of this reassuring approach to understanding the countryside can be seen in the wall chart for Cambridgeshire (see Figure 6.2), a painting undertaken by the well-known East Anglian artist and illustrator, John Nash, which depicts a distant Ely Cathedral, King's College Chapel Cambridge, and a representative fen landscape complete with windmill and dyke. A strong natural history component is evident in the foreground. By numbering some of the painting's elements on the map and in the text, the would-be tourist is guided around the features that the artist has chosen. For example, a numbered drawing of King's College Chapel is suitably placed within the borders of Cambridgeshire. Other items of a more symbolic nature, such as the windmill, are also numbered and placed on the map, although they are not linked to a particular place. At the same time, the brass rubbing of Sir Roger de Trumpington, which does exist in a particular place, is treated in the same fashion as the windmill. Representative and actual landscape features are therefore given the same weight. As a result, both symbolic and actual landscape elements serve to influence people's ideas on the kind of landscape they would expect to see in a specific part of the country. This in turn could dictate the places which tourist authorities decided to develop or conserve. The reflexive character of this process is not always recognized.

Such 'guiding' posters draw upon the learning methods of field studies and Land Utilisation Surveys from the 1930s, approaches which were still being employed in schools in the 1960s, and with which motorists in *their* thirties would have been familiar (Stamp, 1948). Shell was providing the expanding new generation of motorists with an ordered and thus predictable way of accessing the countryside.

The keys which guided the viewer around the motoring landscape were framed by Shell's advertising slogan: 'You can be sure of Shell – The key to the countryside'. This slogan served a dual purpose, putting forward not only the painting as the key to intellectual access of the

Figure 6.2   Wall-chart *Shell Guide to Cambridgeshire*, showing the numbered elements in the text and on the map. Paintng by John Nash (© Shell-Mex and BP Co Ltd)

countryside, but also Shell petrol as the key which physically opened the door to its appreciation.

Shell-Mex and BP Ltd also published a wide selection of books about the countryside during the 1950s and 1960s: the range of publications which usually springs to mind is that of the 'County Guides'. These hardback books were first commissioned in the 1930s, following an idea submitted to Shell by John Betjeman, who was thereafter employed as their editor. They gave Betjeman and his friend, the artist John Piper, the opportunity to indulge in their favourite pastime, that of driving round the countryside looking at villages, and in particular the vernacular architecture to be found there. The guides continued to be published, with a short break for World War II, until the 1980s, during which time John Piper took over as sole editor. However, these somewhat idiosyncratic guides were not designed for a mass audience – a typical print run would only have been around 10,000 copies. To discover the more popular end of the Shell motor-touring market in the 1960s, we must look at the series called the 'Shilling Guides', and the compendium volume which gathered together all the 'Shilling Guides' to form *The Shell and BP Guide to Britain* (Boumphrey, 1964). A million copies of the 'Shilling Guides' were sold in the first sixteen months of issue beginning in 1963, and 50,000 copies of the *Shell and BP Guide to Britain* were sold within ten months of its publication in 1964. These were, therefore, reaching about 13 per cent of the car-owning public, and as such would have had an appreciable impact upon what and where the motor tourists were visiting (Shell-Mex and BP Ltd, 1964b, p. 16; Shell-Mex and BP Ltd, 1964c, p. 8; Plowden, 1971, p. 482).

The principle behind the 'Shilling Guides', according to their publishers, was to provide 'a modern, reliable, well illustrated and accurate motoring guide',[3] in the cheapest and handiest form, which would cover the whole country. The last point is significant, for the hardback series of Shell 'County Guides' never did get to the point when every county had been described. The selection of counties covered reflected the personal choice of the editors and Shell's publicity department, and had no other clear geographical logic.

The cover designs of the 'Shilling Guides' were also taken from the original Shell 'counties paintings', and inside the front cover of each guide a shorter version of the wall chart key was reproduced, although this time without the map. Figure 6.3 shows the cover of the Berkshire 'Shilling Guide' (Boumphrey, 1963), which was painted by Barbara Jones, then a well-known mural artist. Apart from constructing specific cultural landscapes, this, and many of the other 'counties paintings', had the effect of telescoping both natural and cultural landscape features into a small area. For example, it would not be possible for the motorist to see both Windsor Castle and the atomic research centre at Harwell at the same time, as is shown in this landscape. One of the implications of this was that all the places were within easy reach of each other, thereby developing a reassuring but false sense of their accessibility. Perhaps another was that motorists were being encouraged to visit as many places as possible whilst out on their tours. The 'Shilling Guides' were intended to be sold locally through Shell or BP Service Stations in the relevant counties, with a selection of guides for adjoining counties also being available. *The Shell and BP Guide to Britain* was, however, sold through bookshops.

The text of the 'Shilling Guides' consisted of a short introduction to the county or counties involved, usually containing a brief description of the history, geography, geology, buildings and settlements of the region. A road map and a gazeteer followed, and all was interspersed with black-and-white photographs of both buildings and views which were considered of interest. The Berkshire guide, for example, began with a photograph of an Elizabethan manor house and included a view

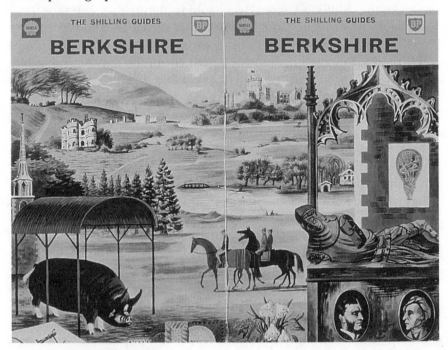

Figure 6.3   Cover of the *Shilling Guide for Berkshire.* Painting by Barbara Jones
(© Shell-Mex and BP Co Ltd)

of the White Horse near Uffington. Details of architectural interest were often included, a practice probably inherited by the editor, Geoffrey Boumphrey, from the Johns (both Betjeman and Piper), who had a passion for this subject. The entries in the gazeteer unfailingly centred around the church or cathedral of each location, again probably a legacy from John Betjeman, who, as he compiled some of the early hardback guides, stated 'We always thought looking at a village meant looking at the church' (Ingrams and Piper, 1983, p. 47). The style and content of the 'Shilling Guides' were, therefore, developed from a very personal and often idiosyncratic perspective.

Shell-Mex/BP also sponsored a series of television programmes as part of its promotion of motor touring in Britain. In 1955, Independent Television broadcast a series of 26 programmes on Friday evenings, featuring such places as Mereworth Castle in Kent and the gardens and house at Stourhead in Wiltshire. The programmes were narrated by John Betjeman (in his unique style) and were produced in conjunction with the Institute of Contemporary Arts. A range of pamphlets was issued to accompany them, including maps detailing the location of each place of interest. The films lasted about two and a half minutes, each of them beginning with the Shell logo opening up to a view motorists would see when driving down a country lane. This was a pioneering venture in the use of indirect television advertising. It is difficult to assess its impact, but the combination of a celebrated public figure with what was, at the time, a fast emerging communications medium would certainly have made an impact on those fortunate enough to have access to a television, many of whom would, of course, also be those able to run a motor car.

The 1960s Shell list of publications also included *The Shell Nature Book* (Grigson and Fisher, 1964), first published in 1964, which set out to describe the seasons through a series of paintings and keys covering everything from 'The Flowers of the Countryside' to 'Fossils, Insects and Reptiles'. The illustrations in this book often depicted iconic regional landscapes, such as the view of a Scottish Highland croft in September, painted by Maurice Wilson in collaboration with Rowland Hilder. Accompanying numbered keys and text were strongly reminiscent of the 'counties' wall charts and sought to attract the budding natural historian not only to visit but to anticipate a particular kind of landscape. Despite being presented as a book of 'nature', much of the material showed highly cultivated landscapes, including ornamental parklands, with the stately home just out of view. This was a legacy from the 1930s, when eighteenth-century parkland landscapes were drawn

Figure 6.4   Publicity for Shell *Shilling Guides* aimed at Shell and BP dealers, showing the range of marketing approaches (BP Archive Reference B2632, © Shell-Mex and BP Co Ltd)

upon to inform the inter-war, Modernist, planning aesthetic of order and improvement (McCallum, 1945).

Shell-Mex/BP Ltd's marketing strategy appears to have been to make wide use of the same material in a number of different media (see Figure 6.4). The power of such a strategy must have been considerable, not only upon the success of the Shell and BP product range, but also in terms of the lasting images of Britain with which it identified itself. The countryside in this advertising was (often) seen as a map of the past. This 'heritage' landscape, in an extension of the words of David Lowenthal (1985), is 'a focus of personal and national identity and a bulwark against massive and distressing change'. In other words, visiting 'our national heritage' is a way to retain our links with the past and reaffirm our national identity. It is not surprising that such books and images, and the places picked out as destinations for the touring motorist, have come to constitute such a lasting part of our culture.

At the same time, we should be aware of how idiosyncratic many of these publications, programmes and posters were, sometimes themselves drawing on even earlier ways of approaching the countryside, which were just as individual and culturally loaded. Shell-Mex/BP, with its educational, ordered and highly personal stance towards the countryside and modern artistic representations of it, demonstrates how advertising constructed visions of Britain at a key moment in the history of changing access to the countryside.

Notes

[1] 'Bradford-on-Avon but Shell on the Road' was originally published in the *Wiltshire Shell Guide* (April 1935: Architectural Press) edited by Robert Byron (General Editor John Betjeman). It was later used in a revised edition of *Wiltshire Shell Guide* by David Verey (1956: Faber and Faber).

[2] Stanley Roy Badmin (born 1906) was a watercolourist, lithographer and engraver with a special interest in the English countryside and in portraying English village life and architecture. He also illustrated the *Shell Guide to Trees and Shrubs*.

[3] Taken from the proposal for the 'county booklets' prepared by the publishers George Rainbird Ltd (no date).

7

Educated Access: Interpreting Forestry Commission Forest Park Guides

GEORGE REVILL AND CHARLES WATKINS

Introduction

From its inception in 1919 the Forestry Commission produced uncompromisingly commercial landscapes. Large-scale afforestation of previously open moorland and heath resulted in industrial-scale landscapes that were modern, regular, efficient and utilitarian. Within a few years these new productive landscapes began to be widely criticized. Two criticisms received a lot of support: first, the loss of public access over open moorland which had been afforested; and second, the change from a 'wilderness' landscape to a landscape all too consciously managed. The pre-war controversy over afforestation reached a peak with proposals to afforest parts of the Lake District (Symonds, 1936). It was claimed that 'public access to the open fells is endangered' (p. 51) and that the proposed afforestation valued 'the profits of commercial timber more than health and beauty' (p. 16). The Forestry Commissioners eventually reached a compromise with the Council for the Preservation of Rural England (CPRE) and undertook not to afforest the central section of the Lake District. It is within this broad debate between afforestation, public access and landscape that we need to set the invention of National Forest Parks and the publication of the Guides to these Parks.

The Idea of National Forest Parks

The Forestry Commission had only been established for ten years when the Addison Committee was set up in 1929 to examine the feasibility of national parks and improving public recreation in the countryside

(MacEwen and MacEwen, 1982). The Forestry Commission representative on the Committee was Sir John Stirling-Maxwell, a Forestry Commissioner who later became Chairman (1930–32). Forestry Commission internal reports show that there was concern about the potential conflict between increased public access and the preservation of flora and fauna. It was felt, for example, that:

> the erection of Hutment camps around the Forest of Dean might tend to destroy the amenities of the neighbourhood and the process might be completed by ill-disciplined visitors, charabanc parties etc; the institution of a camp for children might imperil a Bird Sanctuary, and so on. (Public Record Office (PRO) F18 162 Forestry Commission Mimeograph 1929)

This mimeograph goes on to report on Lord Bledisloe's ideas for National Parks 'where people of all walks of life can enjoy under proper protection and with reasonable comfort attractive natural surroundings'. Bledisloe's proposals included 'permanent camps provided with water and sanitation, refreshment and entertainment, bungalows, car parks, and, if possible, open air swimming baths, bowling greens, tennis courts etc.'

The National Parks Committee (Addison Report) reported in 1931 and supported the idea of National Parks, although no clear mechanism for their establishment was introduced. The idea of National Parks continued to be debated throughout the 1930s. In 1934 Peter Thomsen, in a paper to the British Association at Aberdeen, suggested that there should be a threefold approach to establishing National Parks (Thomsen 1934). First, areas that were to become National Parks should be scheduled and in those areas 'development' should be 'vetoed'. This was to include the prohibition of 'the cutting of timber, especially old timber'. Second, limited access in the form of 'rest houses' and 'camp sites' should be established; and finally, the government would arrange 'full possession upon purchase' of the National Parks. A copy of Thomsen's paper was read by Sir George Courthope, who sent a copy to Sir Roy Robinson, Chairman (1932–52) of the Forestry Commission, in October 1934:

> Have you seen the enclosed effusion about National Parks? I am sure that you agree that wild schemes of this kind must be nipped in the bud. With this end in view, do you think it would be a good thing to push forward your proposals for recreational facilities in connexion with our forests? (PRO F18 162)

George Loyd Courthope, later first Baron of Whiligh (1877–1955), was an influential landowner and spoke for the Forestry Commissioners in Parliament (Commissioner, 1928–48). He was Unionist MP for Rye (1906–45) and was president or chairman of several agricultural and forestry organizations. His comments demonstrate the close organizational links between private landowners and the Commission, and also show the extent to which both the state-run Commission and private landowners felt threatened by the possible establishment of National Parks, which could limit large-scale afforestation and inhibit the management of established woodland for commercial purposes. It is clear that the Forestry Commissioners were not opposed to the idea of public access, but they and the landowners who supported them were very much opposed to the formation of National Parks run by bodies that would interfere with traditional land management and imperil the large-scale conversion of unproductive land to productive woodland.

In March 1935, a few months after Sir George Courthope wrote to Sir Roy Robinson about 'pushing forward' with 'recreational facilities', the Forestry Commissioners appointed a committee 'to advise how the surplus and unplantable land' on Forestry Commission property in Argyll might be 'put to a use of a public character'. This committee was known as the National Forest Park Committee and its report was published later in 1935 (Forestry Commission, 1935). The Commissioners met representatives of youth hostelling and other associations and societies. The hundred square miles of largely unplantable moorland under consideration was felt ideal for 'the rambler, whose main object is to get into the country and away from motor traffic' (p. 3). Because of the high rainfall it was felt that ramblers would prefer using huts rather than tents. Considerable emphasis was placed on the need to control the behaviour of visitors. Responsible organizations such as the Scottish Association of Boys' Clubs and the Camping Club of Great Britain would enforce bylaws so that 'decent behaviour' could be encouraged. An existing camping site was 'regarded in the neighbourhood as a nuisance' (p. 3) and it was felt that 'the interests of existing house owners' (p. 4) should be taken into account. A model set of bylaws with twelve clauses was presented in the report. It was also noted that the risk of damage could be reduced by the careful design of paths, which should 'pass to the uplands through the afforested lands by easy gradients. This would have the effect of keeping people from trespassing on or causing damage to plantations'.

The Report recommended the establishment of a National Forest Park and that the government should provide £5000 for this purpose, which should not come from the Forestry Fund. It was noted that 'campers should in every case be charged a fee to cover the expenses of the services provided' and the intention was to reclaim this expenditure and the costs of supervision from the users (p. 6). The Committee were keen to point out that the term National Forest Park was 'deliberately intended to denote something different from a National Park as described in the Report of the National Park Committee (p. 2).

The continuing concern of the likely effects of the establishment of National Parks on the ability of the Forestry Commission to afforest land and manage woodland is indicated by an undated internal report written by Sir Roy Robinson for one of the Commissioners, Sir Francis Acland (Commissioner, 1919–39), on the Forestry Commissioners' contributions towards the idea underlying National Parks. As much of the memorandum was used by Colonel Ropner in his contribution to the debate on National Parks in the House of Commons in December 1936, it is likely that the memorandum dates from late 1936. Robinson points out that the Forestry Commissioners 'are thoroughly sympathetic to the idea underlying National Parks in general' but consider that 'proposals to sterilise large tracts of country and especially (from their own particular point of view) to ban plantations on suitable ground in National Parks should be scrutinised very carefully'. He suggests that the country is too small for large National Parks found in 'America and the newer countries generally'. He defends afforestation by asserting that plantations might well be an asset in 'wild country' providing 'shelter for the wayfarer' as well as 'constituting in times of emergency an essential raw material'. Within this context he then describes how the Forestry Commissioners had developed the Argyll National Forest Park as a potential forerunner of a different model of public access:

> The Forestry Commissioners regard the Argyll National Forest Park . . . as something of an experiment. They know from their management of the New Forest, which is the nearest approach to a National Park that we have, what are the difficulties in reconciling the protection of forests with access for the public. They believe that with care the two can be reconciled and the preliminary indication from the Argyll Park already confirms their belief.

In its first year four camp sites and one youth hostel had been established and 10,000 'person nights' had been spent in the Park. Robinson described the visitors' behaviour as 'satisfactory'. An Advisory Committee had been established with Scottish outdoor groups. Robinson noted that the Park allowed full public access to 35,000 acres of wild country and limited access to 15,000 acres of forest or potential forest. This was achieved without the need to appoint additional staff and Robinson felt that the Commission had undertaken the work 'in their stride'. Robinson hoped that following the success of the first park, the Commission would be able to designate several more:

> Assuming, however, that Parliament approves the principle of having National Forest Parks (and indeed they could provide an important contribution to the plans which the government are making for improving the health of the nation) the Forestry Commissioners could increase the number of National Forest Parks to ten or a dozen at comparatively slight expenditure of public money.

He saw Forest Parks as a 'by-product' of the Forestry Commission's primary function of timber production, but a by-product 'which it may well pay the country to develop'. The Commission already held 333,000 acres of unplantable land and was 'constantly acquiring land in various parts of Great Britain'. It frequently heard of 'impending sales suitable for' the provision of public access and 'if the House decided that it was desirable to give a bias in suitable districts towards acquisitions for National Forest Park purposes, it would be a simple and easy thing to do'.

National Parks were supported by the Council for the Protection of Rural England (CPRE) and the Ramblers' Association and a Joint Standing Committee for National Parks was established in 1936. Mac-Ewen and MacEwen (1982) point out: 'Under the chairmanship of Sir Norman Birkett KC, it rapidly became a formidable organisation' with support from the middle class CPRE and Friends of the Lake District and the Ramblers' Association 'which had working class and Labour associations'. A debate on National Parks took place in the House of Commons in December 1936. Interestingly, the Argyll National Forest Park was used by the main government speaker, R. S. Hudson, Parliamentary Secretary to the Ministry of Health, as in his own words 'a useful way out' (Hansard, 9 December 1936, 2105) of the problem of establishing 'national reserves'. To this end he suggested that the work of the Forestry Commission, the National Trust, the CPRE and 'various youth movements and youth hostels' should be co-ordinated. Indeed, he was able to use the existence of the Argyll National Forest Park as a means of side-stepping the issue of establishing a new authority to oversee the formation of National Parks. The Government's view continued to be that National Parks or reserves should be the responsibility

of local authorities and not central government. Sir George Courthope's scheme to nip the idea of National Parks in the bud certainly
seems to have borne fruit in this Parliamentary debate.

At a meeting of the Forestry Commissioners only a month after the
debate, in January 1937, Sir Roy Robinson proposed the establishment,
subject to agreement with CPRE, of a National Forest Park in Snowdonia. Sir Francis Acland said that the debate on Mr Mander's motion on
National Parks had been disappointing 'to those interested' in the
formation of National Parks and 'what they wanted was something
more than that which could be done by the Commission'. Notwithstanding this concern, it was decided to establish a Snowdonia National
Forest Park, and the next year (1938) a National Forest Park was
proposed for the Forest of Dean.[1] In February 1938 a letter was sent to
a wide variety of organizations by the secretary to the Forestry Commission, outlining the establishment of advisory committees for National
Forest Parks[2]. It stated that representative committees were being
established following the Report of the National Forest Park Committee (Snowdonia) 1937. The remit of the committee was to advise on the
general conduct of the Snowdonia National Forest Park and other
National Forest Parks which might be established in England and Wales
in the future. The idea was to follow procedures adopted in Scotland
with the Argyll National Forest Park where a large advisory committee
met from time to time and a small executive committee supervised
work.[3]

National Forest Park Guides

The *Report of the National Forest Park Committee (Forest of Dean)* (Forestry
Commission, 1938) suggested the publication of 'a suitable guide book
... for the use of visitors' (p. 7). This matter was raised at the second
meeting of the National Forest Parks Advisory Committee (England
and Wales) on 17 July 1939, when the idea of producing descriptive
booklets for Snowdonia and the Forest of Dean was discussed. There
was little discussion concerning the level of popularity of the guides, but
there appeared to be general agreement that the booklets should be
informative and educational. Dr Wheeler, described as a 'leading
archaeologist', was to provide an account of Dean 'in prehistoric times
and deal with medieval history', while the Secretary of the Cotteswold
Naturalists' Trust was writing the section on plants. Similar experts were
chosen to write on Snowdonia. It was decided that the guides should
include footpath maps and for Snowdonia it was felt that the Ramblers'

Association 'might be prepared to define such routes and the particular points of interest – consideration being given to the routes in Snowdonia which are most accessible for the ordinary "man in the street" '. Concern over the cost of the guides was indicated by the YHA representative, who suggested that 'others would be encouraged to publish cheap leaflets' for the walker.

The Forestry Commission already had a tradition of producing a significant body of literature, mostly instructive and educational, but all of which has constructed a range of images of the British landscape perhaps only equalled by the British Transport Commission or the New Town Corporations. An examination of the National Forest Park Guides enables us to look at how the Forestry Commission justified a particular conception of landscape. It also allows us to understand how the Commission as a state organization conceptualized its constituency and by doing this articulated a particular role for itself within the rural landscape and within the United Kingdom as a welfare state.

Three different kinds of National Forest Park guides were produced by the Forestry Commission. National Park Guides were substantial booklets of around one hundred pages. The first was published in 1938 for the Argyll National Forest Park; publication of additional guides was delayed by the war. The second Guide, for the Forest of Dean, was not published until 1947, closely followed by that for Snowdonia Forest Park in 1948. Forestry Commission Guides were thematically and visually similar to the Forest Park Guides but describe Forestry Commission forests which were not designated Forest Parks. Finally, a series of short guides, under the title 'Britain's Forests', was published from 1948. The first was a 'descriptive leaflet' on the Forest of Ae, 'the first in a series of popular accounts of individual forests'. These short guides are in fact rather technical in content. Each focuses on a specific forest and explains the conversion of land to forestry, techniques used to manage woodland and the use and destination of timber and timber products.

Each National Forest Park Guide had a similar format. There are cultural chapters on the history and antiquities of the area and on literary associations; topographical chapters on geology, mountains and rivers; naturalist chapters on plant life, mammals, birds and insects; and a chapter dealing with forestry and woodland management. Finally there are maps showing the extent of the Park and the footpaths and information about camping facilities. All Guides, other than the first, were edited by Herbert Edlin. They are illustrated with photographs, line drawings and woodcuts. Many of the illustrations are by artists such as Lennox Patterson, George Macley and C. F. Tunnicliffe with national and regional reputations for nature illustrations and rustic scenes (Peppin and Micklethwaite, 1983; Spalding, 1986; Yorke, 1988).

Peopling the Forest, the Reworking of Tradition

The New Forest in particular, but also the Forest of Dean, were given as models for the new National Forest Parks. This relationship was stated explicitly by The Forestry Commission in its Annual Report (1939), as part of a section devoted to the Commission's role in promoting amenity and access through the institution of National Forest Parks. In the search for examples of previous practice by which these might be established, the Commission claimed: 'With its extensive open heaths and recreational facilities, New Forest was the nearest approach to a National Park in Great Britain' (Forestry Commission, 1940, p. 77). The New Forest is always included in publications and descriptions of National Forest Parks even though it was never officially designated as a Forest Park. It is a strange model to choose as an example of good practice, given that the sites for the new forest parks were almost exclusively in sparsely populated upland and moorland areas of high-land and northern Britain. The New Forest is located in southern England on an area of lowland heath, whilst the Forest of Dean is located in a relatively densely populated, industrialized area on the border of South Wales. However, these two areas have at least one thing in common: they had both been designated forests under Nor-man rule in the twelfth century and continued to operate under some form of forest law, controlled through a court of commoners with historical rights. The history of these 'ancient' forests feature largely in Forestry Commission literature. The new Forestry Commission forests located on areas of marginal mountain and moorland had no such history.

That the New Forest became a model for Forest Parks may be interpreted as merely a matter of expediency. The New Forest and Forest of Dean were the only extensive pieces of ancient woodland inherited by the Forestry Commission from the Office of Woods, and therefore it might be thought quite unremarkable that they became associated with the new Forest Parks. However, evidence suggests this was more than an attempt to justify new practices by invoking ancient ones and that their influence was more than superficial. A number of years later Herbert Edlin wrote regretting the adoption of lowland models of forestry by bureaucrats planning new forests in the high-lights, which he believed inappropriate and inefficient in these environments (Edlin, 1963). There is also evidence to suggest that the lowland forests played a deeper role in justifying Forestry Commission access and amenity policy. The history of these lowland southern Forests and the resources of the English landscape tradition were actively reworked and adopted to justify the work of the Forestry Commission in upland areas. In 1939 W. L. Taylor, a close colleague of Robinson within the Forestry Commission, articulated this position in his presidential address to the British Society of Foresters. It suggests a rather different line of reasoning from that adopted by Sir George Courthope:

> I think that it is possible to trace the decline of British forestry (in the sense that we use the term) to the coming of the Normans. We know what they meant by a forest and that they valued venison more highly than vert. We know also that the common people of England were not encouraged in those regions legally declared to be forest ... The wood-land warning 'Beware of man-traps and spring guns' will still be within the memory of some of us. (Taylor, 1939, p. 100)

Taylor justifies current forestry practice by contrasting it with the history of the Royal Forests. He sets out a plan for highland Britain founded on a history which is exclusively English, substantially lowland and southern. He traces a history of forestry from the imposed rule of the Normans to the punitive game laws of the eighteenth century as a history of exclusion. Significantly, denial of access is linked to a concern with the management and exploitation of game, those who 'valued venison more highly than vert'. The declining fortunes of a strategic resource of national importance are directly linked to the unproductive activities of a leisured elite. With forestry in the care of professional foresters working for the state, the forest is restored as an economic resource and a public domain after a thousand years of expropriation and neglect. This is a bold statement of the kind of corporate welfarism that was to become common after World War II. It is not insignificant that Forestry Commission woodlands were called State Forests from the 1930s through into the 1960s, and that this was done without apology for the associations this term might have (Forestry Commission, 1937). An interesting inversion of the argument that National Forest Parks were preferable to National Parks because they did not lock up large tracts of the privately owned countryside was made by Herbert Edlin in 1969. He suggested that the advantage of the Forest Park model over the National Park model stemmed precisely from the benefits of single ownership and executive control:

> [The] first Forest Park was opened in 1935 and was 15 years ahead of the first of the larger National Parks established by the independent National Parks Commission. That Commission was always hampered by lack of land ownership; it controlled developments but could not promote them effectively ... (Edlin, 1969, p. 125)

In his speech of 1939, Taylor was most concerned to stake out 'the psychological value of forests as a national possession' and as such foresters had a duty to inform and educate the public of the importance, purposes and benefits of their shared asset. The concern for education became a major focus of the Forest Guides. In one sense making people aware of the rules of the forest is a merely practical endeavour, particularly given the potential for fire damage. However, it does not explain the Guide's exhaustive detail concerning the activities and processes of forestry, particularly given that the Shorter Guides are almost exclusively concerned with the products and processes of particular forests. These guides, though apparently written for lay visitors, sometimes even carried advertisements for Forestry Commission technical literature. This is reflected visually particularly in the Shorter Guides, which give many illustrations of working forestry practices. Sometimes this adopts a form of imagery reminiscent of the heroic modernism of 1930s Soviet Realism, or New Deal America. As early as 1934, Dallimore had suggested the 'preservation' of areas of modern forest for instructional purposes, something he linked directly to the amenity value of woodland. It is also true that since the controversy over afforestation in the Lake District, the Forestry Commission had realized the need to convince the public of the argument for establishment of intensive forestry, and in this context Herbert Edlin, appointed in 1947 as publicity officer, was a principal proponent of educational literature and of the propaganda value of the Forest Guide series. The rationale for this appointment was given in the Forestry Commission Annual Report for 1949:

> While the Commissioners have consistently striven to keep the public informed of their objectives and of the progress of their forest operations, they have found it no easy matter to get the facts across to the man in the street. (Forestry Commission, 1950, p. 87)

Activities included special forestry broadcasts on the BBC, the development of educational material for schools, youth clubs and other community and special interest organizations such as the Rotary and Young

Farmers clubs. Indicating the position of the Forestry Commission as an agency of national government, at least some lectures during the early post-war period were given on behalf of the Forestry Commission by speakers provided by the Central Office of Information (Forestry Commission, 1951, p. 44). At the Festival of Britain in 1951 the Forestry Commission displayed scale models of the Snowdonia National Forest Park and Keilder Forest village alongside scale models of modern forestry practice from Culbin Forest in Morayshire and Dudmaston in Shropshire (Forestry Commission, 1952, p. 50). The National Forest and Forest Park Guides were developed very largely within a post-war institutional context of government-directed economic and social reconstruction and development.

By producing a detailed explanation of the economic and strategic role of forestry for the visitor, the Guide Books make connections between the economic and amenity values of Forestry Commission land. This both echoes Taylor's speech to the British Society of Foresters and amplifies the stated aims and objectives of the Forestry Commission. It is a notion of access in the broadest sense, it involves bringing new employment, housing and services into the countryside at the same time that rural areas are opened up for urban visitors, ramblers and trekkers. It is more than a notion of coniferous monoculture with separate amenity areas, rather, a more or less vague concept of peopling the forest. This is reflected in the policy to establish, in addition to smaller residential developments, completely new forest villages such as those constructed at Kielder on the Scottish border and Llwyn-y-Gog in North Wales. Edlin expressed this in a paper about Forest Villages:

> It is fair to ask the acutely aesthetic minded not to take the short view, but to look ahead to the mature forests of future years, to a forest industry and the busy and increasing community of forest workers who have already begun to find a home and livelihood within afforested areas, and also to the welfare of the generality of the people of Britain who will find healthy recreation in and about the forest and in the National Forest Parks on which a start has been made, as the peoples of other nations are finding it in theirs. (Edlin, 1953, p. 151)

Later, looking back on the success of Forest Parks, Edlin again made the connection between tourist access and residential access:

> When the Forest Park was conceived it was believed that the tending of the Border Forests would require a large resident labour force, which in its turn would lead to the establishment of bus routes, shops and public services generally. Several Forest Villages were planned, and three were

in fact built. It then became apparent that modern labour-saving methods would enable the forests to be planted, and their timber harvested, with a far smaller force of men. At the same time, ownership of cars led to a growing proportion of these men to travel in from distant homes, rather than to live in the new Forest Villages . . . With the development of public transport, forest housing and tourist accommodation at a standstill, it is hard to see how this particular Forest Park can progress . . . (Edlin, 1969, p. 124)

The visual imagery of the Guide Books reflects this theme very strongly, frequently featuring the Forestry Commission's new housing schemes, characterizing them as modern, clean, bright and efficient in a manner typical of the new towns literature. The drawing of two young hikers walking towards new houses in a forest village from the Border Forest Park Guide is a good illustration of this (Figure 7.1). The picture conveys the sense of a bright future, shared by residents and visitors alike: a future built on the technical expertise of the Forestry Commission. The new clean healthy environment of the forest village as a place to raise a family is represented by the woman resident pushing a pram. The two young hikers look towards the woman with the pram in what constitutes a rather heavy-handed visual gesture. This indicates both the future of the young couple, the suggestion that they are on the brink of

THE LAND AND THE PEOPLE

BY H. L. EDLIN

Figure 7.1 Walkers and a new Forestry Commission village (© Crown Copyright. Reproduced by permission of the Controller of HMSO and the Forestry Commission)

adulthood with its expectations of family formation and the importance of hiking as a healthy outdoor pursuit in which the Forestry Commission plays its part in the creation of a strong, healthy and fertile nation. Two forms of access policy, alternately for residents and visitors, are juxtaposed in this image and visually connected by a message which stresses a commonality in the interests of Forestry Commission, forestry workers and the wider populous, an investment for the nation as a whole.

It is as if State Forests were to imitate the idea of a commonly owned rule-governed multiple use landscape more reminiscent of commoning in ancient woodland. Images of forest landscapes often demonstrate an ambiguity between the coniferous monoculture, the regular and efficient ideal of Forestry Commission planting policy and the open deciduous woodland model, which formed the ideal for access policy. This is evident in the cover for the North Yorkshire Forests Guide, which depicts a mixed forested landscape, in a semi-primitive style reminiscent of Paul Nash (Figure 7.2). Two people rest besides a road and consult a map; they occupy an open hillside site overlooking a diverse landscape of mixed lowland farming. The closed densely packed coniferous plantations clothing the hill slopes are pushed into the distance, and nearby hills have a mix of grassland, deciduous and coniferous cover. The farm nestling in the valley and the small irregular fields suggest this is very much a domesticated landscape and is much more reminiscent of the New Forest or the Forest of Dean than the new northern upland plantations. One may perhaps view this as a brave attempt by the Forestry Commission publications and publicity to show in a most advantageous light a landscape which Herbert Edlin in his more reflective moments could only see as less than attractive for the visitor. In his review of fifty years of National Forest Parks, Edlin could only write of the Kielder Forest:

> Spruce woods on soggy peat, stretching over rounded hills that are often misty or cloud-capped, are not ideal for outdoor enjoyment; and the fact that they go on for further than anyone can walk is more daunting than encouraging. (Edlin, 1969, p. 125)

However, the North Yorkshire Forest picture represents a landscape ideal which complements the Forestry Commission's aim to create rural employment and its desire not to alienate a farming community afraid of compulsory purchase and concerned to limit direct government intervention in agricultural production. It is also a landscape that refers to an English 'tradition' of individualism, the independence of the

Figure 7.2   Cover of *North Yorkshire Forests* guide (© Crown Copyright. Reproduced by permission of the Controller of HMSO and the Forestry Commission)

family farm, the numerous views of lone pairs of male and female hikers suggesting nascent nuclear families. It is not without significance that the Forestry Commission's early settlement policy for forest workers was based on the provision of individual smallholdings. These are amply represented by photographs in the Guide Books and forge associations with the independent cottager of the medieval lowland forest, as well as modern smallholding and land grant schemes linked both to democratic ideology in the nineteenth century and post-World War I. The very design of the Forest Villages by Thomas Sharp conveys this fusion of tradition and modernity. A 'traditional' village structure of church, pub and single family cottages ranged around an open space reminiscent of a village green are adopted to serve a welfare state ideology. In this context these landscape elements could be reinterpreted in a new language, encouraging a sense of community through the provision of social and educational institutions, efficient, affordable, family housing and adequate public open space.

Photographic representations of Forest access clearly convey a sense of modernity. The Guide Books emphasize the importance of the new forest roads and tracks by which amenity access is improved through commercial management policy. A photograph from the Short Guide to the Forest of Ae (Forestry Commission, 1948) exemplifies numerous photographs from the Shorter Guides depicting broad roads, regular plots and straight fire breaks. In this view a new car travels through a recently planted landscape; it is juxtaposed on the page with a bold statement declaring the national importance of the Forestry Commission (Figure 7.3). The photograph, like the writing above it, is unapologetic and totally lacking in nostalgia. It does not deny the new landscapes created by a national need for timber; nor does it deny new ways of experiencing the Forest created by private transport. It might be argued that the two are closely linked by the ethos of post-war reconstruction. A rather different perspective on modern Forestry is conveyed by the photograph of a 'planting gang' from the cover of the Shorter Guide to Strathyre Forest (Forestry Commission 1951) (Figure 7.4). At first glance it is antithetical to the dehumanized landscape of the Forest of Ae which legitimates forestry at the level of national strategy. However, it can be interpreted as quite complementary in the sense that it is able to socialize and thereby justify state forestry on a human scale. In this picture a group of forest workers prepare to set off by boat to across Loch Lubnaig with bags of young saplings for planting. The predominantly female composition of the group suggests this is a wartime view in which the happy, smiling faces of the party convey a sense of stoic resistance. Yet, recycled in a post-war context and placed close by a picture on page 1 of the Guide showing visitors lounging with a boat by the side of Loch Voil, the picture takes on additional meaning (Figure 7.5). Now the workers themselves become tourists enjoying the

Twice in the present century Britain's woodlands have been drastically overcut to meet war needs. During the last war, two-thirds of all the timber standing in 1939 was felled, and reserves were sacrificed to save shipping space. This resulted in the gravest timber shortage the country has known and, because trees need time to grow and there are difficulties in the way of adequate importation, the shortage is likely to persist for some years.

Meanwhile there is no doubt as to the need for large-scale remedial action. To enable the country to grow, eventually, one-third of its timber requirements, and to provide a reserve against emergency, H.M. Forestry Commission, as the State forest authority, seeks to bring into being five million acres of productive woodlands in the next fifty years. This will involve State planting of three million acres of bare ground, and the re-stocking, mainly by private owners, of Britain's existing two million acres of woodlands.

The planting by the Commission of the Forest of Ae is representative of similar work which is going on all over Britain.

Looking south down the road from Closeburn to Ae Bridge, traversing the Forest in the valley of the Windyhill Burn.

Figure 7.3   New plantation (© Crown Copyright. Reproduced by permission of the Controller of HMSO and the Forestry Commission)

highland scenery; socially responsible labour and post-war leisure are seen to be close allies in the struggle for access and amenity.

Coniferous Aesthetics

The massive use of coniferous trees by the Forestry Commission resulted in new large-scale landscapes for which there was little precedent. Coniferous plantations had been made since the eighteenth century, and although extensive tracts of land were afforested with, for example, pines in the Dukeries of Nottinghamshire and larches at Hafod near Aberystwyth by Thomas Johnes (Moore-Colyer, 1992), most plantations were relatively small. Critics such as Uvedale Price (1810) were concerned more about how such coniferous trees fitted in with existing woodland, than the aesthetic effect of whole new coniferous landscapes (Daniels and Watkins, 1991). William Wordsworth (1835), however, was famously critical of the effect of larch plantations on the landscape of the Lake District:

> ... a moment's thought will show that, if ten thousand of this spiky tree, the larch, are stuck in at once upon the side of a hill, they can grow up into nothing but deformity; that, while they are suffered to stand, we shall

Figure 7.4   Planting gang (© Crown Copyright. Reproduced by permission of the Controller of HMSO and the Forestry Commission)

Figure 7.5 Visitors at Loch Voil (© Crown Copyright. Reproduced by permission of the Controller of HMSO and the Forestry Commission)

> look in vain for any of those appearances which are the chief sources of beauty in a natural wood. (1988 edition, p. 57)

Between 1920 and 1938 the area of land under forest crops held by the Forestry Commission increased from 1,393 to 400,712 thousand acres. The landscapes of such diverse forested areas as Argyll, Snowdonia, and Sherwood were transformed. The great bulk of this afforestation was coniferous and Hadfield (1967, p. 181) notes that during the inter-war period:

> a sense of urgency and enthusiasm unusual in any government-controlled body inevitably led to many mistakes and plantings that were both unsightly and unsatisfactory, both by the Commission and the landowners it assisted.

The visual intrusion of coniferous plantations was never far from the thought of Forestry Commission publicity. As late as 1969, well over thirty years after the Lake District controversy, Edlin was pleased to observe that many visitors enjoyed walking in the plantations of Snowdonia:

> These forests are surrounded by the grandest mountains of England and Wales, and stand close to long sandy beaches, yet on every fine summer's day they are filled with visitors who could go elsewhere, but prefer to seek

the peaceful fascinations of growing timber crops. The prophesies of
critics who declared that people would shun the 'dark, dreary, dismal
conifers' have been confounded. (Edlin, 1969, 117)

The National Forest Park Guides, therefore, had the difficult job of
encouraging public appreciation of huge new afforestation schemes.
This was particularly difficult where there were few older plantations.
Edlin explains that at Gwydyr Forest in Snowdonia the woods 'clothe
the side of steep valleys and extend over rugged foothills studded with
still lakes. The whole has been steadily afforested, during the ensuing
half century, with plantations of larch, pine, spruce and Douglas fir that
now look entirely natural' (Edlin, 1969, p. 116). Unfortunately for the
Forestry Commission, such areas with long established plantations were
quite rare.

In addition to many photographs of young coniferous plantations,
the Guides include a range of artists' impressions of forest and forestry,
some of which have been previously discussed. Artistic representations
include line drawings, watercolours and, most characteristically, a series
of woodcuts and wood engravings. Given the hostility experienced by
the Forestry Commission over the visual qualities of its young plantations and the absence of mature plantations to photograph, this is
perhaps not surprising. The Guides and associated literature frequently
implore the wider public to respond imaginatively when faced with vast
stands of young saplings. It is consistent with this request that the
Forestry Commission should resort to 'artistic impressions' of mature
forested land in order to sell the Forest Parks to visitors.

However, it is not at all clear to what extent those responsible for
Forestry Commission publicity were able to sympathize with or even
understand public dislike of large-scale coniferous plantations. Rather
than regarding all the publicity material as an attempt to ameliorate
and apologize for the landscape of commercial forestry, it is possible to
interpret at least one current within the Guide Book literature as an
attempt to impose an alternative view of forestry, one that is very
different from that common in the UK. In his essay on amenity
planting, Edlin suggests a preference for the gothic drama of the
northern European coniferous forest rather than the loose open deciduous woodland of Britain:

> ... there is little or no 'foreign competition' in amenity values. Even if we
> concede that the pines of the Black Forest in Germany, or the spruce and
> birch of the Norwegian hills, are more lovely to look at than our own oak
> and beech, we know that we can gaze upon them for only a few weeks in
> each year. (Edlin, 1963, p. 88)

Edlin's fascination with northern European forest landscapes suggests more than just a recognition of the greater emphasis placed in these countries on the economic or social value of the forester. More too than simply a concern with vital, varied or exotic ecosystems: in addition to these it was also an expression of a coniferous aesthetic, an emotional response to the sublime grandeur of forestry on a vast scale. Edlin speaks of this not for the first time in respect of the Argyll Forest Park, where a sense of 'forest' is created by 'thousands of acres of timber crops'. The wilderness quality of The Argyll Forest Park had been remarked upon by in the Report of the Forest Park Committee, 1935, at which time this idea was used to justify an approach to public access so highly restrained as to render it almost invisible.

> It is difficult to estimate how many people could make use of the area which is the subject of our report, for recreation, without destroying the sense of remoteness and solitude which is its chief attraction. We recommend, therefore, that the Commissioners should proceed cautiously and refrain from drawing undue public attention to what they are doing. The experience gained here should be of use in other areas belonging to the Commission. (Forestry Commission, 1935, p. 5)

'In the Sprucewoods' (by George Mackley: Forestry Commission, 1962) is typical of images celebrating coniferous forestry whilst drawing on a distinctly northern European imagery (Figure 7.6). The woodcut is a uniquely appropriate, not to say organic, means of representing living timber. The history of the woodcut is closely linked to the development of printing and publishing in Germany from the sixteenth century. In addition to this, the history of the medium in illustrating northern European folk themes may be significant. Also, its adoption by twentieth-century artists who endeavoured to forge links between traditional iconographies and modern abstract art indicates the power of this medium as a means of justifying the coniferous landscape as deeply rooted yet vigorously youthful. The picture shows a range of different aged stands surrounding a farmstead and mill besides a rustic stone arched bridge. The detail of the woodcut emphasizes the textural variety of the scene in a conventionally picturesque formulation: the rough cobbled road, the angular stony embankment, the smooth surface of the water. Yet the nature of woodcut as a medium lends emphasis to structural qualities in the natural shapes of trees, rocks and human forms and declares a modernist abstract aesthetic of organic form. The young plantation on the hill indicates a landscape newly transformed by afforestation, whilst the farm claims this as an old landscape with a long history. Yet the picture itself seems to refer to a northern European narrative tradition of folklore and fairy tale. The

Figure 7.6 'In the Sprucewoods' (© Crown Copyright. Reproduced by permission of the Controller of HMSO and the Forestry Commission)

farm nestling under the trees by the stream, suggests the 'cottage in the woods'. The roadway, which divides over the bridge, has forks alternatively skirting and entering the forest giving enticing glimpses of the road ahead. Perhaps this suggests the critical decisions characteristic of folk tales often symbolized by the narrative device of a dividing path, as well as the open and various opportunities for the modern-day walker to experience the forest.

Educated Access?

It is very difficult to know quite who the Forestry Commission and its publicity department had in mind when they produced the National Forest Park Guides. Forests are represented, on the one hand, as varied habitats for flora and fauna for the serious naturalist, delightful and diverse landscapes for the casual visitor; and on the other, the site of an efficient, uniform and modern productive forest for the appreciation of the good citizen or grand expanses of wilderness for the 'serious' walker. Yet the published literature does not adequately service any one of these imagined constituencies. The Guides were not widely enough available to gain a large following amongst a potential or actual readership of casual visitors, for whom they were also much too dry and detailed. The absence of good maps and practical information for walkers gave them limited use for those committed to exploring the forest, even though the Forestry Commission claimed that the maps were suitable for ramblers (Forestry Commission, 1950, p. 87).

The Commission's policy with respect to developing public amenity and access suggests a similar ambiguity, if not to say ambivalence. The development of facilities for visitors, like the publication of Guide Books, proceeded relatively slowly after establishment of the first parks in the late 1930s. World War II was most certainly an important factor in this, as overnight stays within at least some Forest Parks were not allowed during the conflict. However, by 1950 all six Forest Parks had Guide Books and all except Hardknott boasted official camping grounds. Facilities provided by the Forestry Commission were rather spartan, typically just one or two camping grounds in each park often comprising only the most basic of facilities in terms of running water and sanitation. The Forestry Commission were reluctant to provide any accommodation in the Forest Parks, if as in the case of Snowdonia, the Commission considered there to be sufficient independently maintained lodging in the form of youth hostels, hotels, bed and breakfast accommodation and such like. The *Report of the National Forest Park*

Committee (Forest of Dean) (Forestry Commission, 1938) outlines three different types of camping accommodation necessary to provide for visitors:

(a) Huts and chalets, with dining and recreation hut and the provision of meals.
(b) Tents to be supplied at a reasonable charge, campers to provide their own meals.
(c) Sites for visitors carrying their own equipment and providing their own meals. (Forestry Commission, 1938, p. 4)

It is clear that even the Forestry Commission recognized the importance of the independent day trippers, particularly those who were travelling by motor car; for example, in the Forest of Dean they highlighted the importance of providing ' "pull-ins" for motorists' (p. 5). They recognized that in certain areas it would be difficult to get people off the beaten track and out into the woods. The Commissioners also recognized the need to construct vehicular roads and footpaths into the forest parks to give increased access and leisure opportunities for visitors. This had been recognized in the report of the Forest Park Committee for the Forest of Dean when discussing the woods along the valley of the River Wye:

> These areas are on hilly land and the paths are rough and, generally speaking, the public do not wander far into them although the area is available to those who desire it . . . These valleys, beautiful in themselves, lead to high ground with an elevation of as much as 1,000 feet and we think that the public will, in the course of time, wish to explore these places and that consequently improved access will be necessary. (Forestry Commission, 1938, p. 6)

The Forestry Commission Annual Reports from the late 1940s and early 1950s certainly emphasized 'measures taken to encourage public access to the Forest Parks include the improvement of roads and footpaths, the provision of public camping sites, and co-operation with the Youth Hostels Associations and similar bodies in providing accommodation' (Forestry Commission, 1950, p. 87).

Yet in spite of the fine words, it is clear that the Forestry Commission was very reluctant to commit itself to any but the most minimal of facilities. This approach could be justified on the grounds of cost, because of the intervention of the war and the stringencies of post-war austerity, on the grounds of a careful and judicious learning process, or on the grounds of limiting the environmental intrusion of tourist facilities. It is reflected in an access policy through which, on the one hand, the Forestry Commission wanted to retain very close control of the public on Commission land. On the other hand, they wished to promote the idea of the forest as a wilderness to be freely explored by a citizenry who understood the workings of the countryside. This dilemma was summarized by Roy Robinson in 1936 as the difficulty 'in reconciling the protection of forests with access for the public'. The report of the Commissioners into the Argyll Forest Park had raised this very issue:

> We consider that something should be done to indicate routes which may safely be followed by the normal pedestrian. This would not involve the construction of definite tracks, but would necessitate the marking of feasible routes by occasional cairns or whitened stones, or distinctive waysigns or symbols ... Many walkers and climbers equipped with maps will prefer to choose their own routes, and should be allowed to do so once the planted land is passed through ... (Forestry Commission, 1935, p. 5)

Here the Forestry Commission's definition of an 'ordinary pedestrian' does not require the construction of definite tracks for walkers, only occasional way markers. Given the few concessions which the Guide Books make for the walker, it is all the more interesting that the Forestry Commission should assume that even casual walkers would have the resources to navigate themselves across wild terrain.

There are numerous illustrations in the Guide Books showing visitors and tourists within the Forest Parks. Photographs, drawings and watercolours show either organized groups picnicking, pony trekking or mountaineering, or lone couples walking, picnicking or consulting a map. There is little place in the visual scheme of things for either single visitors or small independent groups. This reflects the Forestry Commission's longstanding preference for encouraging organized groups and those affiliated to national institutions such as the Youth Hostel Association.

In spite of the Forestry Commission's apparent reluctance to declare open house, the Forest Parks rapidly increased in popularity. Overall the estimated number of visits rose from 18,755 in 1949 to 53,600 in 1951. However, by the early 1960s the Forestry Commission's access policy and particularly its Guide Book literature were to come in for very severe criticism. Most notable in this regard were the findings of the visitor survey undertaken in a selected number of the Commission's forests under the directorship of W.E.S. Mutch during the summers of 1963 and 1964. In *Public Recreation in National Forests: a Factual Survey* (1968, p. 83) he says:

There is an obvious risk that the interests of the forest manager, which commonly may lean towards natural history, tend to be magnified in the assumed demands and interests of the public users. This is readily apparent in the form and content of the guide book publications of the Forestry Commission. The guides are lengthy and descriptive, botanical, zoological and archaeological in matter, and are intended for use in conjunction with a 1-inch or larger scale map. Undoubtably they are absorbingly interesting guide books for the fairly small proportion of walking-holiday visitors, but they make an insignificant impact on the car-driving, day-visiting family parties who form the majority of the present visitors.

Most damningly, he highlighted the inadequacies of the Forestry Commission Guide Books as a means of informing the public of recreational opportunities. At Allerston Forest he found that in spite of the recent publication of a Guide Book, one-quarter of one per cent had come to the forest as the result of a Forestry Commission publication (p. 92).

The commitment of Forestry Commission officers such as publicity officer Herbert Edlin to public access and education cannot be doubted. Yet it remains true that the Commission were unclear as to what particular constituency they were directing their access policy and aiming their publicity material. This is particularly so as the inter-war conception of the ideal visitor as a member of an organized party driven by a desire to stimulate the mind and exercise the body was replaced by a reality of relatively affluent, sedentary, car-bound picnickers. It is of course, highly debatable whether this pre-war visitor model ever existed as much more than wishful thinking in the minds of concerned middle-class liberal professionals. However, its pervasiveness does say something important.

Firstly, about the need to justify the Forestry Commission to the wider public. A public conceived of as a constituency of active citizens – something very closely related to the development of the Forestry Commission as an institution of the welfare state. By this means the pre-war conception of a highly regulated, fit, healthy, organized citizenry is perhaps linked to a post-war conception of rather less highly regulated, socially responsible democratic individualism.

Secondly, it may say something about the Forestry Commission's approach to the landscapes under its charge. The need to regulate and control was practical – to create an efficient working landscape safe from fire risk. But derived from this there is also an aesthetic sense of value in a well ordered landscape, one in which wilderness and civilization exist in close proximity. More particularly and reflecting the technological and scientific background of the forestry officers concerned, it is one in which wilderness or disorder is carefully managed and rule-governed. Areas of land are set aside as free wilderness, hedged in and controlled by modern management practices. Visitors are encouraged to explore the forest as free agents, yet carefully constrained by rules and codes of practice to ensure regular behaviour. The aesthetic appeal of the ordered forest landscape may be seen in the wood engraving by Norman Wilson of Loch Achray and Ben Venue, near Brig o' Turk in the Queen Elizabeth Forest Park (Figure 7.7). This is a clearly zoned landscape; a belt of deciduous trees around the loch provide a rich diverse habitat. The encircling stands of pine trees are lightened and penetrable close to the seated couple, dense enough to provide a pervasive 'sense of forest', though manageable enough to provide open shelter for a landscape of leisure. The people relaxing in front of the view watch birds circle over the water and recreational fishermen out on the water. At a safe distance beyond the coniferous plantation the wilderness is visible – the uncultivable uplands and mountains. It is perhaps interesting that so many of these pictures

Figure 7.7   Loch Achrae and Ben Venue near Brig o'Turk (© Crown Copyright. Reproduced by permission of the Controller of HMSO and the Forestry Commission)

depict views out from the lowland of the cultivated forest into the wild uplands, indicating a view of nature always controlled by the regular manmade landscape of the commercial forest. For the visitor it is a view of wilderness directed by the regulations and expectations of the Forestry Commission, a taste of freedom set within clear limits.

If anything, perhaps Mutch's attack on Forestry Commission amenity and access policy hit hardest at the publicity officer Herbert Edlin, who responded to the criticism in a more or less overt way on a number of occasions. Edlin claimed that the Guide Books were written for the naturalist walker. Yet it is still difficult to conceive that even this individual would wish to make special detours in order to view specific examples of good practice in coniferous nursery management. In trying to justify the Guide Books, it is obvious from Edlin's writing that the Commission had little idea how many people were using their amenity provision, let alone who these people were. In the absence of any other model it would certainly appear that the personification of this individual was Edlin himself. His own writing on the aesthetic justifications for amenity woodland produced a line of argument which aptly complements the structure of the Guides in their, eclectic anti-quarianism and their expectations of technical interest, as for example in the following:

> But the attraction of the eye is itself no simple thing. It is compounded of various elements: form, expressed in the varied shapes of rounded crowns of foliage on oak or elm, spires of Lombardy poplar, pyramids of spruce, or broad flat planes of Lebanon cedar; colour whether it be of golden laburnum blossom or the rich autumn tints enlivening the fading foliage of beech or liquidambar (L. styraciflua); movement when the wind sways the birches; or the change that comes with winter, silvering every branch and leaf with snow and rime. (Edlin, 1963, p. 67)

The unselfconscious resort to specialist knowledge, the conjunction of a comfortable middlebrow poetics with the compulsive charm of botanical classification in this passage, certainly reflects the style of the Forest Guides; this perspective is also reproduced in some of the images. The wood engraving from the Glen More and Cairngorms Forest Park Guide by Conrad McKenna, 'Cairngorm scene: crag, loch, pinewood, capercailzie and roe deer', is most appropriate (Figure 7.8). The picture illustrates various flora and fauna, which the interested and concerned layperson, the 'naturalist walker', might look out for whilst in the park. It is a highly compartmentalized view, each element in the picture occupying an appropriate place like a specimen for classification purposes in a recognition manual. This picture was made by a

Scottish artist, yet it seems a peculiarly lowland if not English image of the Highland landscape replete with almost every imaginable cliché of the Highlands, a perfect example of antiquarian eclecticism. Not least

Figure 7.8   Cairngorm scene: crag, lock, pinewood, capercailzie and roe deer (© Crown Copyright. Reproduced by permission of the Controller of HMSO and the Forestry Commission)

amongst the stereotypes here are the two people, set in a pose which reinforces patriarchal gender relationships, man pointing, woman following his directions, the couple wearing a highly romanticized and regularized version of highland dress. It is an image which appears to confirm the criticisms by W.E.S. Mutch of an organization which ultimately did not really know who its visitors were; it was perhaps important to generate an image of the 'ideal' visitor as something much easier to stabilize than the actual physical presence of visitors within the carefully ordered environment of the forested landscape.

Notes

[1.] For a full discussion of the involvement of the important role of the Treasury in the development of National Forest Parks, see John Sheail (1981) *Rural Conservation in Inter-war Britain*. Oxford: Clarendon Press, Chapter 10.

[2.] PRO F18 217 National Parks Advisory Committee, 1938–9

[3.] The committee was established and made up of representatives from many organizations including the AA; Commons, Open Spaces and Foot Paths Society; Camping Club; National Playing Fields Association; YHA; CPRE; SPNR; NT; Girl Guides; Society for the Preservation of Fauna of the Empire; National Advisory Council for Physical Training; Cyclists Touring Club; CPRW; Ramblers' Association; Boy Scouts; Caravan Club; Juvenile Organisations Committee of National Advisory Council.

8

Access and Alignment: A Passport to Rutlandshire

SIMON RYCROFT

The politics of access to the countryside are not simply matters of adequate footpath provision, of local conflict over restrictive measures, of a general consensus on rights and negotiations with landowning and governmental agencies. Recent research has emphasized the powerful socio-cultural dimensions of access to nature, landscape and environment, and its constitution of identities, from the personal to the transnational (Cosgrove, Roscoe and Rycroft, 1994; Daniels, 1993; Matless, 1994). Our experiences of the 'countryside' are prescribed in a complex manner, suggesting that the discourses of access are as restrictive as they are enabling, and can be located within the processes through which the countryside comes to signify citizenship and community at all scales. Here, then, 'access' is defined as both a physical and a discursive process, a process which demands the correct cultural and material equipment to experience the countryside.

This research was carried out for a European Commission project on the semiotics of nature, environment and landscape in the modern period; its principal conclusions are that rights of access, particularly to iconic national territories, are expressions of citizenship, community and attachment, and, similarly, the process of controlling or defining the grounds of that access, through enclosure, restriction and education, serves to produce order and define identities (Cosgrove, Roscoe and Rycroft, 1994; Cosgrove, 1995). The case of Rutland County and the design of the reservoir Rutland Water highlight the changing cultural politics of access in the post-war period, contoured by social and physical planning, and later, by an emergent modern environmental consciousness. This chapter addresses the debates concerning structured coherence in the countryside, identifying a period in which such coherence should have been in the process of collapsing and later reformulating under different terms of reference (see Cloke and Goodwin, 1992). It is clear, however, that despite transition to a modern redrawn county (Leicestershire) and the concurrent construction of a very modern engineering scheme (Rutland Water), a series of very coherent and highly ordered continuities are apparent. Both structures and their longevity, therefore, are not simply the expression of social formation, but also a reflection of discursive strategy and the ability of powerful local discourses to graft on to widely different social orders.

Rutland Identity

Rutland Water was built to meet the water supply requirements of planned urban growth after the 1965 New Towns Act approved the expansion of Northampton, Peterborough, Daventry, Wellingborough and Corby. It was placed within the rational post-war planning process, guided by urban-industrial requirements, and sited in the smallest county in England, Rutland, at the moment of its official demise as an independent locality (Knight, 1982). The county is often evoked as a slice of quintessential lowland English rurality and, since 1945, had been resisting amalgamation into a larger region under a series of proposed local government reorganizations. Rutland Water was planned to complement this iconic local identity, careful attention being paid to landscape and architectural design around the shores, the preservation of endangered local landmarks, environmental conservation and educated access to each of these. Architects and landscape architects were involved with the reservoir proposal through to commissioning and beyond, formulating a long-term environmental aesthetic for the area which dictates the grounds of access to this day.

For W.G. Hoskins, author of *Rutland: A Shell Guide* (1963), Rutland remained largely 'untouched', although at the time of writing it was under threat from the 'urban theorists who seem to dominate planning today.' He recommended that Rutland be set aside as a 'Human Conservancy', which would operate like a nature reserve, protecting its people against 'incessant noise, speed, and all the other acids of modernity.' Rutland had always boasted a peculiar local identity. In the post-war period and in the light of the threat to its existence, a series of texts have been written on this identity, from the significance of local dialects and local words to the cosmic alignment of Rutland (Wordsworth, 1891; Traylen, 1977). Hoskins (1963, pp. 7–14) wrote of the freedom of leisurely and slow motoring its geography afforded, without the hassles of fast roads and young impatient drivers. The geographer and Rutland local activist Bryan Waites in a letter to the *Daily Telegraph* (8 February 1972), reiterated Hoskins's plea in a critique of the proposals for local government reorganization in the early 1970s (Waites, 1972). An independent Rutland was important to the fibre of the nation and even, it seems, its biotechnic well-being; Rutland was an 'historic and viable unit satisfying the people's need for the reoccupation and replenishment of the environment as a source of essential values in a balanced life.'[1]

For Bryan Waites, Rutland exhibited the 'right kind of regionalism', that of Vidal de la Blache, a strong organic attachment of community to place after Lewis Mumford, and as a unit, operated at a natural pace and scale. This unity did not derive from physical geography or 'racial affinity', but from 'historical continuity within a small area which, like an island encourages local patriotism'. Writing in 1983, long after the various battles over Rutland, Waites believed that it was the strength of this patriotism which absorbed radical change 'because it eventually cuts things down to the personal, family size' (Waites, 1983, pp. 133–4). Scale was the universal solution to the acids of modernity.

The amalgamation of the county of Rutland into a larger administrative unit was first proposed in 1947 and was accompanied by immediate condemnation from Rutland residents and supporters country- and worldwide, many of whom emphasized its independence and its long and continuous history of isolation from the turbulent forces that shaped the nation, especially industrialization and civil war. On 1 November 1947 *Illustrated* magazine featured the threatened county: 'As the boundary men decide what should be the future of England's smallest county, the "tups" [the folk of Rutland] have joined battle with Whitehall.' The 'tups' had, in October, descended on Westminster singing 'Rutland is our county: Shall our county die? Twenty thousand Rutlandmen will know the reason why' (Jackson, 1947, p. 19). Apart from the threat to their existence, what was so irksome to the Rutland oligarchy, a group of councillors, local dignitaries and business people, including the brewer Kenneth Ruddle and landowner Lord Gainsborough, was the founding rationale that Rutland was not fit to function as part of a reconstructing and modern nation. The Local Government Boundary Commission Act of 1945 had just this agenda: to enable the nation as a whole to develop and integrate the infrastructures, which would ensure its united economic and social well-being. Rutland had neither the resources nor the population to provide 'adequate' local government; some services that

might reasonably be expected to be provided by a county were in-
adequately, or not, provided, particularly in the more recent concerns
of the capitalist, modernist welfare state: health, childcare and education.[2]

Rutland's post-war supporters began rehearsing the arguments that
would become central to later campaigns over the county's independence and that recognized the iconic position of Rutland as integral to
the nation's historic identity. The longstanding discourse of Rutland
identity and the grounds of access were thus reaffirmed in a period of
massive social and structural change. A series of events were orchestrated to gain support for the county. Many, like the landlocked *HMS
Rutland,* seen aiming its guns on targets throughout the county in 1960,
provided symbolic attacks on bureaucracy. Other tactics reinforced
boundaries, including the erection of signs on the highways at Rutland's borders, reading 'Rutland Fights For Minority Rights' and 'The
Rat-Race Ends Here'. A series of local publications outlining the case
for Rutland were also produced in the early 1960s, a central tenet of
which was the notion that, as Bryan Waites implied, the scale of the
county's administration was in proportion to the local scale of human
activity. For this, the failure of a post-war vision of urbanity was frequently counterposed to the more bucolic social order of England's
smallest county.[3]

From the outset, this was a battle against the forces of a modernizing
government who, it was feared, sought to impose a regularized, urba-
nized management of life. Rutland was seen as a unique county, passed
over by the Industrial Revolution and modern commercial and technological developments. Population shifts, new and developing centres of
industry (including the East Midlands), expanding and new towns did
make old boundaries anachronistic and created planning problems.
But the argument was that Rutland in 1962 had remained unchanged
since 1888.[4]

The Council were cautious not to give the impression that Rutland
was a backwater. The tone of the County's campaign mixed both the
rhetoric of local iconic distinctiveness and the rationale of modernity
and efficiency in current and planned county services. Following the
original announcement, Rutland began to develop itself as a viable
administrative area under the government's terms. Local planners were
anxious to attract light industry into the county providing an economic
base upon which planned public improvement schemes could draw
without adversely affecting one of the lowest rates in the country. The
publicity which attended the independence campaign 'put the county

on the map' and even after the withdrawal of the Boundary Commission's recommendations in 1963 the processes of modernizing the county continued so as to avert any future threat.[5] The county, however, eventually became a second-tier authority beneath Leicestershire in 1974 under administrative changes which explicitly sought to rationalize local services in line with the 'pattern of life and work in modern society'.[6]

Whilst Rutland in its struggle for independence aligned itself to the idea of a modern nation, it also outlined its position as a natural and national territory, one whose landscape and social order affirmed a nostalgic construction of a broader English identity, 'the very fibre that has made England the great country it is today'.[7] In both senses, Rutland had, by the 1960s, become a functioning, connected and accessible territory whose historical and symbolic links along with its structural and economic position reached well beyond the county's ancient boundaries. The processes of structural modernization, reconstruction and local resistance therefore had the contradictory effects of opening the county's ancient boundaries economically and iconographically, but also securing the exclusivity of the territory. And these confused cultural politics of 'access' worked themselves out in the design and landscaping of the new reservoir environment.

Rutland Water: Managing the Scale of Human Affairs

Similar arguments of scale, rurality and tradition characterized local resistance to the Empingham reservoir (later renamed Rutland Water). The reservoir covers three-and-a-half per cent of Rutland's total acreage, and it was the scale of the enterprise and the ways in which that scale would affect traditional rural culture which worried the same local grandees who had orchestrated earlier battles. Positions forged in the battle for independence were recalled in the much smaller dispute over the reservoir. Meeting ambitious plans for urban growth, dictated a reservoir construction in a self-consciously rural area 'which had little sympathy with the needs of the towns and cities where the demand for water was concentrated' (Lawson, 1982, p. 19). However, for a county which had proven its modern credentials in the battle to retain independence, the siting of a very modern water regulation scheme to supply the expanding urban areas of the East Midlands would seem less controversial in 1968 than were it proposed twenty years earlier. Despite this, local pressure groups convened to fight the plans, which, it was felt, would further integrate Rutland into an efficiently functioning nation, and the local branches of the National Farmers Union, the Country Landowners Association, the newly established Rutland CPRE and the County Council shared the goal of challenging the suitability of the reservoir.

It was hoped, however, that in a concern for landscape aesthetics at all scales, including the biological, the reservoir would complement and enhance the iconic position of Rutland. Landscaping was central to the management of the new environment and remains one of the major recognized achievements of the scheme. Even local activists who had vehemently opposed the ceding of the county to a larger territory saw the potential of the reservoir to re-create Rutland as 'part of a grand strategy' for the region and the nation. What was happening to Rutland could be seen as a 'formula of change for other areas too ... it reflects national changes' (Waites, 1973, p. 71). In short, the reservoir would serve as symbol and source of local and national advancement, at once both distinctly Rutland and definitively England.

In 1968, the landscape architects Dame Sylvia Crowe and Associates were engaged by the Welland and Nene River Authority to consult on various aspects of the scheme's aesthetics. In line with the philosophy of some inter- and post-war planning and design (Stamp, 1946; Stamp, 1960; Rycroft and Cosgrove, 1994), Crowe believed that the character of a landscape was largely the product of physical geography and human evolution; of the 'configuration of the ground and the scale of its variation; the existing type and pattern of vegetation and land use and the prevailing colour of rock, soil and structures' (Crowe, 1978, p. 7). Existing landscape patterns had evolved from past land use, which in turn was based upon climatic and geological constraints. As a base-line for any project which sought to alter the environment, so affecting access, amenity and conservation, distilling and understanding the 'essential character' of that landscape was central. At interest here was not the conservation of the physical landscape *per se*, but the conservation of local landscape values, which related to the history of land-use evolution and practices in a region. Employing this approach, any existing elements which lent beauty or distinction to a landscape could be identified in a detailed and qualitative site analysis so that any land-use change would not diminish it. Similarly, existing features which degraded a landscape's character should be screened. In short, a design for a scheme which noted local character and landscape values would actually enhance the beauty of the scene and provide a coherent landscape experience for those accessing the reservoir and Rutland generally. The site's physical geography and the ways in which it dictated modes of intervention complemented Crowe's aesthetics. Rutland Water was a very different proposition to other large reservoir schemes. Since the majority of materials in the major works were reclaimed from the landscape itself, engineering parameters were as flexible as possible to allow for unforeseen obstacles. Natural limitations, therefore, dictated the morphology of the scheme. Its design was pragmatic, particularly for the dam, and relied largely upon local geology (Atkinson, 1973, pp. 32–3). From the outset, the scheme was, in a sense, more open to a sympathetic approach to landscape design that would blend both new and existing environments.

Sylvia Crowe was concerned to harmonize with the existing landscape features and integrate new ones. The shape of the reservoir was a particular inspiration, with the Hambleton peninsula forming an 'attractive landscape', a feature which was to be seen from all sides of the reservoir and one which partly solved the problem of scale (Crowe, 1974, p. 11). Indeed, Crowe felt the essence of Rutland's character was of 'human scale and tranquillity rather than drama' (Crowe, 1982, p. 43). She felt that although the surrounding countryside was 'attractive', with villages set in well farmed land, hedgerows and small woodlands, this landscape posed problems for integrating a vast expanse of water and particularly the associated recreational facilities that should also be provided. This had to be balanced, in the light of local opposition, with the need to retain the characteristic rural peace of Rutland. Car parks and other sites for access to the reservoir were accordingly positioned and landscaped to maximise access and minimise disruption to local life. The scheme's landscape design was based upon the guiding principle that the reservoir, its works and recreation facilities had to form a 'unified landscape' ... whose components come together into an overall composition with the surrounding countryside, without visible boundaries or jarring notes' (Crowe, 1974, p. 12).[8] Early co-operation between engineers, architects and landscape architects ensured this unity. Excavated soil from the bed of the reservoir was contoured to scale down works buildings and other infrastructures, knitting them into the scale of the surrounding landscape, which had 'small-scale undulations' as a defining character (Crowe, 1982, p. 45). A canalized stream was designed 'on easy curves' instead of straight lines and the mono slabs of concrete and grass along the dam with the grass on the downstream slope provided a continuous visual sweep up to the wave wall, with planted trees to 'relate' the dam to the surrounding landscape (Crowe, 1974, p. 44). Car parks received 'special attention' so that the 'glittering masses of cars' would not be seen from across the water, being hidden by trees and bunds. To ensure a continuous landscape aesthetic from the new environment to the old, local methods of restricting access were employed: agricultural fences of wooden post and rail, supplemented where desirable by thorn-field hedging. All of these measures were, therefore, 'in accordance with the policy of excluding urban elements from the reservoir, keeping the whole development in character with its surroundings', a policy which Crowe felt would need to be maintained to ensure that visitor pressure would not lead to unsuitable developments: 'The demand will ... be insatiable, and the determining factor should be the site's capability of absorption without losing its character as a magnificent sheet of water set in a landscape neither wild nor grand, but representing the best of rural England' (Crowe, 1974).

Whilst protecting traditional landscape values and preserving the county's iconic position, the landscaping scheme also catered for a different and more recent culture of access. By the late 1960s, a concern for the environment had become integral to landscape design and particularly to the landscape planning of water management schemes. An increase in the acreage of water surface partially compensated for the drainage of wetlands elsewhere in Britain, providing habitats for fast disappearing flora and fauna, and regional water companies were charged with the responsibility of conserving wildlife and ensuring recreation facilities. An increase in the demand for water-related recreation was matched by an increase in public interest for wildlife conservation. By 1981 Sylvia Crowe's insistence on an active policy of environmental 'conservation' at Empingham had attracted so many new species of wildfowl that Rutland Water was declared a site of Special Scientific Interest (Moore and Driver, 1989, pp. 203–12). The Nature Conservancy and local Naturalists' Trusts co-operated with Crowe in the planning of the nature reserve at the shallow west end of the reservoir's southern arm. Islands, bunds and lagoons were formed during construction to encourage wildlife and provide nesting sites for wildfowl. Different types of habitat were developed for a wide range of species: creeks, marshes, mud flats, reeds, osiers, pasture, undergrowth and woodland. Away from the water line, tree belts were planted to give shelter. Other spots were left unplanted, including a medieval meadow. Indigenous plant communities were established, oak, ash and lime[9] and flora was transplanted from the woodland in the area to be flooded

(Crowe, 1974, pp. 10–11). Environmental conservation schemes had aesthetic benefits, allowing the merging of old and new landscapes. The planting of trees and hedgerows on the edge of the water was complemented by the planting of semi-aquatic plants in apposite sites so as to avoid the 'hard line' formed at high-water level and appearance of mud flats at low-water mark (Crowe, 1982, pp. 43–4).

Changes in the technology of water purification had reduced the need to exclude the public from recreating and ushered in a concept of 'multiple use', actually facilitating the 'conservation' of 'fine landscape' and long-held land-use values. Reservoirs could now become 'beautiful features' and need no longer be 'hideous disfigurements of natural scenery' designed with the single purpose of economic efficiency (Colvin, 1970, pp. 236–7). It was decided at Rutland that any recreational and leisure facilities would reflect the essentially rural character of the surrounding countryside with maximum use being made of existing buildings and infrastructures (Adams, 1983, p. 137). Water skiing, power boating and caravan camps, therefore, were deemed unsuitable pursuits in such a landscape (Crowe, 1982, p. 45). The grounds of access to the reservoir were effectively dictated by a selfconscious construction of the county as a slice of quintessential Englishness. Whilst this iconography clearly refers beyond the local and is widely accessible, its exclusivity is very apparent. Through both design and management the new environment restricted the means of access to those activities considered in harmony with rurality.

Indeed, there was a great deal of opposition towards the reservoir as a recreational resource. Like the fight for independence before it, those who opposed the reservoir were worried about the change in ways of life that might be encouraged by the development of amenities. It was regarded as an 'urban intrusion' by the Labour MP for High Peak, Peter Jackson, who considered the type of landscaping proposed not to be suitable for the character and tradition of Rutland. Furthermore, the two bodies whose primary concern was for the amenity of the countryside, the Council for the Protection of Rural England (CPRE) and the Ramblers' Association, were both totally opposed to the Bill.[10] Local Ramblers paid a last visit to the reservoir site in 1971 before 'technocracy' dammed the valley and filled it with an 'iconoclastic lake'.[11] Local senior clergy met planners to discuss future social problems in the region, and, along with difficulties in new towns and changing village life, identified the recreational facilities at the reservoir as a possible source of social change and conflict.[12]

To allay these fears Sylvia Crowe held a public meeting in Oakham sponsored by the local CPRE where she outlined all of the landscaping and amenity plans and was at pains to point out the care that would be taken in blending the reservoir both physically and culturally into the landscape.[16] She placed local values at the centre of the her agenda; striking accord with the preservationists, she rejected the vision of Rutland-on-Sea: 'You don't want neon lights, strings of flags, advertisements and cheapjack souvenir shops. Let's keep the place quiet, seemly and welcome. If you want to know how to do that you have only got to go to Scandinavia or Switzerland.'[17] Crowe also located the scheme within an emergent global environmental concern, outlining the international importance of the nature reserve as an amenable asset.

For some, these cultural politics of access took on a wider significance. Rutland's struggle against the 'twentieth-century environmental juggernaut' in the form of a reservoir was focused upon the notion of the county as a microcosm of rural England in landscape and society. Whilst it stressed its independence from the great revolutions and battles in the nation's history, it also constructed its own evolution as an epitome of the 'greater theme of the nation's developing unification' (Waites, 1983, pp. 133–4). By the 1960s, with the growth of industrial cities in the East Midlands, the extension of road and rail links to Rutland, increased house building and the wider provision of electricity and water, the county became attractive to commuters and a restructured rural society emerged. Accounts in local newspapers suggest that newcomers were vociferous in their support for the preservation of local identity suggesting that, perhaps, regardless of broader structural changes, the discourses of identity are not necessarily mutable, nor can they be easily extrapolated from the economic base.

By asserting a specific regional identity and by delineating its place within a modern post-war Britain, however, Rutland had also accepted a functional position within the territorial order of the nation. The reservoir was in the national interest, and, despite local opposition, was eventually accepted as such, particularly with the change to a Conservative government in 1971. But the reservoir was also envisioned and planned in a period of decreasing faith in the effectiveness of modern planning, particularly in a large-scale schemes which seemed to have little regard for local identities, and at a time of increasing environmental awareness. Consequently, conservation issues, environmental issues and landscape issues loomed large in the execution of the 'Rutland Project'. Such sympathetic planning reflected not simply a local concern for the quality of landscape and way of life, but also national trends towards pragmatic planning, motivated more by a doubt in modern planning than by any coherent vision of social or environmental order.

Rutland Water, as it was renamed following another local campaign in 1977, became not so much a memorial to the old county, but a centrepiece, putting Rutland back on the map: 'Rutland will be famous for its reservoir, as it has been for its peace; its lanes; its churches; its horseshoes, and its fox-hunting. In many ways Rutland will be re-created' (Waites, 1973, p. 61). Bryan Waites was, eventually, a strong supporter of the reservoir to reinvigorate an organic regional identity. In his bid to realize W.G. Hoskins' vision of Rutland as a 'human conservancy', he advocated that the reservoir should be 'seized on as a wonderful opportunity to create a new environment for the 21st century', one which would serve as a 'vast open-air laboratory promoting environmental education for adults and children as a community' (Waites, 1972, p. 41). Rutland Water would encourage a 'special awareness' and appreciation of the environment, so that its workings could be understood and acted upon. Moreover, it could fulfil a 'natural' aesthetic and emotional need in the landscape, a psychological requirement which was beyond scenic value alone. Drawing on Lewis Mumford's notion of the landscape as a source of essential values for a balanced life, Waites hoped that the reservoir, as an integrated scheme evolving an environment which brought into focus 'planning, sociological, biological, ecological and educational issues on grand scale', would become a 'hand-specimen of a new landscape for the mind issuing from the old', a realized human conservancy promoting bio-technic well-being to all who accessed (Waites, 1972, p. 41).[18] Discourses of access, therefore, even when based upon the science of environment, are still considered central to the construction of identities.

Today, the reservoir has, perhaps, realized that vision. It is widely acknowledged as the county's best resource, attracting a level of economic activity into the district that other rural districts in the East Midlands have missed, particularly with the decline in coal mining. In a contradiction of the fears voiced by reservoir protesters in the past, the recent re-establishment of the county once again in control all of its affairs might, in part, be due to this success. The reservoir is an important site for environmental education and conservation, Olympic-class sailing, trout fishing, rambling and sightseeing. The combination of conservation and change embodied in the scheme appears to have been successful: 'it is easier now to lead a full life in

Rutland. ... the future has arrived, but it has not destroyed the past' (Waites, 1980, p. 18). But the reservoir seems to have enhanced the prevailing image of Rutland, and the grounds of access are effectively dictated by discourses of local and iconic national identity.

Notes

1. This quote draws on Lewis Mumford word-for-word and is written up in numerous other pieces by Waites (e.g. 1972, pp. 48–9). Bryan Waites, a lecturer in geography at Leicester College of Education, had only been resident in Rutlandshire for six years at this point. He supervised a historical geography fieldwork project on the villages of Rutland in 1972, in which questions were asked of local residents concerning the independence of Rutland. The results were sent to the Boundaries Commission, 'People of Rutland Say "Keep Status": Students' Survey', *Rutland Mercury*, 9 June 1972.

2. 1960: 'Name of Rutland Will not Vanish – Chairman: Boundary Commission Give an Assurance', *Leicester Evening Mail*, 1 July 1960.

3. Information on the independence battle and the various strategies employed by the council described throughout this chapter is taken from the County Council minute books and various Committee Reports. These are held at the Leicestershire County Public Records Office.

4. Ritson, E.H. (1962) *Ministry of Housing and Local Government, East Midlands Review Area: Report of the Inspector appointed by the Minister of Housing and Local Government to hear objections to the proposed amalgamation of Leicestershire and Rutland, and to the recommendation that the area of the present County of Rutland (subject to minor boundary adjustments) should form a single rural district.* HMSO: London, p. 5.

5. 'Independent Rutland', *The Leicester Graphic: Special Rutland Supplement*, Vol. 14, No. 112, August 1964.

6. Quote from Government White Paper in 'Merger Proposal For Lincolnshire: Rutland to Lose County Status?', *Lincoln, Rutland and Stamford Mercury*, 19 February 1971.

7. From *The Case For Rutland: A 'Fight For Rutland' Official Production*, 6 July 1962, p. 11. These feelings were expressed by Alan Bond, the Council clerk, in a publication sponsored by the Fighting Fund for Rutland. It was produced as a supplement to the *Lincoln, Rutland and Stamford Mercury*, the county buying 2000 extra copies for distribution to members of the House of Commons and House of Lords. Local Government Reorganisation Committee reports for the County Council meeting of 28 July 1962 indicate that it was hoped the production cost of £420 would be offset by £300 income from advertisers. Advertisements contained in the supplement seem to jar with the rural image, however, including those for fast cars and fashionable boutiques.

8. This perspective is echoed in the advice of landscape architect Brenda Colvin for the treatment of landscapes around reservoirs. She stressed that 'new forms' should be linked to the surrounding land-use pattern by using local flora and contouring the land: in Colvin, B. (1970) *Land and Landscape: Evolution, Design and Control*, London: John Murray, pp. 340–44.

9. Sylvia Crowe drew on her experience as landscape consultant to the Forestry Commission for the Rutland Project.

10. 'Rutland Does Not Want to be a Towpath Round a Lake, Says MP', 1969 (un-attributed and undated clipping from Rutland County Local Studies Library).

11. 'Ramblers Visit an About-to-be-Drowned Valley', *Melton and Rutland Journal*, 2 April 1971.

12. 'Rutland Reservoir May Radically Change Social Structure of the County', *Melton and Rutland Journal*, 22 January 1971.

16. 'Oakham Meeting On Reservoir Amenities', *Stamford Mercury*, 11 September 1970; 'Reservoir Accommodation for 3,000 Cars Planned', *Rutland Journal*, 9 October 1970.

17. 'New Life and Prosperity With the Reservoir', *Lincoln, Rutland and Stamford Mercury*, 23 October 1970.

18. Waites, B. (1972) 'Rutland: Human Conservancy?', *Leicester-Rutland Topic*, June 1972, p. 49; 'World Famous and Historic County Seems to be Silently Fading Away', *Grantham Journal*, 11 February 1972; 'Name Dam Rutland?', *Lincoln, Rutland and Stamford Mercury*, 28 January 1972.

9

Accessing the Attractive Coast: Conflicts and Co-operation in the Swedish Coastal Landscape during the Twentieth Century

BJÖRN SEGRELL

Introduction

The coastal areas of Sweden, covering a distance of some 7600 kilometres (including the bays and main islands) have, during various parts of history, played a significant role in the economic and social development of the country. Settlements spread along the shores where farming, fishery and hunting were stimulated by the comparatively easy access to transport. During a large part of the industrial era, however, the cores of economic and social activity gradually became established in urban centres. Many of these have a coastal location in Sweden, but the urban–industrial influence on the coastal areas as such was rather limited. Concurrently with urban growth, extensive coastal areas became depopulated and the importance of traditional trades decreased. For part of the industrial era much of the coastal landscape in Sweden stood somewhat on the periphery.

Gradually, however, several interest groups have increasingly focused their attention on the coastal areas. For industries and waste-treatment activities, coastal locations offer superior transport and recipient conditions. During the 1950s and 1960s, large-scale industries expanded rapidly and established themselves in locations along the coast that previously were neither used nor intended for these kind of activities. Parallel with this expansion, the improvement in welfare had given ordinary people more spare time and better economic opportunities to spend it outside the cities. As early as the end of the nineteenth century, the Swedish coastal areas became a place for recreation and holiday activities; however, this was confined to persons of means, thus to a small group in society. During the twentieth century, large parts of the

Swedish coast have become accessible for many more people, as areas of major importance for recreational activities. Finally, the coastal zone includes areas and resources that are increasingly considered to be of prime national importance both in terms of their cultural as well as their natural features. Taken together, these new activities and interests have radically affected and changed the landscape (Swedish Ministry of Housing, 1988, p. 8.).

The Swedish landscape has been radically affected by economic and social changes. One includes the gradual transfer, in a broad sense, of the population from the rural areas and rural-based occupations to urban living. At the turn of the twentieth century, about 80 per cent of the population was found in rural environments. In the 1940s about half of the population was urban, and today the rural population constitutes less than 5 per cent. These figures hide some changes that are of basic importance for the evolution of the landscape. We often forget that the urban population does, of course, shape the rural landscape and lives from its produce as much as its rural counterparts. The indirect impact that is a result of this purchasing power, the expansion of industries and the spread of various forms of urban services, central control and administration, are significant forces behind the evolution of the rural landscape. In many respects the appearance of rural areas mirrors urban-based interests and control (Segrell and Lundqvist, 1993).

The transfer of people from the rural to the urban areas does not necessarily lead to immediate changes in perceptions and world views. Until fairly recently the great majority of the urban population was not born in urban milieus, and their roots were in their original environments. When holiday periods were expanded from the late 1930s and the urban population could afford to spend more of their leisure time in the countryside, a large proportion did, in fact, return to a milieu whose values they probably shared and respected. Today, however, the great majority of the urban population is also born in urban areas.

This chapter portrays the changing role and importance of the coastal zone in Sweden during the last half-century or so, as expressed by various interest groups and representatives of society. It focuses on who controls the transformation and the use of the landscape, as well as on the response of the changing role of the coastal landscape to the Swedish public in terms of access or non-access. The coastal zone cannot easily be demarcated in geographical or administrative terms, but according to the most narrow definition used in the Riparian Law, it includes an area of 100 to 300 metres from the shore line. A more wide and flexible definition refers to the demarcations by the individual county councils, according to the Natural Resource Act, which protect certain areas because of their importance for public outdoor life, scenes of natural beauty or other environmental or cultural values. The County Council of Östergötland, for instance, has drawn a general line between 500 and 1,000 metres from the shore line along the coast to demarcate such areas.

Demands for Access and Conflicts

The tension resulting from a very rapid increase in the demand for limited but attractive locations and resources was very much at the centre of debate in the 1960s. At that time, industrial expansion along the west coast was particularly rapid and threatened recreational interests (Forsberg, 1992a). No less than 20 nuclear power plants (today the number is 12), a number of new pulp industries, oil refineries, chemical and other heavy industries were envisaged as future locations along the coast, especially in southern and central Sweden. The industrial expansion was based on strong economic interests, both private and public, but at the same time the authorities also supported public recreation interests, above all outdoor activities, in coastal areas. Other water- and land-use conflicts during this period were between urban expansion and farming, summer houses and outdoor activities as well as between spare-time activities and the preservation of nature (Swedish Commission Report 1979; p. 13, Forsberg, 1992b). The number of summer houses increased rapidly during the 1960s (see Figure 9.1) and this development was seen as a serious threat above all to the public's access to attractive recreational areas. The authorities responded with measures that were ratified through the *Fysisk riksplanering*, the Swedish National Land-Use Planning system, established in 1972. However, the *Fysisk riksplanering* did not became a law in a strict sense. It was a broad guideline for planning authorities at different levels, which needed to be specified and developed at regional and local levels. By 1972 it was proposed that a confirmation of the regulations should be carried out, but at that time such confirmation had to wait, because of the ongoing work with the proposal for a new Swedish Planning and Building Act (Official Parliamentary Publications, Bill no. 1985/86: 3, 8). It was not until 1987 that the National Land-Use Planning regulations were transformed into the *Naturresurslagen*, the Natural Resource Act.

The main principle of the Natural Resource Act is that land and water areas shall be used in a way which 'they are best suited for' (Swedish

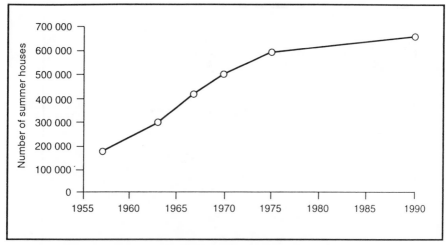

Figure 9.1   Summer house expansion in Sweden, 1957–90.
Source: Commission Report, 1979; Government Bill, 1990/91:90, Appendix A:76.

National Environment Protection Board (SNV), 1990b, p. 43). In practice this means that the land- and water-use planning at all levels shall aim to create a situation where different activities dominate in different areas. However, in the Natural Resource Act, there are also concrete directions for certain areas of national importance, *riksintressen*, because of environmental and cultural values. They are more strongly protected against exploitation and the central authorities control their use. However, urban growth, local trade and industry and the Swedish national defence are not restrained by the *riksintressen* regulations; mostly it covers coastal and mountain areas, and also some rivers classed (Eliason, Hellström and Johansson, 1987, pp. 10–14; see Figure 9.2).

Conflicts and Co-operation at the National Level – The Riparian Law

From preservation to conservation

In the 1930s, politicians and other groups in society, for instance the Swedish Society for the Conservation of Nature, *Naturskyddsföreningen*, started to discuss the use of coastal areas, primarily for outdoor recreational activities. These discussions were an important part of the transition in the view on the relationship between Man and Nature in Sweden; from preservation to conservation of nature, to use Passmore's (1974) definition. When the preservationists wanted to stop all use or

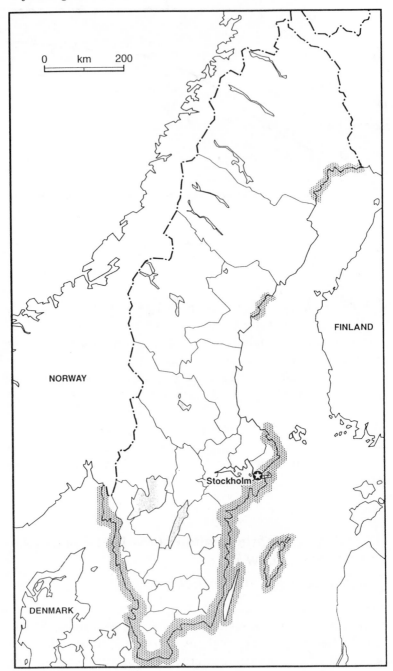

Figure 9.2 Coastal areas, classified as being of national importance (*riksintressen*) because of considerable natural and cultural values, according to the Natural Resource Act (SFS 1987:12).

development in some areas, on the basis that these areas and their resources were too valuable to be used, the conservationists encouraged careful husbandry of resources. In other words, when preservation aimed at protecting nature areas *from* humans, conservation aimed at doing the same, but *for* humans (Passmore, 1974, p. 73; Haraldsson, 1987, p. 13; Hillmo and Lohm, 1990, p. 101). Sweden had been the first country in Europe to establish national parks in 1909, in connection with the first Nature Protection Act. Most of these were in mountain areas in the north and far away from urban areas (Cutter, Renwick and Renwick, 1991, pp. 34–6; SNV, 1989, pp. 15–16; Ödmann, Bucht and Nordström, 1982, p. 79). Opportunities for ordinary people to visit the national parks were, therefore, quite limited.

Industrialization, urbanization, democratization, economic growth and technical development necessitated a new attitude towards Nature and corresponding arrangements to meet the emerging new needs and demands. The conservation ideology became the response to a new geographical dimension of the socio-economic situation. From the turn of the century to 1930 the farming population decreased from 80 to 35 per cent of the total population and during the same period the industrial population increased from 10 to 40 per cent. More and more people moved to the cities and were, in a sense, parted from Nature. The demand and, indeed, the need for outdoor recreation and 'away-but-near-to-town' activities and arrangements increased rapidly. Areas where such activities could be developed were, however, also under pressure from other interests, mainly urban and industrial expansion. Land-use conflicts arose and preservation of certain nature areas in the vicinity of cities was discussed as one way of handling the new situation.

The interest from a growing urban population for recreation outside cities and industrial centres was stimulated by the introduction of the first Holiday Act of 1938 (two weeks' paid holiday for all employees). Changes in settlement patterns, employment structure and economic opportunity contributed to a strengthening of the social dimension in the use of natural resources.

Nature as Compensation

The first official expression of these new thoughts were two parliamentary motions in 1936, where an 'idea of compensation' was well defined. Three Social Democrat members of parliament argued that modern industrial society and the urbanization process created increasing strain and stress, physically and psychologically, for the working population in the cities. Therefore, the need for compensation in the form of recreation and open-air activities increased. The authorities should secure the possibilities for open-air activities, especially for the urban population. Open-air bathing was considered to be one of the best counter-balances to stress and strain in modern working life, and the motion writers suggested that public recreation areas, including beaches by the sea and lakes, should be established.

In the 1930s, before the general holiday reforms and the breakthrough for private motoring in Sweden, the need for recreation areas was perceived as a local issue. The proposed public areas should be easily accessible to the urban population, and therefore they had to be located near the cities in areas where competition with other land-use interests was very severe. According to the parliamentary motions the public recreation areas should solve differing problems, not only giving common people the right to meaningful spare time, but also protecting other areas, for instance, land owned by farmers, from damage.

The Right of Public Access

The famous Swedish *allemansrätten*, the Right of Public Access, was not mentioned in the parliamentary motions of 1936. *Allemansrätten* is not a legal right in a strict sense, but a practice with its roots in the Middle Ages. Briefly, this 'public access' gives everyone the right, under certain conditions, to stay temporarily on private land and, for instance, pick wild berries, flowers or mushrooms. In fact, if the ideas in the motions had materialized it is likely that access to nature would have been quite different from the actual, subsequent development. If special recreational areas had been created, the public would have had much less access to other parts of the countryside. In other words, the Right of Public Access, as we know it today, might have been severely curtailed.

However, at the end of the 1930s, when the question of public recreation and open-air activities had been under debate for some years, it became obvious that it would not be sufficient to establish public recreation areas on domains already owned by the state or the municipalities, if the ideas in the parliamentary motions were to be realized. To satisfy the increasing demand for areas for recreation and outdoor activities the authorities also had to buy privately-owned land on a large scale, and this would be possible only at a very large cost to society (Swedish Commission Report, 1940). This was not realistic at the time and, in this context, the Right of Public Access was put forward as an alternative solution to the problem. By 'dusting off' this old practice and making it commonly accepted, almost any countryside area became accessible for public outdoor life, and at no real cost to the state or the municipalities. The private landowners had little chance to oppose *allemansrätten*. It was put forward at a time characterized by strong nationalism and need for national unity, and it was difficult to criticize it for historical and nationalistic reasons. The most important reason, however, was that the Right of Public Access did not provoke any dominant economic interests, neither private nor public. It did not, for instance, lead to any real reduction of the land ownership.

However, the *allemansrätten* that was discussed in the 1930s had completely different motives from the old common right in pre-industrial Sweden, when long distances and poor communications in a sparsely populated country made it necessary to have the possibility of walking across other people's land, staying there temporarily, for instance overnight, and making a fire, picking berries, etc. Now the Right of Public Access would make recreation and outdoor activities possible for everyone. Despite the landowners' will, people would be able to ramble, exercise, bathe, etc. almost everywhere, although according to certain regulations. The question as to whether camping was to be allowed was uncertain, as it was a new outdoor activity in Sweden in the 1930s (Swedish Commission Report, 1940, appendix 2).

Through the common acceptance of the new aim of the Right of Public Access at the end of the 1930s and the beginning of the 1940s, the proposal to reserve certain areas for public outdoor life was really no longer relevant. However, in some beach areas, by lakes and along the coasts, public outdoor life was threatened in spite of the Right of Public Access. Other interests, manifested above all by summer house expansion, competed with the public outdoor activities in attractive areas. This was first noticed in the Stockholm archipelago in the mid 1930s and later in other parts of the country (Romell, 1936; Lindman and Påhlman, 1936). As such a development was commonly considered a serious problem at the time, demands were raised for some sort of legislation that would support and interact with the *allemansrätten* in order to ensure the possibilities of outdoor activities for the public.

The Big Threat – Summer-House Expansion

The parliamentary motions in 1936 initiated the first official leisure-time report in 1937 (Swedish Commission Report, 1940). However, in

1938 an official report suggested that a special Riparian Law should be drafted. According to this law no buildings, especially not summer houses, should be allowed in a 500-metre-wide zone along the coast and by the larger lakes (Swedish Commission Report, 1938). This law, together with *allemansrätten*, would secure public access to the beaches. The fact that the summer-house expansion was considered as a severe problem was based mainly on the situation in the Stockholm archipelago, where, since the turn of the century, uncontrolled summer-house building had occupied more and more attractive beaches. In other areas public access was almost completely eradicated by this development, and several county architects demanded some sort of beach protection (Swedish Commission Report, 1938, pp. 50–66).

Reference was given to Denmark, where the Nature Protection Act of 1937 did not allow new buildings in a 100-metre-wide zone and the public had general access to the beaches by foot. In Germany, restrictions for houses and other buildings in beach areas were introduced as early as in 1922, and along the shores of the North Sea and the Baltic Sea a general prohibition against building activities in a 100-metre-wide zone was in force (Swedish Commission Reports, 1938, 1940).

New Age – Old Problems

However, the official leisure time report did not initiate any legislation. The proposal of public recreation areas owned by the authorities was, as mentioned earlier, already undermined when the report was presented in 1940. Concerning the question of the summer house expansion, World War II postponed the issue for the time being. The economic consequences of the war led to a crisis in the building trade, which among other things negatively affected the summer-house expansion (Swedish Commission Report, 1952, p. 1160). Thus, for the moment the problem was dissolved rather than resolved. But in 1949 the discussion about a beach protection law returned, this time through an initiative from the Social Democratic government. A proposal with the aim of securing public access to the beaches was worked out by the Ministry of Justice: the county administrative boards were to decide that no building was allowed in a maximum 300-metre-wide zone along certain beaches. This protection was selective and therefore weaker than the proposal from the official report of 1938. Two economic aspects are of special interest: buildings needed for farming, forestry, fishery, communications and military defence should be exempted from the law; and landowners who got their right of disposal restricted by the beach protection law should not get any economic compensation (Swedish Commission Report, 1951).

The law was meant to be temporary for two years; meanwhile a proposal for a permanent law should be worked out. The need for a temporary law was motivated by the Ministry of Justice under the presumption that the 1950s would see a more intense summer-house expansion than ever before, and beaches that still were accessible to the public would be seriously threatened (Swedish Official Parliamentary Publications, Bill no. 223/1950). However, the first estimate of the number of summer houses at a national level was not carried out until 1957 (Figure 9.1). The lack of compensation to the landowners raised furious opposition in parliament, mainly from the Conservative party *Högerpartiet* and the Farmers' party *Bondeförbundet.* Despite this opposition the proposal was accepted by parliament in 1950 (Swedish Official Parliamentary Publications, record AK no. 32: 103/1950).

In 1952, a proposal for a permanent beach protection law, The Riparian Law, was presented to parliament. In the main, this was the same as the temporary law, but regulations about economic compensation to landowners were now included.

Therefore opposition was not anything similar to that two years earlier and the permanent beach protection law was passed with great support in parliament (Swedish Official Parliamentary Publications, Bill no. 187/1952; record AK no. 22, FK no. 21/1952; Swedish Code of Statutes (SFS) 1952: 382). As in the 1930s, the aim was conservation, and not preservation, of the beaches and summer-house expansion was considered as the big threat against the public's opportunity for meaningful spare time and recreation activities. At the end of 1961 the county administrative boards had put a total of over 13,700 kilometres of beach under the law, of which 7000 kilometres were in coastal areas (Swedish Commission Report, 1962). In 1964, the beach protection regulations were included in the new Nature Conservation Act, without any significant changes (Swedish Code of Statutes (SFS) 1964: 822).

From Selective to General Beach Protection

The selective beach protection regulations from 1950/52 were in force until 1975, when the section concerning beach protection in the Nature Conservation Act was rewritten. Because of the continuing increase of pressure against the beaches, the Social Democratic Government wanted to tighten up the regulations, and once again priority was given to the public's outdoor activities. Therefore the regulations were now automatically in force along all beaches in a 100-metre-wide zone, with the possibility of expanding the zone up to 300 metres. However, the county administrative boards could decide to abrogate the regulations in certain areas that obviously had no importance for public recreational activities. Furthermore, buildings necessary for farming, forestry, fishery and reindeer breeding would not be affected by the regulations. In addition, it was possible for the county administrative boards to grant exemptions for summer houses and other buildings, when 'special circumstances' existed (SFS 1974: 1025). Moreover, the new rules allowed the county administrative boards to delegate the possibility to grant exemptions to the municipalities, in full or partly, although in many cases the county administrative boards retained control over the attractive coastal areas (Swedish Commission Report, 1990, p. 380; 1993, p. 490).

These beach protection regulations are still in force and since 1 July 1994 are amplified by ecological motives to protect living conditions for plants and animals (Swedish Official Parliamentary Publications, Bill no. 1993/94: 229). In 1988 an official report reviewed the Nature Conservation Act and came to the conclusion that beach protection worked satisfactorily (Swedish Commission Report, 1990). However, in parliament the Conservative party, *Moderata Samlingspartiet,* has opposed the general regulation, preferring a selective beach protection that allows a differentiated application. Their main argument is that the general law is too bureaucratic and not in accordance with real conditions (Swedish Official Parliamentary Publications, motion no. Jo752/ 1988/89; Jo713/1989/90; Segrell, 1993). However, a differentiated application of the beach protection regulations, adjusted to local conditions in various parts of the country, has not yet come into practice.

Exemptions and Appeals

Between 3000 and 4000 exemptions from general beach protection are currently granted each year. Most are motivated as cases with 'special circumstances', for instance, a new summer-house to replace an old one or a new outhouse, complementary to a house on an established plot (SNV 1990a). However, from 1987 onwards the number of exemptions against which the Swedish National Environment Protection Board (*Statens Naturvårdsverk*) has appealed increased rapidly, and currently, 50–60 appeals are made each year. *Statens Naturvårdsverk* argues that the appealed exemptions are a threat against the public access to the beaches, and therefore they are not in accordance with the beach protection regulations (SNV, 1991a). From a local point of view, the exemptions are looked upon as one planning instrument among others, necessary to guarantee a 'living countryside'. For example, exemptions can be granted by local authorities with the purpose of making good housing conditions possible for local people or to attract investors, especially in thinly populated areas of the country. In addition, in these areas public outdoor activity is often not very extensive. However, most exemptions do not concern houses for permanent living, but summer houses (SNV, 1991a).

Conflicts and Co-operation at the Local Level – the National Park in the Sankt Anna Archipelago

From a national point of view, the Swedish coastal areas have considerable natural, cultural and recreational values. According to the Natural Resource Act, almost 80 per cent of the coastal areas in general are classified as being of national importance, *riksintressen*, for nature conservation and outdoor life (see Figure 9.2). In this respect the question of public access to attractive coastal areas is of great importance. For national authorities it is desirable to protect various coastal areas from different kinds of exploitation, in order to satisfy 'the need by individuals and society' to experience unspoiled and accessible nature. In practice, this can be done through nature reserves, national parks, etc. (SNV, 1991b, 6, 12). However, it is not always the case that centrally initiated environmental protection measures are accepted at the local level.

Outside urban areas, the Swedish coastal landscape is nowadays mostly sparsely populated. The people who still live in these peripheral areas are above all occupied in traditional activities, such as small-scale farming and fishing. They demand, not unexpectedly, maintenance of their economic activities (Boverket, 1993, p. 55, Swedish Commission Report, 1994, pp. 115–18). But protection measures, for instance the establishment of nature reserves as well as public recreation activities, or for that matter industrial expansion, often lead to restrictions in primary activities. Controls over forestry, hunting and building can be the consequence for the local landowners of a nature reserve. However, this does not mean that local people are against protection of nature in general. On the contrary, they are often engaged in the protection of local natural and cultural heritage. The question is rather how a specific area shall be protected in the best way and who will have the responsibility. From the local perspective it is better that local people, with detailed knowledge, manage the nature protection at the local level, as they always have done (Segrell, 1994).

'A system of national parks covering the entire country'

At the end of the 1980s a strategy for a new Swedish national park system was constructed by the National Environmental Protection Board, in order to 'determine which areas should be included in a system of national parks covering the entire country' (SNV, 1989, p. 121). The plan included a proposal for twenty new national parks, reconstruction of four existing parks and transformation of four existing parks into nature reserves. These last four are early established parks of a quality that does not match up to today's standards. Thirteen of the existing parks should remain unchanged. Thus, according to the plan Sweden will have 37 national parks (SNV, 1989, p. 122).

In the national park plan the importance of coastal areas, especially the archipelagos, was put forward. Among the existing parks the archipelagos were poorly represented, in spite of their very high natural and recreational values (SNV, 1989, p. 22; Miljöaktuellt no. 5/1989). Furthermore, the Swedish archipelagos were presented as unique from a European perspective. Only the Finnish archipelagos could be considered as comparable. So, both from a national and international point of view, it was important that national parks were established in these areas (SNV, 1989, pp. 22, 85). It is obvious that the National Environmental Protection Board's strategy also aimed at giving Sweden more international prestige in the field of environmental protection. Through the new national park system, nature in Sweden would be well known abroad and attract foreign tourists, and as a consequence, make various parts of the Swedish countryside more accessible for visitors from other countries. (SNV, 1989, pp. 12, 22, 85).

The National Park in the Sankt Anna Archipelago

According to the national park plan, five new parks should be established in island areas along the Swedish coast. For one, a location in the Sankt Anna archipelago on the east coast, in the province of Östergötland and the municipality of Söderköping, was suggested (Figure 9.3). This is an illustrative example of implications of centrally initiated

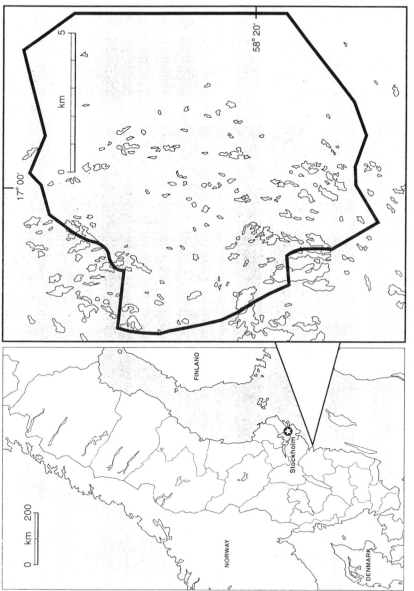

Figure 9.3   Proposed national park area in the Sankt Anna Archipelago, according to the National Park Plan (SNV, 1989)

protection measures, related to the question of public access to attractive coastal areas, at the local level. The Sankt Anna archipelago is no exception from the general picture in coastal areas concerning structure of the population and economy. The islands in particular are sparsely populated and primary activities dominate. The number of summer-houses in the area is rather large.

The proposed national park area will cover about 10,000 hectares, of which 400 are land; parts are already protected as nature reserves and by special bird protection rules. This area is regarded by the National Environmental Protection Board as a typical east coast archipelago, with finely chiselled gneiss bedrock and coniferous forest. As important characteristics of the area, 'outer and middle location, comparatively difficult to reach and undisturbed, countless small islets' are mentioned (SNV, 1989, p. 125). There are no summer-houses in the park area, only some small hunting cottages. However, parts of the planned national park are currently used for rather intensive sea-based recreational activities in the summer, in accordance with the Right of Public Access, and local small-scale fishing and hunting all year around. Still, the major part of the area is owned by local people, occupied in fishing and farming. To be able to establish the national park at all, the National Environmental Protection Board needs to own the whole area. Up to now, this authority has bought 25–30 per cent, mainly former municipality-owned areas. So far the private owners have refused to sell (SNV, 1989, pp. 88–90; Segrell, 1994).

Local Opposition

Among local people there is strong opposition for the national park proposal, primarily based on worries about the possibilities of carrying on traditional activities in the future. The wish to hand over a cultural and traditional heritage to future generations is also of importance, especially for those landowners whose properties have been owned by the same families for a long time. But there are also other arguments, connected to the questions of nature protection and public access to the countryside. The local inhabitants share the National Environmental Protection Board's opinion that it is necessary to protect the area from different types of exploitation. However, local people argue that a national park is not the best way of doing this, because of the distanced control it would lead to. From their point of view it is much better that local people handle the protection, since they have the best knowledge about the natural and cultural values in the area. The inhabitants have protected the area up to now in that it does not contain any summer houses; in fact, local people claim that this is the main reason for the interest in the area by the national authorities. Besides, the proposed park area is already satisfactorily protected through nature reserves, bird sanctuaries, regulations in the Riparian Law and as being of national importance, *riksintresse*, according to the Natural Resource Act (Segrell, 1994). In this viewpoint the local inhabitants are supported by the local authorities (Söderköpings Kommun, 1991).

Regarding the question of access, local people claim that a national park would lead to increasing environmental damage and exploitation, both inside and outside the park area. Because of its national park status the Sankt Anna archipelago would be well known in Sweden and abroad, and more visitors would result in increasing exploitation in the form of sea-based outdoor activities and nature tourism. Local people argue that if tough restrictions to public access were in force in the park, other parts of the Sankt Anna archipelago would be exposed to pressure from outdoor and tourist interests, with littering, wear and tear, disturbance to birds and so forth as a consequence (Segrell, 1994).

From a local point of view, it is better that the national authorities improve the possibilities for the local inhabitants to continue to live permanently and make a living in the Sankt Anna archipelago instead of establishing the national park, not only for the local people but for the natural and cultural values in the area (Segrell, 1994). It has also been pointed out that 'a living archipelago' is very important for most of the recreational and touristic activities, as much of the attraction, both of a natural and cultural kind, is connected to the people who have lived and live there (Boverket, 1993, p. 55).

Obviously, the National Environmental Protection Board and the inhabitants in the Sankt Anna archipelago have the same goal: to protect the area from exploitation and to preserve it for the future. For the national authority it is important to satisfy the public's need for access to attractive nature areas along the coasts, and to be able internationally to show a type of nature landscape that does not exist anywere else in Europe. From their point of view, the best and most effective way to achieve these goals is to establish a national park, or, in other words, to use the strongest nature protection instrument that the legislation provides. From the local perspective, however, the protection concerns an area that is a part of a landscape where local people live and work and is consequently both a natural and cultural habitat. Therefore, the best thing to do is to support the local inhabitant's way of life to which a historical heritage and a special native-born feeling for the home area belong.

The discrepancy between these two viewpoints explains why the implementation of the Sankt Anna national park has met with such little success. The National Environmental Protection Board believes that a complete realization of the plan lies far ahead in the future, and the Sankt Anna national park will probably be one of the last established according to the national park plan, in about the year 2010. However, this presupposes that the authority has acquired the whole area by then (Segrell, 1994).

Access to the Countryside in a Changing Geographical/Political Context

Today's discussion about public outdoor activities and the Right of Public Access has a striking resemblance to the debate in the 1930s, but the geographical/political context is another matter. Then, the conflict scenario was confined to city (Stockholm) versus countryside. Now it is Europe versus Sweden, but the arguments and demands for restrictions, as well as the fear of littering and damage imposed on the landscape and the environment and disturbances for the inhabitants, are much the same.

An important question for further studies concerns the application of the Right of Public Access, *allemansrätten*, in the future, especially from the perspective of Swedish membership in the European Union. This right allows not only Swedish people but also tourists from other countries to roam about freely or to go camping in the countryside. Some people fear a 'tourist invasion' from Germany, England and other densely-populated European countries in the near future, with resulting negative environmental consequences in attractive areas. To prevent this, the transformation of *allemansrätten* into a real law applying only to Swedish citizens and foreigners with a permanent address in Sweden (Westerlund, 1991, pp. 148–50, Miljöaktuellt no. 6 and 7/1991) has been debated; representatives for the National Environmental Protection Board oppose this, arguing that this would only lead to a limitation of public access, and it would be inhospitable to exclude foreign tourists from it (Miljöaktuellt no. 6 and 7/1991).

In the debate the Right of Public Access has been defined as 'the free space left' between the restrictions of economic interests, privacy, conservation and increasing specialization and rationalization of the landscape (Sandell, 1991). The last-mentioned factor is connected to the 'industrialization' of agriculture and forestry, which has created a landscape with monocultural field and forest blocks, and few intermediate zones in between. This has made it physically more complicated to roam about in the landscape (Sandell, 1991). The summerhouse expansion and the national park plan described in this chapter can be regarded as examples of threats to the *allemansrätten.*

In recent years a new, non-industrial economic interest, closely connected to the question of public access itself, has come into focus. It is a commercialized form of nature tourism, in which organized groups, often from Denmark and Germany, roam, camp and paddle canoes in attractive nature areas. Travel agencies that organize these activities often use the *allemansrätten* in their advertising. However, according to the origin and tradition of the Right of Public Access, it presupposes individual, small-scale and non-commercial utilization. It is, therefore, being discussed if organized nature tourism is consistent with the Right of Public Access at all (for example, see Lagerqvist and Lundberg, 1993 and Ahlström, 1993). In some parts of Sweden, where these activities have led to littering and damage to vegetation, as well as disturbances for local people, local authorities have introduced charges for visiting groups. Local authorities also try to control these activities by preparing certain camping sites, where the outdoor activities are accommodated. Income via these charges will partly compensate affected landowners and partly finance the local authorities' costs for cleaning and management of the nature camping sites. Obviously, these measures are not in accordance with the Right of Public Access, but, as mentioned, the question is if commercial nature tourism is either. Despite this, the problem often is described in the press as the consequence of foreigners' utilization of the Swedish *allemansrätten,* and demands for restrictions are being raised.

Conclusions

During the twentieth century, the Swedish coastal zone has increasingly come under pressure from different interest groups. As a result, conflicts have occurred in attractive coastal areas. A complex pattern of conflicts has emerged where the various interests can be referred to as a centre–periphery dimension or a national–local dimension. Some important trends are noticeable in this respect: one is the growing relative influence of the centre on resource management and environmental considerations with regard to the coastal zones. Another is that during the period studied in this article, conflicts between different centre-connected interests have become more pronounced than conflicts between the interests of the centre and the periphery. An illustrative example within the sphere of the centre's interest is the conflict between public outdoor life and summer-house expansion. Another important conflict is concerned with rapid industrial expansion. Increasing influence from the centre has taken place concurrently with a weakening of the communities in coastal areas. Through migration and changing economic conditions, the local communities have become more exposed to influence from outside. However, as described in this article, there are centrally initiated measures, in the interest of 'the whole Swedish people', that still meet with strong opposition at the local level, measures which are considered as an inappropriate remote control, and almost an injustice, by local people and local authorities.

The complex pattern of conflict can partly be related to ideological positions translated into political action, partly to a dynamic socio-economic transformation of society. Public outdoor life was thus given priority by the authorities in the 1930s at the expense, above all, of private summer houses. Formally, this was handled through the Riparian Law. Thereby the protection regulations in the law also became an important support to the Right of Public Access. However, due to changes in economic conditions and communications during the post-war period the number of summer-houses has increased so rapidly that summer-house life has become an important public, urban-connected interest. Today about 650,000 summer-houses exist in Sweden, most of them located in, or close to, beach areas (Swedish Official Parliamentary Publications, Bill no. 1990/91:90, appendix A. 76). Simultaneously, extensive coastal areas have been depopulated and transformed into a periphery, used mainly for leisure activities during the summer season.

The ideology of the 1930s has survived, although its significance has, to some extent, been lost. The priority of public outdoor life has thus continued, which, among other things was manifested through the introduction of general beach protection in 1975 and the national park plan in 1989. The national park plan can be seen as an example of the centre's continued attempts to control and regulate resource management, irrespective of local opinions and demands. The National Environmental Protection Board's priority of 'the public and society', as well as the aim of giving Sweden international prestige, obviously contrasts with local interests, in which possibilities for primary trades and permanent living are fundamental parts.

From a peripheral perspective, the general beach protection can also be seen as an obstacle for local interests. It is a fact that the pressure against the beaches is not uniform in the whole country. General beach protection is to a great extent a response to the strained situation in the Stockholm archipelago and along the west coast. In other areas, and especially in sparsely-populated rural districts in northern parts of Sweden, the stretches of unexploited beaches are quite extensive, and the pressure is relatively low. From this viewpoint, local authorities see the general regulations as an unneeded and unjustified central involvement. More flexible management, in line with local conditions, has been requested and to some extent this has been responded to by the government. In practice this means opportunities to attract investors and permanent residents with housing near beaches. To what extent such flexible management has apparent regional development effects, and if it is possible without extensive exploitation of attractive beach areas, are questions for future studies.

Acknowledgements

The research reported in this article has been carried out with the help of grants provided by the Swedish Council for Planning and Coordination of Research (*Forskningsrådsnämnden*) and the Swedish Council for Building Research (*Byggforskningsrådet*). Special thanks to Lindy P. Gustavsson for improving the English in this chapter.

10

Conflict and Co-operation over Ethnic Minority Access to the Countryside: The Black Environment Network and the Countryside Commission

PHIL KINSMAN

In this chapter I would briefly like to describe one aspect of the work of an organization called the Black Environment Network (BEN); that is, their promotion of the use of the countryside as a leisure resource by ethnic minority[1] groups. This must be seen in the context of an argument about race,[2] landscape and national identity. I would argue that not only is landscape imagery and ideology a powerful means of articulating national identity (Daniels, 1993), especially in Britain (Lowenthal, 1991, p. 213), but that ideas of race form an implicit part of the articulation of that identity. These categories can all be seen as contested territories, which are constantly reshaped in a process of negotiation (Kinsman, 1995). It is that process in which I am interested, illustrated here by what I have called the discursive environment of BEN as an organization (Figure 10.1), a map of the exchanges in a variety of media which have constituted their engagement with these issues.

The Black Environment Network

BEN is an organization which seeks to facilitate the increased participation of ethnic minority groups within the environmental movement. It has particular characteristics as a political organization, which bear some comparison to existing environmental organizations (Lowe and Goyder, 1983) but depart from them in other ways. I am interested in examining the ways in which it has created and developed a particular political niche, and how it has initiated change not through having a popular mandate, but rather through its deployment of particular moral and ideological categories.

One of the issues in which it has seen its greatest impact has been that of access to the countryside, in a novel form, and this is one strand of what I have called its ideological project, which has involved it developing a relationship with the Countryside Commission during the period 1988–92.

Julian Agyeman, BEN's co-founder and chair, was developing a critique of the environmental and conservation movements when he

---

Access to the Countryside and the Countryside Commission.

AGYEMAN, J. (1989a) Black people, white landscape, *Town and Country Planning*, 58, 12: 336-338

AGYEMAN, J. (1989b) A snails pace, *New Statesman and Society*, 2, 35: 30-31

AGYEMAN, J. (1990a) Black people in a white landscape: social and environmental justice, *Built Environment*, 16, 3: 232-236

AGYEMAN, J. (1990c) A positive image, *Countryside Commission News*, 45: 3

AGYEMAN, J., WARBURTON, D. & WONG, J.L. (1991) *The Black Environment Network Report: working for ethnic minority participation in the environment* (BEN, London)

BRITISH TRUST FOR CONSERVATION VOLUNTEERS/THAKRAR, N. (1994) *Ethnic participation in Community Forest Activities: a report for the Countryside Commission*, BTCV, Manchester

CLOKE, P. (1990) *Analysis of responses to 'Training for toworrow's countryside': results of the consultation on the Countryside Staff Training Advisory Group's report,* CCP 313 (Countryside Commission, Cheltenham)

COSTER, G. (1991) Another country, *Weekend Guardian*, 1-2 June 1991: 4-6

COUNTRYSIDE COMMISSION (1987a) *Policies for enjoying the countryside*, CCP 234 (The Countryside Commission, Cheltenham)

COUNTRYSIDE COMMISSION (1987b) *Enjoying the countryside: priorities for action*, CCP 235 (The Countryside Commission, Cheltenham)

COUNTRYSIDE COMMISSION (1989a) *A countryside for everyone: an advisory booklet*, CCP 265 (The Countryside Commission, Cheltenham)

COUNTRYSIDE COMMISSION (1989b) *Training for tomorrow's countryside: the report of the Countryside Staff Training Advisory Group (CSTAG)*, CCP 269 (The Countryside Commission, Cheltenham)

COUNTRYSIDE COMMISSION (1991) *Visitors to the countryside*, CCP 341 (The Countryside Commission, Cheltenham)

COUNTRYSIDE COMMISSION (1992) *Enjoying the countryside: policies for people*, CCP 371 (The Countryside Commission, Cheltenham)

COUNTRYSIDE COMMISSION (1995) *Growing in confidence: understanding people's perceptions of urban fringe woodlands*, (Countyside Commission, Cheltenham)

GHODIWALA, A., GOUGH, A., JOHNSON, O. & SAMAT, B. (1993) *The Bolton Initiative: the summary (an evaluation of the Project by Bolton College for the Countryside Commission* (Bolton College)

MOORE, T. (1991) Countryside 'must welcome blacks', *The Daily Telegraph*, 26th April

---

Figure10.1 BEN's discursive environment in relation to the Countryside Commission

was Inner London's only environmental education officer. His argument appeared in a number of environmental and planning publications, and also attracted the attention of the mainstream press. Each article was broadly similar, although the tone and emphasis varied according to the perceived audience and the editorial control exercised over the submitted text.

All the articles in question (Agyeman, 1989a, 1989b, 1990a, 1990b, Agyeman and Hare, 1988) have the same starting-point and similar rhetorical techniques. They begin with the words of a black[3] photographer, Ingrid Pollard (Figure 10.2), from the first panel of an exhibition called 'Pastoral Interludes' (Pollard, 1989, p. 42), although only on one occasion is the text accompanied by one of the pictures from 'Pastoral Interludes' (Agyeman and Hare, 1988, p. 39). Julian Agyeman's own similar experiences of heightened visibility and feeling of discomfort while leading fieldtrips into the Lake District as a geography teacher are also included on two occasions (Agyeman, 1989a, p. 30; 1990b, p. 3).

He goes on to argue that black people are excluded from the environmental movement and from the countryside, and thereby from the nation itself. Part of his critique directly addressed the Countryside Commission and the access of ethnic minority groups to countryside areas. It is BEN's engagement with the Countryside Commission, and their response, which will be examined in some detail below.

The Initial Engagement of BEN with the Countryside Commission

In 1987 the Countryside Commission produced a policy document, *Policies for Enjoying the Countryside* (Countryside Commission, 1987a; CCP 234), which tried to shape the future direction of the Commission's role in encouraging both conservation and greater visitor access. It recognized that 'the countryside is changing – and so is society' (p. 3), and among the social trends the Commission discerned was 'the greater ethnic diversity of our society', which will 'make new and changing demands on the countryside' (p. 6).

From its own research the Commission had found that the one-quarter of the population who visit the countryside rarely, or not at all, 'include the elderly, those on low incomes, the unemployed and ethnic minorities' (p. 9). However, despite this recognition of the under-representation of ethnic minority groups among countryside visitors and the barriers they face (p. 13), the document contained no policy

. . .feeling I don't belong. Walks through leafy glades with a
baseball bat by my side. . .

Figure 10.2 From *Pastoral Interludes* by Ingrid Pollard © 1984 Ingrid Pollard. Used with
permission

suggestions specifically targeted at meeting their needs, and also categorized them among groups regularly perceived as a problem. The Commission also touched upon one of the key barriers to ethnic minority participation in the countryside – confidence – which it sees as increasing with experience and the acquisition of skills such as 'map reading, understanding timetables and appreciating wildlife and the working of the countryside' (*ibid.*). This could also be seen as a process of acculturation and does not recognize the specificity of ethnic minority status as resulting in a particular type of lack of confidence in the countryside.

What the Commission did not offer were specific points of entry for excluded groups, a full recognition of the diversity of 'the general public', or an equal opportunities policy in the recruitment of countryside staff. Also, of the seven photographs of people in the countryside contained in the document, none was of black or other ethnic minority people.

The companion document to *Policies for Enjoying the Countryside,* called *Enjoying the Countryside: Priorities for Action* (Countryside Commission, 1987b; CCP 235) 'sets out the initiatives and support the Countryside Commission intends to bring to the task and the targets we believe should be met' (p. 3), but made no mention of the needs or difficulties of the particular groups referred to in *Policies for Enjoying the Countryside.*

These omissions, coupled with the fact that the Commission's own research had identified the under-representation of ethnic minority groups among people visiting the countryside, opened up a space for BEN to apply pressure to the Commission through Julian Agyeman's critique of the environmental movement generally, and it was through his publications that the public face of this dialogue was carried out.

The publications Agyeman produced in 1988–90 asked questions, albeit ones which he knows the Commission will struggle to answer, rather than directing accusations. They concerned the amount, or rather the lack, of research done by the Commission on ethnic minority access to the countryside, or by other environmental organizations into ethnic minority participation in the environmental movement, or by the Department of Environment on the environmental quality of life enjoyed by black people. Without empirical evidence, he argues, it is hard to elicit official concern, and at this time much of his evidence was circumstantial. However, many of his intuitions about these issues have since begun to be validated by empirical research (Malik, 1992; Jefcoate and Kearney, 1994; Thakrar, 1994).

One of his main levers over the Countryside Commission was the proportion of its budget, £20 million at this time, spent on developing ethnic minority access to the countryside, in the light of the proportion which comes from black people's taxes, which he calculates as around 2 per cent. He further asks to what degree did the Commission involve black people in their deliberations over these issues, expecting the answer of little or not at all (Agyeman, 1989b, p. 337).

The Commission exists within the tension of the two roles of preservation and access, which are often seen respectively as elite and popular, even conservative and radical. It is under Section 2(2)c of the 1968 Countryside Act (Figure 10.3) which defines their role of promoting universal access that BEN finds the possibility of exerting some leverage over the Commission.

Partnership with the Countryside Commission

In *The Black Environment Network Report,* the Countryside Commission is described as one of its major national partners, with the Commission funding Ethnic Minority Awards Scheme (EMAS, BEN's subsidiary which distributes funds and organizes specific projects) projects to enable ethnic minority groups to go on visits to the countryside, and in turn 'the Countryside Commission has been pleased with the results in encouraging a wider range of people to understand and value the

---

Section 2(2)

The Commission shall keep under review *all matters* relating to:

(a) the provision and maintenance of facilities for the enjoyment of the countryside;

(b) the conservation and enhancement of the natural beauty of the countryside; and

(c) *the need to secure public access to the countryside for the purpose of open-air recreation.*

and shall consult with such local planning authorities and *other bodies* as appear to the Commission to have an interest in those matters.

Figure 10.3 Section 2(2) of the 1968 Countryside Act (emphasis added)

countryside, and to use it more for recreation' (Agyeman, Warburton and Wong, 1991, p. 17). This is part of BEN's strategy, 'to link ethnic minority groups interested in environmental issues with existing environmental organisations, and to help those organisations be more responsive to the needs and wishes of ethnic minority groups' (*ibid.*), rather than set up another environmental group competing for a specific niche of support. Countryside trips to promote ethnic minority access to the countryside have been an important component of BEN's work, with 31 per cent of their award money going on such trips between 1987 and 1989 (Taylor, 1993, p. 277).

Their funding raises questions of their relationships with environmental organizations, as they are both funded by them and yet publicly critical of them. This has been argued by Dorceta Taylor as resulting in a process of accommodation and de-radicalization for BEN through being drawn into the network of government-sponsored environmental organizations, which means that only Agyeman as a private individual, and not BEN itself, is critical of its funders. She stresses their financial reliance on a small number of institutionally powerful funders including the Commission (*ibid.*, p. 289), but the figures BEN published in their 1991 report differ substantially, as funders seem to make one short-term commitment (annual), and during 1990–1991 the Commission gave BEN and EMAS £4000 out of total receipts of approximately £65,000: 6 per cent. BEN seems to be dependent on different funders from one year to the next, although they have been trying to secure corporate sponsorship to diversify their funding base.

The majority of articles Agyeman has published have declared his affiliation to BEN, while at the same time being critical of bodies such as the Commission, so it is not the case that BEN is being simply and unproblematically institutionalized. Also, BEN does not necessarily see itself as a confrontational and radical organization, although Agyeman is concerned that it should not lose its radical edge. It should perhaps be seen instead as involved in a process of negotiation within the defined boundaries of a civil society, even if at times its greater goals run contrary to this dominant, orthodox political vision.

The public face of partnership runs in parallel to the public pressure described above, but the two are not contradictory. Rather, they are the way relationships between environmental organizations are often negotiated (Lowe and Goyder, 1983). Moreover, the way in which this relationship has been established and initiated exemplifies the tension upon which BEN plays. Part of their behind-the-scenes strategy is to develop relationships with people at middle-management levels in the organizations with which they establish relationships, in this instance Peter Ashcroft from the Commission's Recreation and Access Branch.

By 1991 BEN was one of the Commission's partners, and was one of the 457 organizations consulted by them through their consultation paper, *Visitors to the Countryside* (Countryside Commission, 1991; CCP 341). The paper specifically mentions the special difficulties of ethnic minorities alongside other groups who experience difficulty gaining access to the countryside, such as the young, the elderly and the disabled (p. 3). It mentions ethnic minorities on four further occasions, and 'minorities' twice, in the context of the need to enhance the confidence of certain visitor groups (p. 10), the need to increase a sense of customer care among countryside staff (p. 14) and the presentation of information in a relevant way (p. 19).

A number of proposals for comment, which address all the issues BEN raised, were offered in the paper (Figure 10.4), and, moreover, the Commission set itself and other countryside agencies specific proposed targets, one of which was 'One per cent of countryside staff employed in front-line recreation provision to be of ethnic minority origin by 1995, rising to two per cent by the year 2000' (p. 15). Despite these positive steps, BEN took the opportunity of the launch of this document to place more pressure on the Commission.

---

13. Basic training for countryside staff should include customer care, and ensure that it gives *recognition to the cultural and social diversity for modern society.*

14. Colleges, career councillors, employers and trainers of countryside staff should *enhance the representation of ethnic minority people among front-line countryside staff*, through the positive promotion of accessible training opportunities.

15. Would an 'equal recreation opportunities charter' – an award scheme to recognise local authorities who take positive steps to develop confidence across their entire population – encourage action on this front?

16. All originators of countryside leaflets and information should *encourage a greater presence of, and reference to, minority groups.*

Figure 10.4: Proposals for comment from *Visitors to the Countryside* (Countryside Commission, 1991c), p. 14 (emphasis added)

White people in rural areas must stop staring at black visitors and making them feel unwelcome, the Countryside Commission said yesterday at the start of a campaign to encourage members of ethnic minority groups from the inner cities to venture beyond the urban landscape . . .

It also wants to encourage people of West Indian descent who live in areas such as Brixton, south London, to learn traditional rural crafts.

Figure 10.5: Countryside 'must welcome blacks' (Moore, 1991)

Pressure in the mass media

The press launch resulted in an article in *The Daily Telegraph* called 'Countryside must welcome blacks' (Moore, 1991), which begins in a somewhat credulous tone (Figure 10.5). It does go on to report the basic elements of the Commission's initiative, but in a way which trivializes the issues of black people's experiences of the English countryside. The Commission were left looking as if they were worrying about issues beyond their scope of concern.

Consequently, Agyeman wrote to Peter Ashcroft, expressing disappointment in the partnership BEN was supposed to be having with the Commission, although he was at the same time impressed with what he saw as the progress the Commission had made over these issues. He argues that the tone of the article in *The Daily Telegraph* was inevitable, without BEN being there to present the issues in their complexity and demonstrate that these are issues of genuine concern to black people.

During 1991 and 1992 Julian Agyeman and Judy Ling Wong represented BEN in a number of regional and national television programmes, and in which the Commission was often the object of specific criticism. They brought together issues which are not normally seen as related within what are well-defined boundaries in the medium of television. In one of them, *Countryfile*, Agyeman is further able to articulate his understanding of the exclusiveness of the English countryside. While walking round a gymkhana, a 'white event', as he puts it, he describes the countryside as 'a cultural club with its own rules, etiquette and traditions'. His final words, over the strains of *Jerusalem*, are interesting as an imperative for access (Figure 10.6). Citizenship is not enough: some kind of belonging born of personal knowledge of Britain is required to avoid estrangement from the nation. However,

Britain prides itself on being a multi-cultural society, yet out here in the countryside that's far from the truth. I believe that being British means more than owning a British passport. We need to feel confident that we can explore every corner of it, but until then, we'll continue to feel like strangers in our own land.

Figure 10.6 Julian Agyeman's closing words from *Countrywide*, BBC2, 1 August 1992.

this is a utopian vision as no one in Britain has this degree of freedom of access to the land.

In an edition of *Birthrights* a component of the BBC's minority programming, the Commission is taken to task for the same short-comings Julian Agyeman identified. They replied through Jeremy Worth, Head of the Recreation and Access Branch, and he repeated the target of 40 out of 2000 countryside staff being drawn from ethnic minority groups by the year 2000, although he anticipated that this would be difficult, as competition for such jobs is intense and black people did not tend to apply for them.

The issues were inevitably represented within both the constraints of time and the genres within which they were working. BEN and the Countryside Commission were always put into oppositional roles and despite being one of the Commission's members of staff most sym-pathetic to BEN's ideas, Peter Ashcroft was used as the vehicle for what came to look like a standard denial. Interestingly, the issue was con-sistently developed as one intimately linked with notions of national identity, through the ideas expressed but also through the rhetorical and iconographic structure of the programmes. For instance, *Birthrights* opened and closed with a reggae version of *Jerusalem*.

Conclusions

The pressure applied in these ways, both directly to the organization itself and through the media, has had some discernible effects in the policies and attitude of the Countryside Commission, seen in the consultation, policy and advice documents it has subsequently pro-duced.

One of these, *A Countryside for Everyone: An Advisory Booklet* (Country-side Commission, 1989a; CCP 265), 'is based on the experience of a Commission-sponsored experiment that looks for practical solutions and expands on the ideas in *Policies for Enjoying the Countryside'* (Countryside Commission, 1989a, p. 3). The document takes some time making its case for promoting access among specially targeted groups (p. 4), and the reasons the Commission gives for promoting this access are those usually associated with the benefits of experiencing nature firsthand, but mixing them with a sensitivity to contemporary social issues (Figure 10.7). The booklet is aimed at a variety of professionals, including recreation providers, community and youth workers and social workers, and so ties in with the idea of social improvement of the groups it seeks to reach. Black cultures are here included within those

---

Many studies have shown that *fresh air and exercise in natural surroundings is of value to people's physical and spiritual well being.* The countryside is not a panacea for complex personal and social problems, but its place in people's lives can be a significant contributor to the quality of life. *It restores a sense of purpose and perspective and is an antidote to the pressures of modern living.*

Enjoying the countryside is not simply a European, middle class, cultural activity – rooted in cultural values that go back to the Romantic poets and the deeply nostalgic folk-memories underlying much of modern urban culture. The Access movement had its origins in working-class communities in Northern England for whom the mountains were a natural lung to escape into, away from the dingy streets and factories of industrial cities, owing little or nothing to a sentimental view of the past. *The countryside has widespread appeal, which crosses cultural barriers, classes, gender and age.*

It is often assumed that people of ethnic minority origin, particularly of Afro-Caribbean background, do not share traditional British attitudes to the countryside, instead identifying more closely with their own particular cultures. However, *a feeling for the richness and beauty of nature is something endemic in both African and West Indian culture. Second and third-generation British people of both Afro-Caribbean and Asian ethnic origin tend to identify with their host culture and now see visiting the countryside as something relevant and to be enjoyed regularly.*

Figure 10.7 *Why bother?* the Commission's position on ethnic minority attitudes to the countryside, from *A Countryside for Everyone: An Advisory Booklet* (CCP 265) (Countryside Commission 1989a, pp.5–6) (emphasis added).

that are able to achieve the distance from nature necessary to appreciate it, although in the past these cultures themselves have often been constructed as totally natural, at no distance from nature. It also tries to establish countryside appreciation as a classless, even radical, activity, referring to the early activities of the Ramblers' Association. However, this is merely an inclusive mythology, a multicultural version which erases the conflicts which exist between the visions of the 'Romantic poets' and the 'Access movement'. It is an attempt to render invisible the very process of conflict and accommodation in which it is actually engaging with BEN.

The document also gets tied up in linguistic problems in trying to define these unreached 'customers', problems which it readily acknowledges, but which remain substantially unresolved. It ends up using the ACORN classification system of residential areas, so that black people, as well as the other problem groups, are defined by four pictures of different types of housing, in which no people appear. This demonstrates the intangible nature of the category of race and how the Commission were not equipped at that time to deal with it as an issue.

However, the change in the Commission prompted by BEN's attentions has gathered momentum. This is seen in the end result of their consultative process, which had begun in 1987, namely the policy statement *Enjoying the Countryside: Policies for People* (Countryside Commission, 1992; CCP 371), which was based on 'a substantial and overwhelmingly positive response' from 457 individuals and organizations, BEN among them.

It is a people-oriented document, which seeks to enable the enjoyment of the countryside. Its policies are set out under three headings: creating opportunities, tackling the problems and sharing the benefits. With the first heading, in a section entitled 'Confidence', it suggests a policy that 'literature and leaflets concerned with countryside issues (not just those promoting recreation provision) should make positive reference to all sections of society' and 'recreation services need to reflect the diversity of people's interest in the countryside' (p. 3). It is stressed several times that information should be 'made relevant to the intended audience' (p. 4), and as part of their 'Agenda for Action' they make a commitment that the Commission will 'extend the scope of its sponsored training for countryside staff to include issues of customer care, and social and cultural awareness' (p. 7). The Commission urges that local authorities should 'review their employment, training and student placement practices to enable a better representation of all social groups among their countryside staff' (p. 8). This is a coded response, where direct references to ethnic minority participation are absent but implied.

These, however, are the extent of its propositions. There is no mention of the specific employment goals found in *Visitors to the Countryside* (Countryside Comission, 1991c CCP 341) and mentioned publicly elsewhere as an answer to some of BEN's criticisms. When I asked why this goal had been withdrawn, Peter Ashcroft explained that it would have been impossible to monitor, but that the Commission plans 'to experiment with some tester employment courses aimed at a number of missing groups but we expect the greatest benefit to come when the confidence of black people to enjoy the countryside is improved' (Figure 10.8). He does not make clear how that is to come about, although the Commission is still involved with BEN in promoting first-experience trips to the countryside by ethnic minority groups.

This explanation represents the Commission's position on an issue that they were not expecting to face and that must have caused some upheaval within a fairly conservative organization, which at a basic institutional level would not seem to perceive itself as embroiled in

---

The target you mention of '1 per cent of countryside staff to be from ethnic minority background' was raised in our consultation paper and was aimed at local authorities who employ the vast majority of countryside staff. You are correct in that *the target did not eventually appear in our final policy statement 'Policies for People' (PFP) largely because we had no way of monitoring it.* However, we did make it clear in the Agenda for Action section that we wanted to see a better representation of all social groups among countryside staff. *We plan to experiment with some taster employment courses aimed at a number of missing groups but we expect the greatest benefit to come when the confidence of black people to enjoy the countryside is improved.* This is important because pleasurable contact with the countryside in peoples [*sic*] leisure time often becomes, in later life, a key motivator for people to seek employment in countryside work.

Figure 10.8 reasons for the withdrawal of the 1 per cent employment goal.
Source: Personal correspondence with Peter Ashcroft, 8 January 1993 (emphasis added).

metropolitan politics. Although precise policies have not been implemented, the Commission still has the issue of ethnic minority access on its agenda due to its relationship with BEN, seen in the publication of a number of recent reports. The first, prpared by Bolton College, was an evaluation of the Bolton Countryside Initiative, which included the trips to Moses Gate Country Park featured in the *Birthrights* and *Countryfile* television programmes, which BEN played some part in initiating (Ghodiwala *et al.*, 1993). The second was prepared for the Commission by the British Trust for Conservation Volunteers on the use of community forests by ethnic minority groups (Thakrar, 1994). Despite being planned and executed under fairly severe constraints of time and resources, the report provided the Countryside and Forestry Commissions with an opportunity to heighten the awareness of black and ethnic minority people in this area of the Community Forests venture, and to involve them actively in its planning. Leaflets and advertisements concerning the forest were sensitively translated into Bangladeshi, Chinese and Urdu and distributed via key points within the ethnic minority communities of the area.

Most recently, the Commission has published a technical report, researched and written by Dr Jacquie Burgess, called *Growing in Confidence: Understanding People's Perceptions of Urban Fringe Woodlands* (Countryside Commission, 1995; CCP 457). Two of the seven visitor and discussion groups were composed of women from ethnic minority communities, being Asian and Afro-Caribbean women living in urban/ suburban London (p. 14). Their responses to the woodlands they visited expressed a qualified pleasure in an experience which was new to many of them, but also emphasized a heightened sense of personal visibility due to their ethnicity, which resulted in a fear of racist violence or abuse: 'Fear that people would not assist [in the event of an attack] in woodlands in deep countryside was amplified for the Asian and Afro-Caribbean women by their common experience of racism. Through an enormous range of insulting behaviour and non-verbal cues, they are made to feel "alien" and unwelcome in the countryside' (p. 28). The report recommended that a number of strategies be adopted to build confidence generally among the population in the use of Community Forests, through their design, staffing and working with user groups (pp. 31–6). Under the heading 'Action for disadvantaged groups', 'culturally appropriate events' and an understanding of ethnic minority groups' particular needs by countryside staff were seen as ways of addressing the issues of confidence and under-use by ethnic minority groups (p. 38).

These reports, all of which were sponsored or published by the Countryside Commission, demonstrate the continuing collection of empirical evidence concerning the access of black and ethnic minority people to the countryside, as well as presenting data, policy and promotional information in a representative manner. Both their findings and recommendations have largely echoed BEN's intuitive analysis, although often in a locally more informed way. This is not to say that BEN has been the only group pressing these issues, but it did apply pressure directly to the Commission in a way which has tangibly altered their recommendations and their modes of presentation.

It could be seen as political opportunism by an organization such as BEN to take advantage of the self-consciousness which makes any body, but especially government organizations, highly concerned about their public perception. However, as a political organization, BEN have merely been engaging in a process of negotiation in which they have used the resources and levers at their disposal, but in a way which does not seem to be exploitative of their partners' situations. Also, in the context of a changing political idiom, they are using the emerging language of contemporary civil society, that of the consumption of services and the distribution of resources, predicated upon the payment of tax.

In terms of developing a political strategy, it can be seen as quite discerning for BEN to have approached the Commission in the way that it did. As the government body which is meant to oversee the network of countryside organization in Britain, BEN have been able to reach that network very effectively through the Commission. It also allowed the issues to be brought within the scope of the media by appointing a keeper of the status quo which BEN was taking to task, and as an organization caught in the cleft stick of its own mandates of conservation and access, it contained its own internal pressures and tensions upon which BEN could capitalize. It is a little ironic that a body which came to represent bureaucracy and power within this dialogue is in fact itself a small organization with relatively limited funds at its disposal, and which can often find itself in conflict with other tiers of government.

The Countryside Commission was not the only government body BEN was to engage with, nor the only one with which it was to have this paradoxical relationship. It did, however, set the tone for BEN's encounter with the Nature Conservancy Council for England, albeit over a very different set of issues, which caught the imagination of the more conservative mainstream media and brought BEN more firmly into the public domain.

Julian Agyeman, however, is fairly pleased with the way BEN's engagement with the Countryside Commission has turned out. He is candid about BEN's paradoxical relationship with bodies like the Commission, but does believe that a process of fundamental change has been initiated by influencing people at middle-management levels, and that it can be left to itself now as far as the Countryside Commission is concerned.

Peter Ashcroft also acknowledges that the Commission has seen itself changed, or at least challenged, as a result of BEN's involvement (Figure 10.8). However, it still remains that the Commission was not able to fulfil a public commitment to a form of equal opportunities policy and has not fully accepted the criticisms made by BEN.

Nor are the changes which BEN has initiated merely textual. Other advice from different sources has leaned in the same direction (Figure 10.9; Cloke, 1990). Commission staff have received training around these issues and many ethnic minority groups have visited the countryside and have a high level of re-use (Malik, 1992). BEN has at the same time brought another group of users into the countryside and pressured countryside and environmental organizations to recognize their presence, and even promote it in the near future, and begin to meet their needs. This may in the longer term result in some of the conditions for an ethnic minority presence as countryside staff, which the Commission itself sees as important.

Are any particular groups discriminated against in either securing work or securing training?

'The position of women, *ethnic minorities*, the handicapped, and even the middle and older age groups, needs careful consideration here. Such groups are undoubtedly under-represented in paid employment in environmental work, *and the Commission and others will need to consider policies of positive discrimination, or at least of equal opportunities* (these may amount to similar outcomes).'

Figure 10.9 Other advice to the Commission on the recruitment of staff to environmental organizations.
Source: Cloke (1990), p. 19 (emphasis added).

Notes

1. The term 'ethnic' minorities is used in a very specific way by BEN: 'we chose to use the term "ethnic minorities" to ensure that we did not exclude the Chinese, Latin American and other groups we welcome but who do not often consider themselves black' (Agyeman, Warburton and Wong, 1991, p. 1). They show an awareness of the slippery nature of the terminology of classifying groups according to ethnic criteria and the linguistic pitfalls to which their type of work is so prone. Although the inclusive thrust which has caused them to define 'black' so broadly that it could lose much of its meaning has opened them up to criticism, it was obviously of concern to them to find a name which would be credible with the groups they seek to represent but which would not be exclusive, and they make a commitment to constantly review their terminology in the light of shifting meanings.

2. Race is a concept fraught with conceptual difficulties and will be treated here as an 'essentially contested concept' (Gallie, 1962). It is now widely held to be a meaningless category, a second-order abstraction which uses phenotypical variation to ascribe status and roles rather than allow their achievement (Banton, 1983, p. 8). This does not mean, however, that it can simply be dismissed, as it is an elaborately constructed ideology which releases powerful political forces, and it is the very emptiness of racial signifiers which makes them vulnerable to appropriation, and their contradictions which give them power (Gilroy, 1987, pp. 38–40). As a concept it has a particular history and geography (Banton, 1977, 1983; Livingstone, 1992a, 1992b) which is mutable and contested within specific locations and times (Poliakov, 1974; MacDougall, 1982; Barkan, 1992). It seems to bear close relation with nationalism, even springing from it (Balibar, 1991), as another imagined community which configures identity at a number of scales (Anderson, 1983). It is emphasized here that race is a relative and negotiated process which takes black people outside history, constructing them as problems or victims, paradoxically by reworking past images and ideas within a new context (Gilroy, 1987, pp. 27, 44–69).

3. The term 'black' is used here to denote people of indigenous African, Afro-Caribbean and Asian descent, and therefore as a political grouping rather than as a racial signifier (Miles, 1989).

11

Trespassing Against the Rural Idyll: The Criminal Justice and Public Order Act 1994 and Access to the Countryside

KEITH HALFACREE

> Differences endure or arise on the margins of the homogenized realm, either in the form of resistances or in the form of externalities ... What is different is, to begin with, what is *excluded*: the edges of the city, shanty towns, the spaces of forbidden games, of guerilla war, of war. Sooner or later, however, the existing centre and the forces of homogenization must seek to absorb all such differences ... Abstract space ... asphyxiates whatever is conceived within it and then strives to emerge. (Lefebvre, 1991, pp. 373, 370)

Key determinants of the accessibility of the countryside for specific subgroups within the population are the policies and measures resulting from the attitude of the state towards both these groups and the 'appropriate' use of rural space. This state involvement with accessibility is reflected in a number of measures included in the controversial Criminal Justice and Public Order Act 1994. This Act seeks, *inter alia*, to control the activities of certain semi-nomadic or travelling people within the English and Welsh countryside, to prevent large-scale open-air musical events known as raves, and to discourage the disruptive activities of various environmentally-inclined protestors, such as hunt saboteurs and anti-roads campaigners. Controlling these groups' mobility and their rights of way seeks to make the countryside practically inaccessible to them, at least within the limits of the law, and serve to reinforce the selectivity of the rural experience.

This chapter begins to examine why the state has sought to limit the access of travellers, ravers and environmental protestors to the English and Welsh countryside. Bypassing 'commonsense' explanations of these limitations, which emphasize the New Right's dislike of various 'folk devils' and the longstanding pedigree of Gypsy persecution

(Halfacree, forthcoming), the chapter argues that we must consider the threat posed by these minority groups to the predominant representation of the countryside within 'British' culture – the 'rural idyll'. The first half of the chapter describes briefly the sections dealing with travellers, ravers and environmental protestors contained in the new Act, emphasizing how they build on past legislation, before going on to describe the rise of these 'alternative' groupings. In the second half of the chapter I propose, at a fairly abstract level, reasons why the British state should show a particular hostility towards these groups out of all proportion to their objective nuisance. The spatiality of capitalism is contrasted with the threat to that spatiality posed by these groups through reference to the imaginative geography of the rural idyll.

The Criminal Justice and Public Order Act 1994 and 'Alternative' Groups in the Countryside
The Criminal Justice and Public Order Act 1994

A new Criminal Justice and Public Order Bill was given a First Reading in the House of Commons, having been introduced by the Home Secretary, Michael Howard, on behalf of the Government, on 16 December 1993. It was an extremely wide-ranging Bill, containing what are now well-known measures aimed at removing a suspect's 'right to silence' and dealing with juvenile offenders. However, it also contained a number of clauses concerned with Public Order (Part V) and the perceived disruption of that order by, *inter alia*, a number of 'alternative' minority groups. Although these clauses were initially less familiar to the general public, they gained the spotlight in the summer and autumn of 1994 when large demonstrations against them were held in London (*The Guardian*, 2 May 1994, 25 July 1994, 10 October 1994). There also developed an organized opposition to these clauses, featuring, *inter alia*, Liberty and the Freedom Network. Clearly, for some sections of society at least, these clauses were far from uncontroversial.

After a lengthy and sometimes stormy passage through both Houses of Parliament, where debate concentrated mostly on the Criminal Justice measures, the Criminal Justice and Public Order Act received Royal Assent on 3 November 1994, with all the Public Order clauses largely intact. The main sections of the Act concerning travellers, ravers and environmental protestors are outlined in Table 11.1. There is not space here to go through them in detail, but their net effect is likely to be severe. The Act effectively criminalizes trespass (Fairlie, 1994), taking it out of the civil domain, by building on measures introduced in Section 39 of the Public Order Act 1986. It also removes an official degree of acceptance of the legitimacy of the travelling lifestyle as expressed formally in the Caravan Sites Act 1968. The latter gave local authorities a duty to provide sites for travelling people (see Sibley, 1981,

Table 11.1   Key sections in the Criminal Justice and Public Order Act 1994 affecting travellers, ravers and environmental protestors

Section	Description
61	Enables a senior police officer to direct persons to leave land on which he (*sic.*) 'reasonably believes' they are trespassing with the purpose of residing there for any time, providing the occupier has taken 'reasonable steps' to ask them to leave, *and* if either any of the trespassers has caused damage or if they have been threatening, abusive or insulting, *or* if they have six or more vehicles on the land. Failure to obey such a direction, or returning to the land as a trespasser within three months, is punishable by a fine and/or up to three months imprisonment.
62	Empowers the police to seize and remove vehicles of those failing to comply with Section 61.
63	Enables a senior police officer to direct people to leave or not to attend a gathering on any open land where amplified music is played during the night. Also enables the officer to prevent people preparing such an event. Vehicles and other property can be removed from the land. Failure to comply or returning to the land within seven days is punishable by a fine and/or up to three months imprisonment.
65	Enables the police to define a five mile radius 'exclusion zone' around actual or probable rave sites. Failure to heed the police direction is punishable by a fine.
68	Creates the offence of 'aggravated trespass', whereby it becomes an offence for people to trespass on land with the intention of obstructing, disrupting or intimidating other people involved in any lawful activity on that land or adjoining land. The punishment for this offence is a fine and/or up to three months imprisonment.
69	Allows a police offcer to direct actual or potential aggravated trespassers to leave land. Failure to obey or returning as a trespasser within three months is punishable by a fine and/or up to three months imprisonment.
70	Enhances powers under the Public Order Act 1986 regarding 'trespassory assemblies'. A chief officer of police who reasonably believes that an assembly will be held on land without the occupier's permission *and* which may result in 'serious disruption' to the life of the community *or* damage to a site of historical, architectural, archaeological or scientific importance, may apply for an order prohibiting all such assemblies for up to four days. To organise a prohibited assembly or to incite others to take part in such an assembly is punishable by a fine and/or up to three months imprisonment. Taking part in an illegal assembly is punishable by a fine.
71	Provides a police power to direct persons 'reasonably believed' to be going to a trespassory assembly, up to five miles from such an assembly, not to proceed. Ignoring the police instructions is punishable by a fine.
77	Provides local authorities with the power to direct unauthorised campers to leave land and remove their vehicles and belongings. It is an offence, punishable by a fine, not to comply, or to enter the land again within three months.
78	Provides for magistrates' courts to make orders authorising local authorities to enter land to remove vehicles and other property when a direction under Section 77 has been made. Wilful obstruction of a removal is punishable by a fine.
80	Repeals provisions of the Caravan Sites Act 1968 relating to Gypsy sites, including local authorities' duty to provide sites, and repeals provisions of the Local Government Planning and Land Act 1980 relating to payment of grants for sites.

Source: Criminal Justice and Public Order Act 1994 (HMSO).

chapter 9), a duty which was further encouraged by the granting of 100 per cent government grants to local authorities to take such steps, as expressed in Section 70 of the Local Government, Planning and Land Act 1980. Indeed, Lloyd (1993, p. 84) has gone so far as to argue that: 'The right to travel will be denied by making it impossible to do so, legally'. For ravers, characterized in the new Act as people partying through the night in the open air to 'sounds wholly or predominantly characterised by the emission of a succession of repetitive beats', celebrations can now be shut down and prevented by the police, whether or not they involve trespass. The Act also introduces five-mile exclusion zones around actual or potential rave locations. Finally, for environmental protestors, the new offence of aggravated trespass seeks to curtail the activities of anti-roads campaigners, hunt saboteurs and others, by preventing even the passive disruption of lawful activities such as hunting. For all the new Public Order sections, failure to comply with police instructions is typically punishable by a fine and/or up to three months' imprisonment.

Contemporary Travellers, Ravers and Environmental Protestors: the Beanfield, Castlemorton and Twyford Down

There were a number of immediate reasons why measures dealing with travellers were introduced into the original Criminal Justice and Public Order Bill. On the one hand, there was the perceived failure of the Caravan Sites Act to provide adequate sites for Gypsies, to keep the costs of site provision minimal and to stem the growing numbers of Gypsies (Lloyd, 1993). Here, however, we shall concentrate on the Government's other main concern regarding travellers, namely the growth in the 1980s of the 'New Age' traveller phenomenon. Whilst there were measures in the Public Order Act 1986 which attempted to deal with the perceived public nuisance caused by such people (Dixon, 1987; Williams, 1987), these were felt by the Government to be inadequate to deal with what was perceived as an 'awful problem' (David Maclean, Minister of State at the Home Office, *Hansard*, 8 February 1994, column 531). This concern with travellers spilt over into disquiet with other groups, such as ravers and environmental protestors. This can be illustrated with reference to three key events: the 'Battle of the Beanfield', the Castlemorton festival and the Twyford Down anti-roads actions.

Without wishing to stereotype or essentialize a very diverse group of people (Earle *et al.*, 1994; Hetherington, 1992; Jones, 1993, chapter 8;

Lowe and Shaw, 1993), the 'New Age' travellers emerged in the late 1970s. Their media prominence reached a first peak in 1985, with the events surrounding the infamous 'Battle of the Beanfield' in Savernake Forest, Wiltshire (Earle *et al.*, 1994; Lowe and Shaw, 1993, pp. 68–76; National Council for Civil Liberties (NCCL), 1986). This was a violent confrontation between travellers (then labelled the 'Peace Convoy') and the Wiltshire police, who were attempting to prevent the annual but illegal summer solstice gathering and music festival at Stonehenge (Hetherington, 1992). After this confrontation and the following year's clashes in the same area of southwest England (NCCL, 1986; Rojek, 1988), which prompted the Government to add the traveller-related clauses to the Public Order Act 1986, 'New Age' travellers declined somewhat in media prominence.

However, they reappeared in May 1992 as the result of a gathering of around 50,000 people for another illegal music festival, this time at Castlemorton Common in Hereford and Worcester (New Musical Express, 8 May 1993). In contrast to the Stonehenge festivals, this event involved ravers and rave music as well as travellers, including the involvement of rave 'sound systems', such as 'Spiral Tribe' (Dalton, 1993) and 'Bedlam'. Ravers, who were originally urban-based, were at this time increasingly coveting the open spaces of the countryside as venues for their all-night mass parties, as suitable spaces in the cities were being closed off to them by the police and local authorities in the wake of the drugs and general safety-related 'acid house' scares of the late 1980s.

A key aspect of the often tension-filled intermingling of travellers and ravers at Castlemorton was that it introduced the nationally more numerous but largely apolitical ravers to some of the more 'ecological' politics of the travellers. Consequently, ravers became 'political' for the first time, a politicization which has, paradoxically, been considerably reinforced by the Criminal Justice and Public Order Act's measures. Both groups found a common purpose in opposing the Act.

Whilst Castlemorton witnessed a degree of convergence between travellers and ravers, the link between these two groups and environmental protestors can be symbolized by the attempts in 1992 and 1993 to prevent the construction of part of the M3 motorway at Twyford Down near Winchester in Hampshire (Fairlie, 1993; Vidal, 1992). This piece of road, which had proved controversial for two decades, was a three-mile section aimed to reduce the time of a journey from South-ampton to London by about five minutes. Although Twyford Down was in an Area of Outstanding Natural Beauty, work on the road began in

1992. This prompted a number of protestors to converge on the site over the last six months of that year.

The protestors came to call themselves the 'Donga Tribe' after the Dongas, ancient trackways which converged on Twyford Down. The tribe consisted mostly of young people under 25 but showed a wide range of backgrounds, from former students to ex-carpenters. They were keen to distance themselves from established party politics, fringe groups such as Class War and the mainstream environmental movement, which was regarded as being too tame, comfortable and compromised. Although they succeeded in disrupting the road building for several months, they were finally evicted in December 1992 after having been deserted by the wider anti-Twyford Down M3 groups (Fairlie, 1993; Vidal, 1992). In spite of these evictions, protests over Twyford Down continued well into the summer of 1993. For example, in July there was a mass trespass on the almost completed road (*The Guardian*, 5 July 1993). These actions involved the Dongas as well as other radical groups such as Earth First! (Vidal, 1993).

Whilst Vidal (1992) reported that the Dongas were keen to distinguish themselves from travellers, whom they regarded as being 'selfish', we can see links between the two groupings in terms of their backgrounds and general philosophy. Moreover, subsequent activities involving the Dongas and allied groups, such as the campaign against the Hackney-M11 link in Wanstead, east London (Vidal, 1994a), has typically involved a mixture of travellers, radical environmentalists and ravers (Vidal, 1994b). However, to date, as Fairlie (1993) acknowledges, there has been little academic attention given to the in-depth study of this new radical–environmental constellation.

The Spatiality of Capitalism, the 'Rural Idyll' and Neo-tribalism

The Spatiality of Capitalism and the Rural Idyll

Henri Lefebvre's *The Production of Space* (1991) charts the historical development of space, revealing its increasingly produced character (Smith, 1984), or 'spatiality' (Soja, 1985). With capitalism, absolute space, an integrated everyday experience defined largely by politico–religious forces, is superseded by an abstract space moulded by the capitalist market and characterized by fragmentation. Abstract space is intrinsically bound up with exchange and market forces.

This abstract spatiality of capitalism is alluded to in Robert Sack's work on human territoriality. Sack defines territoriality as:

the attempt by an individual or group to affect, influence, or control people, phenomena, and relationships, by delimiting and asserting control over a geographic area [the territory]. (Sack, 1986, p. 19)

Hence, territoriality is associated with power. Under capitalism, there is the:

repeated and conscious use of territory as an instrument to define, contain, and mold a fluid people and dynamic events [which] leads to a sense of an **abstract emptiable space**. It makes community seem to be artificial; it makes the future appear geographically as a dynamic relationship between people and events on the one hand and territorial molds on the other. And it makes space seem to be only contingently related to events. (Sack 1986, p. 78; my emphasis)

The sheer dynamism of capitalist territoriality – this moulding and re-moulding of space (Smith, 1984) – destroys absolute space's more inherent and established meanings.

The void of spatial meaning resulting from the creative destruction of capitalism can partially be filled by utilizing key features of abstract space, notably the three 'formants' of abstract space described by Lefebvre (1991, pp. 285–6). First, there is the geometric formant, whereby the meaning of space is given by its Euclidian use as a series of reference points. Secondly, the optical or visual formant reduces and simplifies the meaning of space to messages reaching the eyes. Thirdly, there is the phallic formant, whereby perpendicularity represents power and authority. Nonetheless, whilst the latter two formants take some account of the representational spaces of experience, as compared to the formal representation of space apparent in the first formant,[1] they are insufficient to meet the needs of human existence and community.

Lefebvre proceeds to illustrate the need for the qualitative (Lefebvre, 1991, p. 349) with respect to leisure and recreational behaviour (Lefebvre, 1991, pp. 383–5). Although deeply implicated with the market and capitalist production, this behaviour shows a tendency towards surmounting the divisiveness that characterizes abstract space. Thus, as Shields (1991a, chapters 2 and 3) has demonstrated, resorts represent 'liminal' zones partially liberated from the conforming pressures of everyday life. More generally, however, the existential inadequacy of abstract space can be countered by stamping meanings on to space and attempting to sustain and naturalize those imposed meanings. This is achieved through the use of 'social representations'.

Social representations have been defined by Moscovici (1984) as mental constructs which guide us towards what is 'visible' and must be responded to, relate appearance and reality, and even define reality itself. The world is organized, understood and mediated through these basic cognitive units. Social representations consist of both concrete images and abstract concepts. They are organized around 'figurative nuclei', which are 'a complex of images that visibly reproduce ... a complex of ideas' (Moscovici, 1984, p. 38). They perform two major roles: they conventionalize objects, persons and events encountered, and they prescribe and organize subsequent behaviour and responses. Prescription makes social representations not merely neutral and re-active taxonomic devices but also creative and transformative resources, through their usage by people in daily life.

Social representations of space refer to the application of social representational theory to everyday spatial categories. Thus, we can define 'the rural' as one such social representation of space (Halfacree, 1993), in contrast to attempts to define it as a 'locality' (Hoggart, 1990) or a more post-structuralist category of discourse (Pratt, forthcoming). Regarding the social representation of the rural, the (historical) crea-tion of a more-or-less distinct rural space is perceived within British culture predominantly in terms of the 'rural idyll' (Halfacree, 1995; Short, 1991). This imaginative geography posits the countryside as a haven of tranquillity and *gemeinschaft* social relations in contrast to the alienating everyday experience of the city. Moreover, as a 'spatial code', this representation is not solely an aid to perception but also designates a way of understanding, operating within and producing rural space (Lefebvre, 1991, pp. 47–8). This active moment demonstrates the violence of conformity required to sustain social representations of space, since:

> Any determinate and hence demarcated space necessarily embraces some things and excludes others; what it rejects may be relegated to nostalgia or it may be simply forgotten. Such a space asserts, negates and denies. . . . As a body of constraints, stipulations and rules to be followed, social space acquires a normative and repressive efficacy ... that makes the efficacy of mere ideologies and representations pale in comparison. (Lefebvre, 1991, pp. 99, 358)

Thus, in brief, the rural idyll is exclusive in its class, race and status connotations, and in the demands for conformity which it places on its adherents (Philo, 1992). In this sense it is profoundly conservative and poses little threat to the abstract space it serves to disguise.

The Spatiality of Capitalism and the Neo-tribes of Post-modernism

The rural idyll, in spite of its pre-modern heritage, is a modernist 'way of seeing' in its promotion of a 'single' countryside and a 'single' perspective on that countryside. Representing the countryside solely in terms of the contours and shades of the rural idyll denies the multiple identities of (rural) places (Murdoch and Pratt, 1993, p. 421). Such totalizing missions as the rural idyll are, however, increasingly being challenged by post-modern currents within contemporary society. Specifically, the rise of what Bauman (1992, pp. 136–9), following Maffesoli (1988), terms 'neo-tribalism' (see also Deleuze and Guattari, 1987, p. 360; Eder, 1990) suggests an alternative means of filling abstract space to the hegemonic intent of social representations of space such as the rural idyll.

The desire to be in a tribe, a 'neo-tribe', appears as a key existential response to the experience of the post-modernization of society:

> Overall, within massification, processes of condensation are constantly occurring through which more or less ephemeral tribal groupings are organized which cohere on the basis of their own minor values, and which attract and collide with each other in an endless dance, forming themselves into a constellation whose vague boundaries are perfectly fluid. This is the characteristic of postmodern society. (Maffesoli 1991, 12)

Mirroring the experience of abstract space, the disintegration of everyday norms and order which characterizes the post-modern experience (see Giddens, 1990, 1991; Harvey 1989; Lefebvre, 1991) results in an 'obsessive search for community' (Bauman, 1992, p. 136; see also Smart, 1993, chapter 4). A degree of community can be obtained by forming neo-tribes to flee this 'horror of emptiness' (Maffesoli, 1991, p. 14), although Hetherington (1992, p. 93) prefers the term *bund* or communion, since neo-tribes differ from 'historical' tribes in that their membership has to be chosen and involves a constant active self-identification with the tribe. This need to work at being a member of such a tribe eventually undermines that tribe's existence as it exposes the artificiality of the tribe's construction; a neo-tribal community is not 'natural and cosy' (Bauman, 1992, p. 138).

The emergence and current appeal of 'New Age' travellers, 'politicized' ravers and environmental protestors such as the Dongas is representative of the turn to neo-tribalism (Hetherington, 1992). Indeed, as we saw with respect to Castlemorton and Twyford Down, Britain now has some explicitly defined tribes. It can therefore be suggested that we can see the state's current attack on these neo-tribes, through the Criminal Justice and Public Order Act, as being part of the struggle between the dominant modernist social representation of space – the rural idyll – and its post-modern subversion.

Bauman leaves the reproduction of the neo-tribe at a problematic and ultimately doomed level. However, Lefebvre's work suggests how neo-tribes may be capable of prolonging their existence. This is through the production of a distinct space which characterises that neo-tribe:

> Any 'social existence' aspiring or claiming to be 'real', but failing to produce its own space, would be a strange entity, a very peculiar kind of abstraction unable to escape from the ideological or even the 'cultural' realm. It would fall to the level of folklore and sooner or later disappear altogether, thereby immediately losing its identity, its denomination and its feeble degree of reality. (Lefebvre, 1991, p. 53)

Thus, Lefebvre attributes much of the failure of previous communal experiments to their lack of achieving a distinct space. All that they have managed to do is to 'divert' existing spaces to their use, spaces which were inappropriate to the long-term perpetuation of the experiment through the creative reappropriation of that space (Lefebvre, 1991, pp. 379–80). It is this distinctly geographical insight that suggests why there is likely to be a sustained contradiction between the various 'alternative' groupings and the British state – i.e. they represent alternative spatialities. Whilst the neo-tribes adhere to the 'lived spaces' (Shields, 1991b, p. 4) of their self-identified affinities, the British state is concerned with defending the singular space of the rural idyll.

Neo-tribes and the Rural Idyll under Assault

The three 'alternative' groupings discussed in this chapter – travellers, ravers and environmental protestors – all pose a threat to the hegemony of the social representation of the rural idyll. These threats come from a variety of overlapping directions. Travellers represent the nomadic threat of smooth space against the striated space of the sedentary, exposing the rural idyll as being just one way in which meaning can be stamped upon (rural) space; ravers also threaten to efface the rural idyll

stamped upon (rural) space; ravers also threaten to efface the rural idyll and expose the homogeneity of abstract space through carnivalesque reappropriation; whilst environmental protestors, although less directly critical of the rural idyll itself, can expose some of the contradictions of the idyllic representation and delineate an alternative geography to the idyll.

1. Travellers and the Nomadic Threat

Gilles Deleuze and Félix Guattari (1987, chapter 12) regard the nomad as being fundamentally subversive of territorialization in general because s/he is concerned with 'smooth' space rather than with the 'striated' space of the sedentary. For the nomad, life is focused on motion, on paths rather than the points of the sedentary. Hence:

> The water point is reached only to be left behind; every point is a relay and exists only as a relay. A path is always between two points, but the in-between has taken on all the consistency and enjoys both an autonomy and a direction of its own. The life of the nomad is the intermezzo. ...
> [Consequently,] there is a significant difference between the spaces: sedentary space is striated, by walls, enclosures, and roads between enclosures, while nomad space is smooth, marked only by 'traits' that are effaced and displaced by the trajectory. (Deleuze and Guattari, 1987, pp. 380–81)

Nomads are therefore the potential conquerors of the town (Lefebvre, 1991, p. 235) because they are capable of de-territorializing and effacing the meanings imposed by a sedentary society on its striated space. When smooth (nomad) space comes up against the striated (sedentary) space of capitalism, it can expose the void of essential meaning that characterizes abstract space. Hence, the concern to 'purify' residential space and 'to keep things apart' (Sibley, 1988, p. 409) receives added significance under capitalism. This is especially so during periods of large-scale crisis-driven restructuring of abstract space (Smith, 1984, p. 157), such as the present day, when capitalist spatiality is most vulnerable to exposure.

To a greater or lesser extent, travellers can be seen as the modern British equivalent of Deleuze and Guattari's abstract 'nomads' (Halfacree, forthcoming; Melucci, 1989). Consequently, the nomadic 'transgressions' (Cresswell, 1994) of these travellers threaten the complacent permanence of the spatiality of the rural idyll. Travellers' failure to fit into the imaginative settled representation of the rural idyll – indeed, to 'belong nowhere' (Hetherington, 1992, p. 91) – threatens to expose the insubstantial nature of this supposedly historically-entrenched representation of rurality. Travellers trespass against the rural idyll and, as Olsson (1984, p. 75) has recognized, the real sin of trespass lies in the way in which it breaks established definitions.

2. Ravers and the Threat of Exposure

Although not nomadic to the same degree as travellers, ravers also effect the exposure of abstract spatiality. However, unlike travellers or, in particular, environmental protestors, they appear predominantly to strip the rural of meaning and to revel in this lack of meaning rather than to try and re-emboss an alternative meaning on to (rural) space. Ravers' concern with finding a space to party appears as a search for an abstract space rather than a search for a particular place. They seek 'liminality', a 'liberation from the régimes of normative practices and performance codes of mundane life' but a liberation of an 'interstitial nature' (Shields, 1991a, p. 84). This suggests an alignment of the ravers with Baudrillard's (1983) post-modern refuseniks in their resistance of the idea of lasting 'meaningfulness' with regard to rural space.

Evidence to support the Baudrillardian thrust of the ravers' effacement of the rural idyll was reflected at Castlemorton and elsewhere in tensions between them and the travellers (Lowe and Shaw, 1993, pp. 130–81). Such tensions were reported in press stories and were put largely in terms of the travellers' dislike of rave music, the drugs associated with raves (notably Ecstasy) and the lack of respect shown by ravers for the countryside and the environment in general. Ravers, on the other hand, defended their 'right to party' and criticized the old-fashioned 'hippie' character of the travellers. As Simon from the Bedlam sound system put it: 'They [travellers] sit there admiring their crystal and we'll sit there admiring our vinyl . . . ' (Lowe and Shaw, 1993, p. 175). Travellers demonstrated a more engaged relationship with the countryside, whereas ravers were seen as treating Castlemorton Common solely in opportunistic terms: 'For [ravers] it's a night's anarchy then you go home; for the travellers they have to live there and suffer the consequences' (Jeremy from the 'traveller-friendly' band The Levellers, quoted in Lowe and Shaw, 1993, p. 164).

This proposed divide between travellers and ravers has been reduced to some extent as a result of meetings such as Castlemorton and subsequent intermingling during the common resistance of both groups to the Criminal Justice and Public Order Act 1994. Such an increasing tolerance and understanding for both camps is even more necessary when either group encounters the third group discussed here, the environmental protestors.

3. Environmental Protestors and the Threat of Revelation and Challenge

The discussion of ravers suggested that many travellers strive to impose an alternative meaning to rural space and are not just concerned with transgressing and effacing the rural idyll. However, it is the environmental protestors who are making the most effort to re-striate rural space, although it must, of course, be recognized that these protestors do not confine their actions to the rural realm, as the Wanstead events clearly demonstrated. Environmental protestors both challenge the veracity of experience presented by the rural idyll and indicate contours of an alternative representation.

Environmental protestors' challenge to the rural idyll is neither largely nomadic nor nihilistic, but can be seen in terms of exposing the selectivity of the idyllic vision. This can be illustrated with respect to hunt saboteurs, a group reflecting the radicalization of the animal rights campaigns in recent years, where the moral status of animals rather than just their welfare is campaigned for (Garner, 1993). The saboteurs' rejection of hunting is a rejection of a key rural 'embodiment of what we mean by tradition' (Cox, Hallett and Winter, 1994, p. 204). With respect to deer hunting, the social organization and ritual associated with this bloodsport embody a significance of this tradition to the countryside that is valorized and defended by the rural idyll. Thus, whilst discussing the current unpopularity of hunting, Wright (1993) asserts that: 'The harried fox once stood for a settled vision of old England' and the right-wing philosopher Roger Scruton defends hunting by arguing, *inter alia*, that it is conducive to rural harmony. We can thus see the hunt saboteurs' challenge as a challenge to normality of the rural idyll itself.

The hunt saboteurs' critique shades into an alternative spatiality of the rural, suggested by the Dongas and others. There is not the space here to detail this spatiality; suffice to say that it is an ecocentric vision moderated by a cultural valorization of the uniqueness of place. Rather than the centrality of social harmony and the turn to tradition and (human) history espoused by the rural idyll, the Dongas' alternative vision places the environment, especially the physical environment, centre stage and turns to a localized aesthetic of natural beauty and value. The Dongas also espouse an extremely mystical or spiritual vision of the environment rather than a scientific, rational and instrumental vision, hence their resistance to the fundamental principle of damaging Twyford Down irrespective of the more scientific argument for its preservation outlined by mainstream environmental groups. The Dongas challenge many of the existing striations of modern capitalist society, such as the M3 motorway, to recreate what would, in effect, be a new absolute space centred on 'nature' rather than on the religious spaces of history.

Conclusion: Defending the Rural Idyll – 'Trespassers Keep Out'!

Whilst the examples of post-modern neo-tribes discussed here are selective in their membership and attitude, this selectivity is based on an individual's choice rather than on the constraints and hegemonic force which underpins the rural idyll. This makes their political implications potentially extremely threatening for abstract spatiality if this voluntary selectivity develops in a more thorough anti-capitalist direction. In the latter, the difference expressed by the neo-tribe would become a genuinely 'produced' difference rather than an 'induced' difference internal to the system (Lefebvre, 1991, p. 372), as represented by the rural idyll. Such produced alternatives to the abstract spatiality of capitalism ultimately must be suppressed if they are not to pose a threat to that spatiality. They must be reduced by being 'forced back into the system by constraint and violence' (Lefebvre, 1991, p. 382).

Whilst we have come far in this chapter from the detailed measures contained in the Criminal Justice and Public Order Act 1994, these measures in part reflect the issues of spatiality raised above. The threat posed by travellers and their allies to the rural idyll is profoundly disturbing, both for the state, where its alliance with capitalism is threatened, and for many people in the general public, who look to the countryside of the rural idyll for existential inspiration. Overall, both groups have much to lose from any displacement of the rural idyll; both groups thus wish to retain and enhance the current striation of rural space. Hence, access to rural space is controlled by the British state; access must be denied and rights of way must be blocked for those who challenge the rural idyll.

Notes

[1.] Here, reference must be made to Lefebvre's 'conceptual triad' (Lefebvre, 1991, p. 33) of 'spatial practices' (practices reflecting experiences rooted in perceived space), 'representations of space' (formal, academically conceived abstractions of space) and 'representational space' (the symbolic imaginative space of everyday life). Whilst this triad is often somewhat imprecisely delineated (Merrifield, 1993, p. 524), it emphasizes the breadth of Lefebvre's conception of space.

Part III

Management

12

Game Management and Access to the Countryside

GRAHAM COX, CHARLES WATKINS AND MICHAEL WINTER

Popular representations of field sports, and the issue of trespass with which they have long been so closely associated, lead all too easily to the presumption that game preservation and access are always and everywhere fundamentally incompatible. From the Black Act of the early eighteenth century (Thompson, 1975) to the poaching wars of the nineteenth century and beyond (Hopkins, 1985), through to the mass trespass at Kinder Scout in 1932 (Hill, 1980), the image of confrontation with gamekeepers, for instance, has been a key element in the iconography of what has become 'the access issue'.

This has been so much the case that it might reasonably be claimed that shooting has been a perennial leitmotif within the access debate: not always explicitly to the fore, but tending, nonetheless, to be emblematic of the difficulties which those seeking enhanced access are presumed typically to encounter. Cox (1993) emphasizes that such struggles in the post-war period have been played out in a context determined overwhelmingly by the primary concern of government, farmers and landowners alike to harness private property rights to agricultural expansion. But by the 1970s, as Marsden *et al.* (1993, p. 82) point out, this exclusive position has begun to be challenged by a widening range of rural interests.

More recently a shift in the countryside policy agenda has been associated with the movement from a concern with nature conservation and landscape protection towards issues of pollution regulation and access. But although the changes implied by such shifts are profound, we should not lose sight of the acute way in which each set of issues involves questions about how private rights and public responsibilities are to be reconciled. For, as Bromley has noted, 'environmental policy is nothing if not a dispute over the putative rights structure that gives protection to mutually exclusive use of certain environmental resources' (Bromley, 1991, p. 3). Access issues are similarly articulated in terms of such fundamental, and often intractable, concerns: but imbued, if anything, with a more obviously accentuated symbolic significance (see Chapter 1).

Private Rights and Public Responsibilities

In response to the challenges which they have faced in the last two decades, farmers and landowners have been extraordinarily successful in mounting a principled defence of the rights traditionally seen as attaching to private property. They have treated the environmentalists' challenge as a threat to their freedom to manage or use their land as they wish and they have demanded that any restrictions on that freedom be accompanied by adequate compensation to offset loss of income and capital value. Certain long established pre-suppositions have, to that extent, been powerfully affirmed in recent years (Cox, Lowe and Winter, 1988, pp. 328–9).

The view of absolute property rights articulated by John Locke, which has proved congenial to libertarian thinkers, both political and economic, has prevailed. The contrasting view, associated by Bromley (1991) with Kant, which sees social convention as logically prior to real ownership and which presumes that civil society can only exist if there are underlying tacit agreements recognized by all individuals capable of moral judgement, has been only minimally effective. The contrast is marked, in that the Lockean position encourages a view of property rights which sees them as 'some immutable and timeless entitlement that can only be contravened with difficulty, and then only if compensation is paid by the state to make the property holder whole' (Bromley, 1991, p. 7) whereas the Kantian position privileges a more dynamic view which sees property rights as a public trust.

Traditionally in Britain, the public has very few formal rights (in contrast to historic freedoms) over land and the environment. Much is enjoyed by custom rather than by legal right and, as one commentator has noted:

> Public enjoyment of the countryside still depends on a fragile combination of rights and tolerance of land owners ... The public's rights at common law are clearly only few ... *De facto* rights are therefore likely to

remain critical as a means of ameliorating the public's lack of express rights. (Bonyhady, 1987, pp. 18–19)

In present circumstances, when the temptation to market and commoditize access is strong, such *de facto* and customary arrangements might be threatened. The demand, meanwhile, for a generalized right to roam is confronted by the celebrated power of constraint which landed interests continue to exercise with considerable effect.

The presumption that shooting interests are peculiarly inimical to the demands of the access lobby is strongly held. But it rests, often, on information of an essentially anecdotal nature. In this chapter we explore the relationships between different forms of shooting activity and the range of access arrangements which prevail by drawing on the results of the Game Management Project (Cox, Watkins and Winter, 1996). This project, which was funded by the Economic and Social Research Council, involved a postal questionnaire survey in Buckinghamshire, Cumbria, East and Mid Devon, Gloucestershire and Nottinghamshire. These counties were selected to reflect different levels and types of shooting. A sample of 1068 farmers and landowners was selected randomly from *Yellow Pages* and there were 524 respondents. Longitudinal data were collected by resurveying an additional 169 farms and estates which had been surveyed in the 1970s by Helen Piddington for the Country Landowners' Association (CLA) (1981) and 19 of the Nottinghamshire sample were selected because they had been surveyed in the late 1970s by Watkins (1985). We encouraged responses from both shooters and non-shooters by sending two postal questionnaires to each potential respondent. One form was for those whose shooting rights had been used in the year 1990–91 and another for those whose shooting rights had not been used. The success of this technique enables us to make informed comparisons between policies on farms and estates which are, and which are not, shot over.

Table 12.1 shows the number of shooting and non-shooting holdings which responded to the survey. Response rates ranged from 58 per cent for the Piddington sample to 48 per cent in Buckinghamshire, giving a 54 per cent overall response rate. There were 712 respondents, of whom 55 per cent stated that their land was shot over. The survey confirmed that there were clear regional variations in the extent of shooting. Nottinghamshire (60 per cent) and Gloucestershire (55 per cent) had the highest proportion of shooting holdings; Cumbria (38 per cent) had the lowest.

Table 12.1 Farmer and landowner survey: number of shooting and non-shooting holdings

	Shooting holdings		Non-shooting holdings	
	No.	per cent	No.	per cent
Buckinghamshire	46	49	48	51
Cumbria	40	38	66	62
East and Mid-Devon	58	50	58	50
Gloucestershire	64	55	53	45
Nottinghamshire	66	60	44	40
Piddington	119	70	50	30
Total	393	55	319	45

In addition to the postal survey, very detailed information was gathered through personal interviews with 78 of the farmers and landowners evenly distributed between the five counties. We sought, in both the postal and interview questionnaires, detailed information regarding the extent and usage of public rights of way; the impact of such rights of way on the exercise of shooting rights and the extent to which wider public access was allowed. The interviews made possible a more thorough exploration of attitudes towards a wide range of access-related issues. In addition, 122 interviews were carried out with the residents of two small adjoining villages in Gloucestershire and the suburban edges of a small town in Buckinghamshire, each of which was adjacent to a shoot.

Public Access and Game Management

Of considerable significance for the interpretation presented in this section was the fact that of the 91 shooting holdings of 300 hectares or more in size which responded, no fewer than 60 were to be found in the Piddington sample. Indeed, taken together the Piddington and Watkins (PW) sample accounted for 73 per cent of this category. This is accounted for by the fact that the original Piddington sample was of CLA members and the original Watkins sample was of woodland owners. In general terms it should be noted that whilst the *Yellow Pages* (YP) sample falls fairly evenly into shooting and non-shooting holdings, having a ratio of 260:246, the PW sample has a comparable ratio of 132:50.

Shooting holdings are, on average, larger than non-shooting and it is not surprising that whereas 23 per cent of the PW sample released over

1000 pheasants each season, only 5 per cent of the YP sample did so. Indeed, of the 217 YP respondents who provided usable answers, 72 per cent did not release any birds whilst 46 per cent was the comparable figure for the 112 PW respondents. Associated differences in the matter of keepering were similarly marked. It is important to appreciate that the number of keepers has declined dramatically after climbing to a peak of 23,056 between 1871 and 1911. By 1951 there were only 4391 and the best recent estimate puts their numbers, including part-time workers, at about 2000 in England and Wales (Tapper, 1992, p. 17). Some 48 of the PW sample of 124 had some sort of paid keepering (32 at one or more full-time equivalents (FTE) and 16 at less than one FTE). Only 20 of the YP sample had some paid keepering, nine of which had one or more FTE. The perception of poaching being a significant problem was related to area, with 35 per cent of the 82 larger holdings who responded taking that view, as opposed to 14 per cent of the 271 below 300 hectares.

A majority of holdings, ranging from 96.7 per cent of the shooting holdings over 300 hectares to 65.6 per cent of the non-shooting holdings below 300 hectares, had rights of way on their land. Three-quarters of the PW sample report a 'once a week or more' frequency of use of rights of way, whilst the comparable figure for the YP respondents is 64 per cent. Both footpath and bridleway use was reported to be higher on shooting and larger holdings.

We were anxious to ascertain the extent to which the use of public rights of way was seen as affecting in any way the use of shooting rights. A third of the respondents with over 300 hectares claimed that they did, whereas the comparable figure for the below 300 hectare category was 15 per cent. Asked whether they allowed wider public access to any of their land other than on public rights of way, 31 per cent of the PW sample of 126 claimed that they did, whilst 20 per cent of the 223 YP respondents answered in the affirmative. Amongst all shooting holdings, 42 per cent of the larger category and 18 per cent below 300 hectares allowed wider access, whilst the combined figure for all non-shooting holdings was 20 per cent. Interestingly, amongst the shooting holdings permitting wider access were seven respondents – five in the larger category – who nonetheless claimed that this wider access affected their use of their shooting rights.

Before examining some of the implications of these figures, it is necessary to draw attention to the remarkable unanimity amongst

Table 12.2   Farmer and landowner survey: opinion on wider public access; comparison of (a) Piddington/Watkins sample and *Yellow Pages* sample; and (b) holdings which release and do not release pheasants. The figures referred to are percentages.

Opinion on public acess	(a) Sample type		(b) Pheasant release	
	Piddington/ Watkins	*Yellow Pages*	Not released	Released
Strongly agree	2	2	2	2
Agree	18	13	13	16
No opinion	7	11	13	5
Disagree	39	40	44	38
Strongly disagree	34	34	28	39
Total	100	100	100	100

respondents when invited to respond to the question 'In general do you agree that the public should be allowed wider access to uncultivated private land?' (Table 12.2). There is also a remarkable consistency when we turn our attention to the returns provided by the non-shooting sample. Two per cent of the 46 non-shooting PW respondents strongly agreed with wider access, whereas the corresponding figure for the 226 non-shooting YP sample was 0.4 per cent. At the other end of the attitude range, comparability could hardly have been more marked. For no fewer than 76.1 per cent of the PW sample and 74.6 of the YP sample either disagreed or strongly disagreed with the proposition.

Indeed, so marked is this pattern that if we disregard the distinction between the PW and YP samples and return again to our size distribution, we find that for shooting holdings above 300 hectares the percentage disagreeing and strongly disagreeing is 77.4 per cent whilst for holdings below 300 hectares the figure is 73 per cent. Similarly amongst non-shooting holdings in the larger category the figure is 75 per cent and for the below 300 hectares category the percentage disagreeing is 74.5 per cent.

In the face of such a generalized scepticism regarding the advisability of allowing wider access to uncultivated land, it is necessary to return to our seven seemingly aberrant cases who both permit access and consider that it affects their use of their shooting rights. Four are from the Piddington sample, two are from Devon and one is from Gloucestershire. On the question of allowing wider access, their responses include three 'strongly disagree', two 'disagree', one 'strongly agree', and one 'agree'. Such responses are clearly complex as is evidenced by the fact that the two cases where wider permissive public access was allowed over the whole holding produced the one 'strongly agree' and one of the 'strongly disagree' returns.

The extent of wider permissive public access is clearly critical, and when we take account of that variable we find that a claim advanced by Piddington (1981) is in need of some qualification. Piddington suggested, on the basis of her study of a sample of CLA members, that owners of shooting holdings were more likely to allow access to their land than the average owner. But it does not appear from our data, comparing the views of those who release pheasants with the views of those who do not, that the former have greater existing public access than the latter. Whilst it is the case that larger holdings are much more likely to permit wider access than smaller ones, this must be interpreted in the light of the no less apparent observation that it is 'partly shot over' estates that allow such access rather than those where all the land is shot over. If we compare organized shooting holdings (where birds are released), rough shooting holdings and holdings where either no shooting at all or only vermin shooting takes place, we find that the proportions of those allowing wider access are very similar: 26 per cent, 29 per cent and 22 per cent respectively. Contrary to the claim advanced by Piddington, the data from the Game Management Project suggests that shooting activity has no effect either way on the likelihood of permitting wider access. That finding holds, moreover, irrespective of whether the shooting activity involves no release of birds, or rearing and releasing activities at above and below average densities.

There is clearly a need to be circumspect in interpreting the data. The larger estates characterizing the Piddington sample are more easily able to zone different activities such that releasing pheasants and allowing wider access become more readily compatible. But the need for care goes beyond that general point, as is indicated by an estate from our Buckinghamshire sample. The 3000 acre estate, which has been in the same family for over 200 years, included 150 acres of woodland. In the 1992–3 session some 5000 pheasants were released and 16 days of driven shooting were organized. Numerous footpaths crossed the land and the local authority had provided a circular walk. The owner had indicated on the questionnaire that wider access was permitted on all the land. In fact, he proved to be an advocate of 'managed and controlled access'. The wider informal access which he permitted is enjoyed, for the most part, by villagers who are nearly all tenants and who are required to satisfy a number of conditions, one of which is that they are not opposed to field sports.

Effects of Game Management on Public Access: The Views of Residents

The Game Management Project conducted a survey of residents in two contrasting communities: a village and a suburban locality. In total 122 interviews were conducted with residents who lived within walking distance of farms and estates where shooting was known to take place. The aim of the household survey was to assess the importance of country pursuits to the residents and the effect that shooting has on them. One sample was taken from a Gloucestershire village and the other from a small suburban town in Buckinghamshire with easy access to London.

Respondents were asked to list their three most important leisure and hobby activities. Outdoor activities, such as walking and horse riding, were most popular in the village sample. Indeed, this sample (53 per cent) was twice as likely to place an outdoor activity as its main leisure pursuit than those in the suburban sample (23 per cent). 'At home' leisure activities, like gardening and DIY, were more important for the suburban sample, as were indoor sporting activities such as squash and swimming.

When both samples were asked to quantify the importance of the opportunity for access to the countryside, one might expect, on the basis of the response to leisure activities, a contrasting reply. In fact, there was very little difference between the two samples; in both cases over 70 per cent thought it was 'essential'. It has to be noted, however, that the suburban sample was smaller (44) than the village one (78), primarily because a number of suburban respondents felt they had nothing worthwhile to say regarding their use of the countryside and refused to be interviewed.

The sense of paradox is reinforced when the use of local footpaths is assessed. Over ninety per cent of the village sample had used local footpaths, with about two-thirds knowing that they had used the paths near the organized shoot. Comparatively, 70 per cent of the suburban sample used paths in the area and 34 per cent had used the paths near to the neighbouring shoot. These figures correspond closely to those relating to dog walking, where over half the village sample walked a dog, the majority on every occasion that they took a walk. Not surprisingly, respondents from the villages recorded a higher level of walking for any time or day of the week. The difference was particularly marked for weekday evenings.

From the interviews conducted on farms and estates, it was clear that dogs without owners or generally out of control are seen as causing many problems. Indeed the overriding message from the farm and estate interviews appears to be that dogs are considered the most serious problem in terms of disturbance. As far as shoots are concerned, this relates to the summer months, when birds are in a release pen, and the autumn/winter period, when they are fed in holding woods. The breeding season is not of such great concern on those shoots which rely heavily on reared and released birds. This consideration is, however, likely to become more significant if farmers and landowners respond to the encouragement to increase the wild population of pheasants in their stocks.

In the social survey, the perception that the landowner was tolerant of public access was upheld by 77 per cent of the village and 71 per cent of the suburban samples. However, a small but significant number in both village (14 per cent) and suburban (27 per cent) samples felt that most landowners 'disliked' public access. Additional key interviews in the village locality revealed that there had been a tangible shift in the opinions of farmers towards public access over the past decade and most were now less defensive. However, one farmer interviewed in the village sample thought that '90 per cent of the village population are ignorant of farming and use of the countryside'.

A further question in the community survey asked about broader use of the countryside, defined as that away from public footpaths (Table 12.3). Eighty per cent of the village sample affirmed this 'broader use' largely because of the close proximity of a common, which divided the village. In the suburban sample 70 per cent stated that they did not wander. Of those who did leave public footpaths, excluding 'common only' in the village sample, the majority did so without permission of the landowner, 31 per cent in the village and 28 per cent of the suburban

Table 12.3   Residents' survey: informal use of countryside

Type of informal use	Village		Suburb		Total	
	No.	per cent	No.	per cent	No.	per cent
None	16	21	31	70	47	38
Commonland	22	28	0	0	22	18
Permission	13	16	1	2	14	12
No permission	24	31	12	28	36	30
Combination	3	4	0	0	3	2
Total	78	100	44	100	122	100

samples. Those requesting permission formed 16 per cent in the villages and 2 per cent in the suburban location.

Differences in the numbers with shooting experience between the two samples were marked with one-third of the village sample having shot at least once compared to only 11 per cent of the suburban sample (the figures included clay-pigeon shooting). Some 18 respondents from the village but only two from the suburban sample had shot live quarry. It is perhaps surprising therefore that both samples, 92 per cent for village and 80 per cent for suburban, stated that they were aware that shooting took place in the locality. All of the suburban people who were aware of the nearby shoot knew through hearing shots or seeing young pheasants near the road. In the village sample, whilst most were similarly made aware, a number had watched it or were interested in its activities and a further group of respondents participated through beating or picking up. This type of knowledge is possibly a major reason why three-quarters of the village sample knew of local people who shot, compared to only 11 per cent in the suburban sample.

General opinions regarding shooting varied with the almost one-third (31 per cent) of the village sample being in favour of all types of game shooting, compared to only nine per cent of suburban respondents (Table 12.4). Apathy was greater in the suburban sample, with 23 per cent stating that they did not mind, five per cent higher than in the village sample. Those against shooting were more common in the suburban sample (39 per cent) than the village sample (21 per cent), with equal numbers feeling that vermin control was legitimate but game shooting was not.

Results concerning the incidence of shooting affecting the usage of public footpaths also varied between the two locations. A fifth of the village sample stated that shooting had affected their own use of public footpaths either through prior knowledge of organized shooting days

Table 12.4   Residents' survey: Opinions of shooting

Opinion of shooting	Village sample		Suburban sample	
	No.	per cent	No.	per cent
In favour	24	31	4	9
Don't mind	14	18	10	23
Against	16	20	16	36
Vermin only	24	31	13	30
Don't know	0	0	1	2
Total	78	100	44	100

or the sound of rough shooting. However, in the same sample a larger proportion (31 per cent) cited the effect of general occurrences of footpath obstruction; 32 per cent stated that general obstructions occurred infrequently. Figures for the suburban sample were much lower, at seven and 11 per cent respectively. In the suburban area the total number of those affected made up only 11 per cent of the sample, reflecting the low level of knowledge regarding their immediate local area and lower level of use of the countryside. The presence of shooting in the study areas does appear to challenge the right to public access in the study areas but not to the same extent as other obstructions. In relation to organized shoots, the publicity of shoot days results in the local population knowing when to avoid the area. Avoidance of certain areas when shooting is unorganized or rough is more difficult. Such instances may mean a last-minute change in direction away from the area.

The Effects of Public Access on Game Management

The vast majority (84 per cent) of the respondents with shooting holdings stated that their farm or estate had a public right of way. There was a small variation between those who did not release pheasants (79 per cent) and those who did (91 per cent). The probable explanation lies in the size of the farm, which was generally smaller for those not releasing pheasants, thus reducing the likelihood of there being rights of way. The respondents were asked to specify the type of right of way and estimate how frequently it was used by members of the public. With reference to footpaths, 45 per cent of those not releasing peasants claimed that they were used once a week or more, but this figure rose to 61 per cent for those who released pheasants (Table 12.5). A similar type of response is found in the case of bridleways, with only 22 per cent

Table 12.5   Farmer and landowner survey: Use of rights of way by pheasant release

Use of rights of way	Pheasants not released		Pheasants released		Total	
	No.	per cent	No.	per cent	No.	per cent
Footpath: none	20	13	5	4	25	9
Footpath: light	48	30	34	27	82	29
Footpath: heavy	89	57	87	69	176	62
Footpath: total	**157**	**100**	**126**	**100**	**283**	**100**
Bridleway: none	100	64	43	34	143	50
Bridleway: light	14	9	11	9	25	9
Bridleway: heavy	43	27	72	57	115	41
Bridleway: total	**157**	**100**	**126**	**100**	**283**	**100**

of the 'non-releasing' group saying that these rights of way are used once or more, compared to 51 per cent of those who release birds.

The discrepancy is the result of some respondents who are more 'serious' about their shooting, perceiving there to be greater use of rights of way than those who are less serious. The respondents were also asked if the public rights of way affected, in any way, the shooting that occurs. If those in the more serious group perceived there to be more access to their land, it may be that they consider it a problem on their holding. Most respondents, however, stated that there was no conflict between their shooting activities and the public access on their holding, whether pheasants were released or not. Nevertheless, those claiming that there was an effect were more likely to release pheasants (25 per cent of those releasing compared to 11 per cent of those who do not release). This was partly explained by the need to site release pens and drives away from footpaths, to avoid disturbance. In addition, in some instances the position of drives was altered so as to limit nuisance and perceptions of danger by the public. In other cases, action was taken to minimize disruption from those using the rights of way on shooting days, especially where bridleways were regularly frequented by horses.

The most likely explanation for those releasing birds being affected to a greater extent by access is that they are more aware of it. The presence of birds that need protecting or the employment of a keeper with 'policing' responsibilities makes the respondent more aware of those using rights of way. It may not be the case that dogs are more likely to roam in shooting areas but that they are more likely to be seen as a nuisance. Hence those on committed game shooting holdings appear to be more aware of the situation than those who are less serious about their shooting.

We also sought to explore the perceived relationship between rights of way and poaching. This was not seen as a major problem among shooting holdings in four out of the five study areas. The proportion of those with poaching problems ranged from 7 per cent (Buckinghamshire) to 14 per cent (Devon); however, in Nottinghamshire the figure was 34 per cent, higher even than in the Piddington sample. The interview questionnaires conducted in Nottinghamshire appear to identify two causes: proximity to urban areas (including mining villages) and the long tradition of hare coursing in the area.

In nearly all localities the problems were caused by dogs. However, only in Nottinghamshire did there appear to be gang poaching on a large scale. A considerable amount of time was spent by some respondents on night-watching in an attempt to reduce levels of poaching.

One respondent resented the fact that while other shoots worked to a cost of £10 per bird, his costs were considerably higher due to anti-poaching measures. One even concluded that the police were 'frightened' of poachers. The theft of an entire release pen was not unusual. One solution adopted by a respondent to the interview survey was to have a greater number of smaller release pens.

Generally speaking, all the respondents accepted that people wanted to come into the countryside for recreation and leisure and that the vast majority caused no problems. Several interviewees suggested a figure of 10 per cent of visitors causing a disturbance, or damage or left litter, with people not understanding or following the Country Code. Anecdotes relating to major access problems were given by respondents, often relating to other landowners' experiences rather than their own but, according to many of those in the interview survey, most of the problems would not occur if the Country Code was followed. One of the easiest solutions to this from the farmer's point of view was to mark paths clearly and maintain them. Such a policy ensured that the majority of the public passed through without any problems for those concerned.

Local users of paths and bridleways were generally considered to be more responsible than visitors. Exceptions to this occurred in areas where particular recreation activities could be concentrated, like swimming in a river, with locals becoming, from the landowners' perspective, rather proprietorial. Interestingly, the situation relating to organized ramblers was not of great concern. In the opinion of most interviewees they tended to know where they were going, not to have dogs and to respect the Country Code. There were instances of disagreement over footpath changes with organizations such as the Ramblers' Association, but on the whole this did not affect the game management side of the holding.

The postal survey gathered data on the frequency of use for the public rights of way present on the respondent's holding. There was little regional variation with the exception of Devon where use of footpaths and, particularly, bridleways was lower. Overall, two thirds of footpaths were used at least once a week, compared to 40 per cent of bridleways. Those paths and bridleways which are most heavily used tend to be those recognized by owners as having an adverse effect on game management.

Data from the residents' survey (Table 12.3) suggest that whilst the majority of the public keep to public footpaths most of the time, there are a number of people who will knowingly stray from the formal routes. Thus even if landowners site all their game-related features, such as release pens and drives, away from public rights of way, it is quite possible that someone will stray into that area. The effect on breeding is an obviously sensitive issue, for on the one hand the data in this project has shown that shoots are not dependent, even in a small way, on 'wild birds' compared to the dependence on released birds. On the other hand, habitats which effectively hold birds over the winter period share some of the characteristics of those which are successful in the spring for breeding. Breeding is not just for the pheasant populations that survived the shooting season but for other, possibly, non-game species. Any disturbance of the game species is likely to mean disturbance for the non-game species.

In the key interviews, all of the agencies concerned with shooting shared the same progressive typology regarding the dangers presented by the public: the worst scenario is 'walker with dogs not under control'; better is 'walker with dogs under control'; best is 'walker without dogs'. Wildlife and game are not as a general rule frightened by people (Cox, 1993). When a walker is accompanied by a dog the problem is greater as the presence of the dog, a hunting animal by instinct, is alarming to wildlife. Whilst the alarm may not be reduced, the opportunity for damage is, should the dog be on a lead or obedient. If this is not the case then damage in terms of disturbance is of particular concern during the breeding season for all ground-nesting birds, and during the shooting season for commercial shoots. A review of research covering bird communities and specific studies on recreational disturbance found that where public access is concerned, most anxiety has been centred on upland areas (Sidaway, 1990). The evidence of recreational disturbance is not conclusive, but studies assessing this issue were uncommon in Britain and focused on individual species rather than wildlife habitats.

This latter concern for disturbance during the shooting season affects shooting success rates and centres around the undesired 'flushing' of birds away from the wooded or holding area before drives have taken place. Once moved away, a bird may not return and is often lost to other areas. A successful drive moves birds from one holding area over the guns to another holding area. The birds can then either be walked back to their starting point via hedgerows or cover crops or driven from the resting point to a further holding area. Any disturbance which occurs interferes with this process and reduces the number of birds which can be presented to the guns.

Conclusions

The Game Management Project's survey of 712 farms and estates has allowed us to explore in considerable detail the views of owners and occupiers of shooting and non-shooting holdings on the relationship between game management and access to the countryside. The study confirms the continuing hostility of farmers and landowners to wider public access to uncultivated private land. The land agency profession identifies wider public access as contributing to a loss of control and management resulting in damaged sporting facilities (Clifton-Brown, 1992). Those representing landowners are just as equivocal in their stance, stating that there is 'no justification for an unqualified "right to roam" in private woodland' (CLA, 1994).

Our survey results show that this hostility to wider public access is not directly linked with the level of shooting activity. Piddington (1981) suggested that owners of farms and estates where shooting occurred were more likely to allow access than the average owner. It appears that larger farms and estates, which characterized Piddington's sample, are able to exercise a system of zoning. In this way the public are concentrated in areas well away from those used for shooting.

Most of the respondents considered that there was no conflict between their shooting activities and the management of land for game and the public access on their land. Conflict where it occurred was more likely to be found on fairly intensively managed shoots. In these instances, the pheasant release pens, shooting drives and so forth were normally modified to take account of the potential conflict.

The residents' survey showed that the majority of people felt that access to the countryside was essential. Most people had used local footpaths and most people were aware that shooting took place in the locality. A minority of respondents felt that shooting had affected their use of local footpaths. This minority was smaller than the number who had experienced general footpath obstruction caused by growing crops or blocked paths. This is consistent with the results of the Countryside Commission's (1989c) study of rights of way.

Overall, the results of the Game Management Project suggest, perhaps counter-intuitively, that the management of land for game does not significantly reduce the level or quality of public access to the countryside. Owners appear not to allow their shooting activities to interfere with public paths and bridleways, and our findings confirm the political sense of managing public access (Country Landowners'

Association *et al.*, 1994). However, the results also confirm the considerable hostility of the great majority of the farming and landowning community to the idea of wider public access to uncultivated land.

13

Access Opportunities in Community Forests: Public Attitudes and Access Developments in the Marston Vale

CHRIS BULL

In July 1989, the Countryside and Forestry Commissions launched a national programme to create community forests on the fringes of major towns and cities in England and Wales. The idea had first been proposed by the Countryside Commission two years earlier in its major review of countryside recreation policy (Countryside Commission, 1987a) and also adopted in its policy statement on Forestry of the same year (Countryside Commission, 1987d). Forests were planned to cover areas of 30–80 square miles (8000–20,000 hectares) located within the rural–urban fringe and designed to promote the concept of multi-purpose forestry by providing extensive opportunities for a thriving farming and forestry industry, with increased scope for diversification, as well as for recreation, education and new wildlife habitats. Following the initial designation in 1989 of three projects in north-east England, south Staffordshire and east London, nine further areas were designated in February 1991.

From the outset, recreation and leisure have been seen as important features of the community forest vision. The concept was initially proposed in a document concerned with 'policies for enjoying the countryside', where the principal focus was the management of the countryside to facilitate greater access. As stated by the Countryside Commission in its key documentation two years later:

> Community forests will provide a unique environment for many outdoor activities. Set among the woodlands, open grasslands, rivers and lakes will be facilities for all kinds of sports and recreations: active and passive, formal and informal, simple and sophisticated. (Countryside Commission, 1989b).

As Taylor (1989) has suggested, 'community forests are to be designed, developed and managed to provide for the community's leisure needs'.

Community forests offer considerable scope for improving access to countryside areas for substantial numbers of people. By improving overall environmental quality through major tree planting, such areas should become more attractive for leisure. Not only will visual quality be improved but the ability of woodlands to absorb greater visitor numbers than more open areas should greatly increase recreation carrying capacity, especially as in some forest areas the plans are to increase woodland cover from a current figure of 4 per cent to 30 per cent. Community forest schemes, as described in the various plans, also list various specific objectives relating to improving physical access. These include the improvement, rationalization and way marking of existing public rights of way; promoting increased access to existing woodland; establishing new woodland with free public access; the creation of strategic routes with feeder routes to villages and other centres; and the creation of 'gateways' (key sites at the edge of the forest areas providing basic facilities, interpretation, and safe and comprehensible access to the wider countryside). If such objectives are realized, then community forests will have made a major contribution to improving and extending countryside access.

However, while bold and imaginative, the initiative has been criticized for possibly promising too much – for being long on vision but short on the resources and power to ensure success (see, for example, Bishop, 1991 and Tiffin, 1993). Clearly there are a number of constraints, which may limit the potential. As the projects are not going to involve large-scale changes in land ownership but instead rely on the voluntary approach backed up with grant aid (Countryside Commission, 1989b; Bishop, 1991), it might at first appear that community forests have few advantages over anywhere else in terms of increased access potential. There is, as yet, no grant exclusively available for farmers in community forests, although the Farm Woodland Premium Scheme and the Community Woodland Supplement are targeted towards such areas. Even with these grants, however, it has been suggested that farm forestry may not be particularly lucrative (Lorrain-Smith, 1992), which is something that many farmers believe anyway. A recent study by Williams, Lloyd and Watkins (1994) concerned with farmers' attitudes to the planting of new farm woodland in the Greenwood Community Forest area has clearly demonstrated the rather negative attitude of farmers in this respect and provided additional confirmation that farm woodland creation is relatively uneconomic in present circumstances.

In addition, though farmers may be happy to grow more trees, they may not wish to extend access, whereas the grants are often conditional upon woodland with access. In fact, it has been suggested that some farmers are very concerned about the whole concept of community forests, believing that the 'community' label might imply a 'right to roam', something that is anathema to farmers in Britain (Chapter 1). They would thus not wish to provide any encouragement to such developments. However, a preliminary survey of farmers' attitudes carried out in the Marston Vale Community Forest area revealed little evidence of such fears (MVCFP, 1993).

Where land is owned by industrial or commercial interests there is some scope for using the 'planning gain' mechanism to achieve key objectives, although as Bishop (1991) points out, this may well create conflict with existing Green Belt policies. Where most land is owned by farming interests, however, such a strategy is of limited use unless it is linked to some kind of diversified development.

As can be appreciated, in order to win the co-operation of landowners who essentially hold the key to the success of the project, much will rely on the work and skills of the various project teams. As with other rural management initiatives in recent years, a critical element in community forest development is the extent to which these key personnel can change attitudes and persuade landowners of the merits of the scheme. Equally, they need to win wider public support. The vision promoted by the Countryside Commission emphasizes the agreement, enjoyment and participation of local people. They are needed as volunteers for many practical tasks such as tree planting, scrub clearing and fundraising efforts, but their support is also required for lobbying and helping to promote developments as well as for giving the schemes added legitimacy. If local people are not interested, then the project falls far short of its aims. However, as the vision is long-term with gradual improvements rather than dramatic change, there is a danger that people who might initially be interested could become frustrated and disillusioned with consequent dwindling of support. The role of the project team in winning support for the schemes from these two different constituencies of landowners and the general public, however, is a careful balancing act. As suggested earlier, if there is too much emphasis on community, farmers will shy away; but if the public see little happening they may lose interest and the project will equally be flawed.

A final problem for access is that community forest areas are not environmentally attractive, which is of course one key reason why they were designated in the first place. They are typical rural urban fringe landscapes and contain substantial areas of derelict and degraded land. Thus, unless major environmental improvements can be achieved, people may not want access to them anyway. As the Draft Plan for the Marston Vale points out, 'how can landfill, the brickworks, and working clay pits sit comfortably next to sporting and leisure activities ... ?' (MVCFP, 1993). In addition, it has also been suggested that the transformed environments may also be unattractive but in a very different way. Burgess (1994), for example, has shown how some people, especially women, are afraid of using urban fringe woodlands for recreation because of fears about personal safety. Thus, although such projects may improve the visual quality of urban fringe landscapes, they may not necessarily improve access opportunities for certain people in the community.

The extent to which the plans will be successful, therefore, is clearly related to a number of factors, the precise effects of which are uncertain at present. These include financial arrangements; changing attitudes of landowners; public support; and the efforts and initiatives of the project teams in trying to develop the projects in spite of the various constraints. While a certain amount has already been published on the financial aspects and the attitudes of landowners, little has been written about public perceptions of and support for the schemes. Equally, little has been widely published about the work of the project teams concerning initial developments relating to access.

It is the intention of this chapter to examine briefly these two aspects in relation to one particular forest area, the Marston Vale Community Forest near Bedford. It is based on a detailed knowledge of the Marston Vale Community Forest obtained through consultancy work for the project, as well as the results of a number of related surveys of public perceptions and attitudes. These include a large questionnaire survey of 700 households in the area undertaken in 1992 (CRRU/MVA, 1992), a questionnaire survey of public attitudes to the Draft Plan (CRRU, 1993a) and a series of panel meetings designed to discuss key features of the Draft Plan (CRRU, 1993b).

Public Attitudes towards the Marston Vale Community Forest Project

The Marston Vale Community Forest area covers some 61 square miles and contains a population of about 25,000 located within 17 villages

(Figure 13.1). Approximately 145,000 people live on the very edge of the forest, mainly in the urban area of Bedford and Kempston, and 500,000 live within a 20-minute drive. Most of the land within the forest area, a little over 70 per cent, is in agricultural use and just under 10 per cent is affected by the brick-making industry, either awaiting clay extraction, actively being worked or being restored. The present extent of woodland cover is approximately 600 hectares, 4 per cent of the land area, and one of the principal aims of the project is to increase this tree cover to approximately 30 per cent over the next 30 years.

In relation to the various potential problems outlined above, the results of the various surveys of public perceptions and attitudes do provide some grounds for optimism, while at the same time confirming some of the concerns. One of the key results to emerge from the various community surveys and discussions relates to the purposes for which people would want access. Most people interviewed as part of the

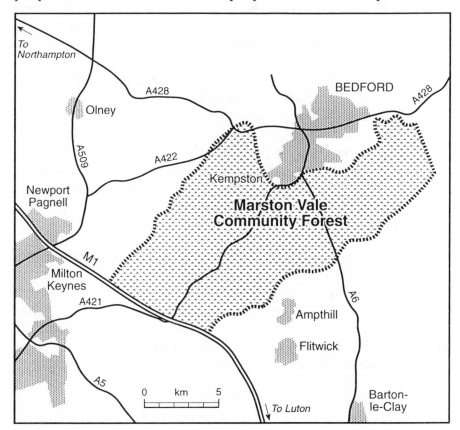

Figure 13.1 Marston Vale Community Forest

Community Survey thought that the community forest would clearly increase their opportunities for taking part in leisure activities, and a substantial majority thought it likely that they would make more use of leisure facilities if opportunities were increased as a result of the project. The increased resources and facilities that people are requesting, however, are not for sport and active recreation but rather for informal, passive leisure – for example, walking, cycling, picnicking. These are essentially the activities in which people tend to be engaging at present and thus the demand is largely for more of the same – for an enhanced version of the status quo. Fifty-seven per cent of the population of the Marston Vale and surrounding area had walked in the countryside in the six months prior to the survey, 27 per cent had cycled for pleasure and 13 per cent had taken picnics. Asked about a range of leisure opportunities that could be provided in community forests, over 80 per cent of respondents recorded walking and rambling in the countryside as being very important, this being the second highest ranking.

Allied to this result, and possibly more significant, was the overall importance placed on wildlife, conservation and educational opportunities. The opportunity with the highest overall score was that of 'information for schools' with 'nature trails/farm trails' being in fourth highest position. 'Nature conservation projects' had the third highest score just behind 'walking/rambling in the country', and 'nature study/bird watching' was fifth. Thus, in terms of the various different components of the forest project, it would seem that the community is placing greatest emphasis on education and conservation aspects. Less importance was placed on sport and leisure except for more opportunities for passive walking, which is often linked to education and wildlife aspects anyway.

These findings were further reinforced by the results of the draft plan consultation survey, which involved people being given a list of 29 statements covering the major elements in the plan and being asked to record their strength of agreement using a 5 point scale ranging from 'strongly agree' to 'strongly disagree'. Once again those proposals with the greatest level of agreement were all concerned with either nature conservation or landscape improvement and tree planting, especially in relation to landfill sites, clay pits and derelict brickworks. As many as 86 per cent strongly agreed with 'the protection and improvement of existing ancient woodland', the proposal ranked first from the list of 29. The next most important proposals were also mainly in the 'landscape and tree planting' and 'nature conservation' categories, with two pro-posals concerned with passive recreation. The proposals concerning 'improving the rights of way network using existing and new routes' and the 'promotion of local circular walks in each parish' were ranked 7th and 9th respectively with 60 per cent and 55 per cent of respondents indicat-ing strong agreement. The proposals which received least support were all concerned with sport and active recreation and accounted for the bottom five ranks in the list. At the very bottom was the proposal concerned with 'provision for small-scale motor sports such as weekend scrambling and airsports' with 'provision of water skiing and "jetski" facilities in the Bedford urban fringe area' being the next least supported.

Thus, despite the opportunities which the community forest might offer for quite major developments in sport and leisure, and of course there are small groups of sports enthusiasts who would clearly welcome such developments, this is not a perception or aspiration held by the public at large. Community forests are clearly seen by the public as very much tied to the 'countryside aesthetic' and prevailing attitudes about what the countryside should be for and how it should be managed.

Another finding which clearly relates to this is the public's attitudes towards the farmers' role, which was an important aspect of the panel group discussions. Most panel groups expressed some scepticism about the likely success of the project, identifying the problem of whether farmers and landowners would co-operate. Despite farmers and land-owners being perceived as a major potential obstacle to increasing access, there was nevertheless considerable sympathy for the farmer's position. Everyone believed the answer to the development of community forests lay in a strictly voluntary approach, with increased financial incentives for landowners. There was a strong feeling that if farmers were expected to play a significant part in the creation of the forest, then they would have to be adequately compensated – 'farmers must not be out of pocket'. When pressed what could be done if it became clear that the voluntary approach was not working, only one of the four groups would condone compulsory purchase and then only as a last resort to obtain land from the large industrial landowners such as Hanson Trust (London Brick) and the landfill operators, Shanks and McEwan. They stressed that they would definitely not condone this in relation to farmers.

Public support for the farmers' situation was also demonstrated in relation to the question of charging for public access. The community survey considered whether leisure activities, including access, should be provided free to users and paid for out of public funds or whether

Table 13.1 Proportion Who Believe Forest Activities Should be Free

	In Vale* per cent	Not in Vale* per cent	Total+ per cent
Free to users	25	40	37
Paid for by users	25	20	21
Some of each	50	40	42

* Columns show the results for those living in the Marston Vale Community Forest area and those living just outside, mainly in the town of Bedford.
+ Overall total is weighted to take account of total populations within the respective areas. These qualifications refer to all tables in this chapter.

people who use them should be expected to pay. As can be seen in Table 13.1, a relatively high proportion of respondents believed that users should pay for either all or at least some activities. The questionnaire also provided various scenarios relating to different activities, and people were asked what they thought would be a reasonable charge for adults and children for different time periods. Table 13.2 lists the mean perceived charges for use of specific leisure facilities (such as the hiring of cycles, fishing, and visiting craft workshops – the examples listed in the question). The results show a mean amount of £2 per hour and £6 per day for an adult with corresponding figures of 96p and £3.25 respectively for a child. Well over 90 per cent of respondents said they would be prepared to pay these charges, and thus the figures suggest a reasonably accurate picture of people's willingness to pay.

In addition to asking about charges for specific recreational activities, all respondents were asked what they thought a reasonable charge would be for people simply to gain access to the Forest, assuming an efficient means of collecting the money could be found. Less than half (44 per cent) thought that access should be free for adults and only 54 per cent thought that access should be free for children. Although the actual level of charge was modest (see Table 13.3), the fact that so many

Table 13.2 Average Perceived Reasonable Charge for Use of Specific Leisure Facilities in Relation to Various Scenarios

	In Vale £	Not in Vale £	Total £
Adult for one hour	1.91	2.02	2.00
Child for one hour	0.78	1.00	0.96
Adult for a day (6 hours)	5.89	6.11	6.08
Child for a day (6 hours)	2.75	3.34	3.25

Table 13.3 Average Perceived Reasonable Charge for Access to the Forest

	In Vale	Not in Vale	Total
For an adult	40p	90p	83p
For a child	14p	52p	47p

people would be prepared to pay for access certainly supports those who have argued for the greater use of market mechanisms in country-side recreation (McCallum and Adams, 1980; Bovaird, Tricker and Stoakes, 1984). Furthermore, it should also be pointed out that in analysing attitudes to charging amongst different social groups, only age and environmental awareness proved to be significant factors. Younger people and the environmentally unaware were more likely to want free facilities than older people and 'extreme greens'; there was, however, no significant difference in attitude amongst different socio-economic groups.

Apart from its relevance to the wider debate on charging for country-side recreation, these results may have much more direct consequences for the development of community forests. As with the earlier findings, they portray attitudes which are sympathetic to the farmers' situation. A public that is not demanding free access but rather one that is willing to pay for both access and other diversified leisure facilities is something that is much more likely to persuade farmers to be more sympathetic to the whole concept.

While farmers may not be so keen, the community survey found almost universal support amongst the general public for the vision and aims of the project and also recorded a high level of willingness to get involved. As many as 16 per cent of local residents and 5 per cent of people from the surrounding sub-region said they would be very likely to undertake some form of voluntary work, with slightly smaller numbers agreeing to undertake fund-raising events and organizing activities which make use of the Forest (see Table 13.4). These figures are

Table 13.4a Likelihood of Supporting the Forest by Undertaking Voluntary Work

	In Vale per cent	Not in Vale per cent	Total per cent
Very likely	6	5	6
Fairly likely	23	20	20

Table 13.4b Likelihood of Supporting the Forest by Undertaking Fund-raising

	In Vale per cent	Not in Vale per cent	Total per cent
Very likely	10	2	3
Fairly likely	25	17	18

Table 13.4c Likelihood of Supporting the Forest by Organizing Activities that Make Use of the Forest

	In Vale per cent	Not in Vale per cent	Total per cent
Very likely	5	4	4
Fairly likely	17	9	14

extremely high and add further emphasis to the overall strength of community support for the Project. Nevertheless, one needs to be somewhat wary about placing too much store on stated intentions. People may be willing to become involved, but the reality of their doing so may be very different, a point which was highlighted by the panel meetings.

All the panel groups referred to the potential problem of disillusionment and also that of the nature of involvement. It was felt that if people were going to become involved, they would need to feel that they had some power and influence in the project rather than just being a source of cheap labour. However, while the panel groups expressed some scepticism, they were also very positive about how local communities might be involved, suggesting various mechanisms for doing so. In this respect the promotion and marketing of the scheme was seen to be very important, and it was felt that in order to sell the project and counter problems of cynicism and apathy, there was a strong need to make it more tangible to people – that it was difficult to market an idea, whereas it was possible to sell something that was specific. It was felt that the marketing had to be positive and focus on the benefits to people and show that developments were actually occurring. Once people could see that the Marston Vale Community Forest was developing in a tangible, visible way, rather than being merely an idea, people would be more likely to support it and become involved. Thus, the panel groups were emphasizing the crucial role of the project team in promoting the project.

Access Developments in the Marston Vale

Although the Plan for the Marston Vale Community Forest was not approved by the Secretary of State until February 1995, a project team has been involved in preparing plans and undertaking preliminary work since 1991. While the overall plan presents a vision to be achieved over the next 30 years, already a number of improvements have occurred in relation to access. The final part of this chapter, therefore, considers some of these developments and, in so doing, re-emphasizes the role of the project and project team as well as that of community involvement.

Although the community forest designation affords no extra powers for increasing access, what it does do is focus attention and resources on the issue. Apart from the project's Community Liaison Officer and her work with local communities, there is also a Rights of Way Officer on the team, who can liaise with landowners and the relevant officers in the local authority. In addition, a working group with representatives of the Highway Authority, local community, user groups and landowners is already established to discuss a wide range of rights-of-way issues, and it is proposed that this will continue as an important part of the Project's development. Most of the achievements that have been made so far are largely the result of these processes and facilities.

For example, local ramblers, encouraged by the project team, have undertaken a complete survey of the state of the 240 km rights of way network (CRRU, 1992) and the project has subsequently stirred up a lot of interest in the villages. This heightening of awareness has led to groups from local villages organizing walks and putting pressure on the County Council to make improvements to the existing system. As a result, many footpaths that were previously impassable have been opened. In addition, local communities, user groups and landowners are also being encouraged to enter schemes such as the Parish Paths Partnership.

The existence of the community forest project has meant that more pressure is being put on landowners to open up existing footpaths and also create new routes. Discussions are taking place with landowners to re-route existing public rights of way and a small number of landowners have also agreed to establish 'permissive' rights of way where access is permitted, even though no statutory right exists. The Forest Plan also proposes incentives to landowners to maintain their paths in better condition, which include 'free structures such as stiles and gates, payments for clearance of headland paths, where agreed, and a 50 per cent contribution towards advertising costs for certain proposals in agreed cases'.

Two strategic footpaths along the Greensand Ridge and the West Bedfordshire Ridge have been improved through surfacing and increased waymarking, and work is under way to join parish footpaths to these strategic routes by means of feeder routes. Furthermore, routes are being publicized and the public is being encouraged to walk them.

In addition to improving access along linear routes, some significant areas of land have also been opened up to provide free access. These include Hulcot Wood, covering almost 100 hectares, which was formerly privately owned but has been bought by the Woodland Trust; and Berry Farm, previously a working farm owned by the local authority, which has now been given over to set-aside and tree planting with free public access. The Woodland Trust is now targeting purchases in community forests, and so once again the designation itself is having a clear influence.

Finally, the project has provided more opportunities for detailed discussions with farmers, with potential opportunities for extending access. The project runs a 'one stop shop' service for farmers where project officers are able to give advice about a range of issues that might affect the farm business, such as grants, tree planting schemes, hedgerow re-instatement, diversification and conservation. While discussing these more 'acceptable' aspects, the opportunity for talking about access also presents itself and thus the potential exists to extend access by means of subtle and sensitive collaboration.

Conclusion

The key results to emerge from the various studies concerning the public's perception of and attitudes to access opportunities in community forests provide significant cause for optimism. While the public may yet be somewhat sceptical that the overall vision will be achieved, they nevertheless value the initiative with substantial numbers willing to volunteer support. The perception of the project in the public's mind, however, is relatively modest, involving little in the way of radical change either in terms of extra leisure opportunities or in terms of enhanced powers to persuade landowners to increase access. Not only do people have considerable sympathy for the farmers, believing that extra grants should be made available to them for the environmental and access improvements that are required; they are also prepared to see landowners charging directly for increased public access, albeit on a modest scale.

While such views are rather depressing to those who would wish to see greater public support for an assault on the power of landowners, they are nevertheless useful for the sensitive environment of community forest promotion. If the requirements of local people are relatively modest, then the chance of delivering the vision is simplified and the chance of public disillusionment and loss of public support will be reduced. In addition, to be able to demonstrate to farmers that the general public does not wish to see the countryside transformed into a free 'people's playground' greatly increases the chances of access agreements being negotiated by the project teams.

Already tangible developments with regard to access are being achieved and, as has been demonstrated, public interest and support is playing a significant role in this respect. Clearly, one of the challenges over the next few years will be not only to retain this initial commitment, but also to extend it.

14

Developing Market Approaches to the Provision of Access

BOB CRABTREE

Introduction

The accompanying measures to Common Agricultural Policy (CAP) Reform (Regulation 2078/92) contain provision for the payment of incentives to farmers in order to increase the supply of public access to the countryside. Paying farmers to provide additional access on their properties represents a new departure in agricultural policy and could be seen as an element in the wider role of farmers in countryside management envisaged in the development of the CAP (Commission of the EC, 1991). The UK government has indicated its approach to policy development for positive environmental management (Ministry of Agriculture, Fisheries and Food (MAFF), 1991). Where market mechanisms do not exist for environmental goods, it envisages the creation of markets by purchasing countryside goods and services on behalf of the public. In relation to access, this implies the procurement of public good output through contracts with farmers as private suppliers. Seen from the viewpoint of the landowner, environmental goods become an additional production opportunity for which government (or its agencies) provide the market outlet.

In the UK the proposals to develop access on set-aside and in ESAs under the CAP Reform measures can be seen as an extension of experimental access provision schemes operated by the countryside agencies in recent years. The prototype Countryside Premium Scheme, operated from 1989–91, was designed to enhance the environmental and recreational output from set-aside (Countryside Commission, 1993c). Within this scheme, which operated in a restricted area in Eastern England, the conversion of set-aside to publicly accessible grassland was one of a number of options aimed at producing public benefits from land taken out of arable production. This first scheme has been followed by further agency schemes aimed at encouraging countryside stewardship by farmers and providing additional recreational access for the public.

This chapter explores three aspects of these developments in national and EC policies: the possible reasons for increased public intervention to provide access; the instruments by which access may be provided, and the effectiveness of the schemes that have been introduced to date.

Intervention in the Provision of Public Access

Several situations can be identified in which public policy may seek to increase the provision of access in the countryside. Some of the more significant, as seen from an economics perspective, are examined here, but in no sense is it intended to be an exhaustive list.

Market Under-provision

One important case for intervention relates to the presence of market failure. If markets for public access cannot develop, for whatever reason, there will be no incentive for landowners to extend the quantity or range of access provision or maintain the quality of any existing public access. Only where access provides an income stream will managers be induced to maintain and possibly extend the supply of access. For the development of a market in recreational access (without a change in landownership) four necessary conditions can be identified:

- a well-defined set of property rights
- limited local free access to reduce the potential for local substitution
- the ability to link use to payment and exclude non-paying users
- a level of income net of transaction costs that produces an acceptable return to investment.

With certain recreational activities, evidence for market failure is slight because these enabling conditions are satisfied. Fishing and shooting are good UK examples where the conditions are met and for which competitive markets have developed. With some other activities (e.g. orienteering, all-terrain vehicles) a form of market provision is increasingly evident, either through permissive arrangements without charges, or through payments by organized groups (Crabtree *et al.*, 1992). These types of recreational activities lend themselves to possible market development because they require specialized sites in order to provide the necessary conditions, together with a degree of security in provision, which needs the involvement of the landowner.

Evidence from surveys of land use for recreational access indicate an increase in the extent to which more formalized 'market' arrangements are developing. For example, in a survey of 800 farmers and estate owners in Scotland (Crabtree *et al.*, 1992) it was found that access had increased substantially in the past ten years. Ten per cent of farms and 36 per cent of larger estates had established at least one arrangement for recreational access by organized groups or the general public. Of these, almost 50 per cent involved payment.

The failure of markets to develop is most obvious on unenclosed land where it is difficult for owners to extract payment, and with activities that can be undertaken independently of the owner's involvement. This occurs principally with walking, cycling and mountaineering, since specific requirements are minimal. In our Scottish survey we were unable to locate any examples of payment for these activities. Landowners face a number of difficulties in creating markets for these types of informal recreation – property rights are fuzzy, the cost associated with exclusion may make exclusion totally infeasible, and even if exclusion is possible, very high transaction costs may be involved in collecting income from those using the access provision. The tradition of property rights that may develop on unenclosed land creates a major barrier to market development, even where increases in the demand for access may provide an additional incentive for landowners to develop income from recreation (Shoard, 1987).

Markets may develop not only for the recreational services that land can provide but also for the land itself. Numerous Conservation, Amenity and Recreation Trusts (CARTs) (Hodge, 1988) have been formed, which engage in land purchase in order to conserve the stock of environmental assets and facilitate use by members. This structural route to the provision of services appears to circumvent the problems of high transaction costs faced by individual farmers and landowners, since CARTs typically receive income directly from membership subscriptions. However, such organizations are still likely to require some exclusivity in use, if for no other reason than to demonstrate benefits to members. This poses problems for the development of those CARTs which aim to provide less specialized countryside recreation.

Excess Utilization

Unrestricted access on sensitive areas may lead to negative externalities from public access in the form of environmental damage. This is the problem of excess use of common property resources (Stevenson, 1991), which is most apparent on popular sites where paths can become eroded and wildlife habitats may be adversely affected. On private land there may be other externalities in terms of impacts on both the business activities of the owners and disturbance of privacy. Options to reduce rates of site utilization are often severely limited since exclusion may not be feasible. However, one indirect approach to excess utilization is to increase the provision of local substitute opportunities. While this will contribute to the overall supply of recreational facilities, little research has been done on the extent to which it can substitute for demand at critical popular sites which have experienced excessive use. Research on other countryside attractions has suggested that the additionality from new provision may be low, indicating a high substitutability between visitor attractions (PACEC, 1990). However, it would seem much more difficult to create new recreational experiences in the countryside that could act as good substitutes for existing popular sites. Certainly, the provision of more farmland access is likely to be a very partial substitute and therefore ineffective in reducing damage in over-utilized areas.

Distributional Issues

A further justification for public access provision occurs when government wishes to ensure that the social welfare benefits associated with countryside recreation are available irrespective of ability to pay. This embraces both merit good provision in relation to the health and welfare of the population in general and the more specific concern for economically disadvantaged social groups (Musgrave and Musgrave, 1976). These arguments for public recreational provision have been rehearsed by Coalter *et al.* (1986). The provision of outdoor recreation for all was an element in the post-war development of National Parks, and this objective clearly underpins local authority provision of free access to urban and peri-urban parks and footpaths. It is an important element in policy in several countries in Europe. Sweden and Norway have *allemansratt* and *allemansretten* polices, which encapsulate the 'countryside for all' ethic, and in Germany there is extensive legislation supporting a freedom-to-roam policy in forests and unenclosed countryside (Scott, 1991). However, it is less obvious that it underpins policy in the UK. There is, for example, little evidence that national policy aims to increase the accessibility of access to social groups not currently engaging in countryside recreation (but, see Chapter 10).

New Opportunities for Access on Farmland

Public intervention to facilitate farmland access in the UK was triggered by the potential for developing new countryside output from set-aside land. New possibilities occurred to increase the opportunity set for rural environmental output in the context of reduced land use for food production. While the development was essentially supply-led, it was a situation in which private sector provision of access was constrained by high transaction costs and difficulties in identifying market opportunities. The response of the public sector has been to identify situations where it believed intervention was justified in order to increase the supply of local public good access.

Instruments for the Provision of New Access

A number of different instruments may be used to extend the provision of access to the countryside, and their effectiveness in the context of countryside conservation has been assessed by Colman *et al.* (1991). The aim here is to summarize briefly the characteristics of different approaches, concentrating on the use of voluntary incentives.

Adjustment of Property Rights through Legislation

Additional access rights could be established for the public through new legislation which gave the public a greater 'freedom to roam'. This, however, poses enormous problems since it would entail uncompensated welfare transfers from existing landowners (see Chapter 1).

Taxation

Several countries use capital or inheritance tax exemption as an instrument for increasing the provision of access to the countryside. Its practical use is highly dependent on the tax arrangements in force, since these determine the benefits to the landowner from exemption. As an instrument, its use tends to be restricted in scope to very large properties where the reductions in tax burden can be substantial and where the quality of the conservation resource is high. It is therefore specialized in its focus. It does, however, provide a means for facilitating public access to areas of high quality countryside and addresses situations where incentive payment approaches are likely to be quite ineffective, given the wealth of the landowners concerned. Unfortunately, research to assess the effectiveness of tax breaks is made extremely difficult in the UK since details of agreements between landowners and the Inland Revenue are confidential. The fact that there is no public information on the location of any additional access resulting from such agreements must bring the effectiveness of the instrument into question.

Cross-compliance

Access to farmland for recreation could be facilitated through cross-compliance mechanisms, which linked the right to receipt of agricultural support with the provision of public access. This type of linkage has been promoted primarily as a mechanism aimed at limiting the external environmental costs of agriculture, although it could be used to link the benefits of farm support programmes to an increasing flow of environmental services from farmers (Batie and Sappington, 1986). One attraction of cross-compliance is that it does not require additional public expenditure in order to achieve an increase in public good output from farmland. It also fits well with the concept of a greater linkage between farm support and the provision of countryside services by farmers.

Cross-compliance mechanisms are most efficient from a cost and administrative point of view if the conditions are readily defined and universally applicable – such as adherence to a minimum set of environmental standards. With recreational access it is more difficult to envisage how a practical compliance scheme could be established because the variability in farm conditions makes it extremely difficult to define what type of access should be provided, and costs would be unevenly distributed across farms. More specific cross-compliance could be envisaged. For example, access on set-aside land could be made a condition of set-aside payments, but this would be inefficient in that on many less accessible sites additional costs would be imposed, yet demand for public use might be very limited. As a route to increasing access provision cross-compliance does appear to have major limitations.

Public Purchase and Access Agreements

Public purchase of access and associated facilities is the most direct route to the enhancement of access. Nevertheless, management agreements in which the price and conditions of access are negotiable have not always performed satisfactorily as an instrument because of the weak bargaining position of the public body and the high administrative costs involved in negotiating agreements with individual landowners. Leonard (1982) envisaged such agreements as a temporary arrangement before a more cost efficient mechanism could be identified. Standardized payments overcome many of the difficulties of the one-to-one approach, since they reduce the negotiation element and hence administrative costs (Crabtree and Chalmers, 1993). However, a standard payment scheme for access would have to incorporate a discretionary component in view of the extreme variability of the benefits from access on farmland. Such discretionary entry into a scheme would necessarily have to take account of anticipated use, which would reflect the recreational characteristics on offer, the proximity to sources of population, and the extent of substitute recreational access in the locality.

Measuring the Effectiveness of Incentive Schemes

How might the effectiveness of an incentive scheme for access be assessed? Any approach would need to identify the use-value created through new access opportunities. The aggregate public benefit could most easily be measured in terms of maximum willingness-to-pay (WTP) using the contingent valuation method. The travel cost method would be less appropriate for a locally specific good. Several estimates of use values for recreation experiences such as forest walks and nature reserves have been made and some UK examples are given in Table 14.1. Estimates of consumer surplus are typically small and less than £2.50 per visit. There are no published estimates for access to farmland for informal recreation but use values may be expected to be no greater than for the more specialized (and less substitutable) experiences listed in Table 14.1. Bateman *et al.* (1994) have recently compared consumer surplus estimates for a range of countryside experiences in relation to the presence or absence of local substitutes. Where many substitutes exist in the local area (typified by beach access), WTP estimates are low and ranged from £2 to £5 per annum. WTP estimates increase only where the number of local substitutes decreases, for example with access to improved river, woodland and heathland sites. There the WTP

Table 14.1 Use-Value Estimates from Informal Recreation in the UK

Good	Method	No of sites	Value (per visit)	Source
Nature reserves/wildlife sites	CVM[+]	3	£1.13–£2.53	Harley and Hanley (1989)
Forest recreation	TCM*	6	£1.20–£2.51	Willis and Benson (1989a)
Forest recreation	CVM	15	£0.43–£0.73	Willis and Benson (1989c)
Botanical sites	CVM	3	£0.07–£0.15	Willis and Benson (1989b)
Botanical sites	TCM	3	£1.59–£1.67	Willis and Benson (1988)
Community forests	CVM	2	£1.00–£1.34	Bishop and Stabler (1991)

[+] Contingent Valuation Method
* Travel Cost Method

estimates range from £10 to £19 per annum. In the context of access, it would be reasonable to conclude that unless the recreational experience was exceptional or no local substitutes existed, WTP expectations for farmland access would be at or beyond the low end of the use-value estimates for recreational experiences reported in the literature.

Public benefits from access need to be assessed in relation to costs of provision. One straightforward approach here is to use the financial costs of provision as a basis for a 'value for money', expenditure-based evaluation. This approach is the one favoured by the countryside agencies (Countryside Commission, 1994a) since it identifies the efficiency with which agency budgets are used to achieve public good benefits. From the national perspective, however, net exchequer costs would be more appropriate.

Experience with Incentive-Based Access Schemes

The first development in this direction occurred under the Countryside Commission's Countryside Premium Scheme, in which access to farmland was an option on set-aside land in certain locations (Countryside Commission, 1993c). Subsequently, the purchase of access management has been incorporated in mixed conservation and access schemes operated in England and Wales. These various schemes, together with a number of local initiatives, are described in detail in Bishop and Phillips (1993). More recently, government has proposed that access payments be incorporated as an option in Environmentally Sensitive Areas (created under Regulations 797/85 and 2328/91) and on set-aside in order to provide benefits from the enhanced public use of farmland (MAFF, 1993b). A parallel development has taken place with respect to Community Forests where planting and management grants are available for the creation of woodland in the proximity of population centres, specifically with the aim of providing an accessible amenity product.

Countryside Premium Scheme

This set-aside add-on scheme used a set of incentive payments to provide public access on set-aside land converted into grassland (Countryside Commission, 1996). The public benefits from this 'Meadowland option' were primarily through the creation of new areas of grassland for quiet enjoyment by the local community, and through the extension of wildlife habitats. With access as the prime objective of this option, it seems reasonable to evaluate the payments only in terms of the use benefits that were produced. In other words, any non-use benefits to landscape and wildlife (which would need to be adjusted to a net basis to account for any wildlife output forgone from set-aside itself) are treated as secondary, and probably quite minor benefits.

The total agency financial costs were £2.15 million over five years (Table 14.2), including both capital payments, annual payments and administrative costs. Administrative costs during the first three years were £313,000, of which 65 per cent can be allocated to the Meadowland option, on the basis of the revenue payments. The total annual cost per farm was thus £2736 for the 157 farms involved, and this gave an average annual cost of £135 per hectare.

Data on the public benefits derived from the access created are limited. Robertson Gould (1992) acting on behalf of MAFF, surveyed a random sample of sites and concluded that sites were not heavily used – on average, 12 people per site per week. This indicates a mean rate of slightly over 600 visitors per site per year, giving a cost per visit of £4.40.

Table 14.2 Payments to Farmers in the Countryside Premium Scheme (Meadowland option, 5 year totals)

	£m
Annual payments	1.766
Capital payments	0.179
Total payments	1.945
Administrative costs	0.203
Total cost	2.148
Total annual cost per farm (157 farms)	£2,736
Cost per visit (600 visits, per year)	£4.40

Source: Countryside Commission (1993c)

Since there is evidence that some sites were used by the public prior to the introduction of the scheme (Robertson Gould, 1992) the cost per net additional visitor would be somewhat higher. This cost per visit is higher than that calculated by Robertson Gould (1992) but their calculations were made before the definitive costs of the scheme were available and appeared to be based on projected rather than actual rates of usage. It is, however, possible that usage rates increased during the life of the scheme, a factor which would reduce the cost per visit. In the Countryside Commission's own evaluation of the scheme (Countryside Commission, 1993c) evidence on the utilization of sites is quite limited. Sixty per cent of the sites were deemed to have no obvious recreational value although 99.7 per cent of respondents surveyed used access created by the scheme. It suggests that use was highly concentrated on better quality or better located sites.

No research has been undertaken to quantify the WTP of access users. However, compared with the estimates given in Table 14.1 and discussed above, it seems inconceivable that the maximum average WTP of users would approach the mean financial cost of access provision in the scheme. This is not to say that on specific sites high rates of usage and/or a high aggregate WTP would not have indicated a satisfactory return to expenditure. What is evident is that sites were extremely variable, depending on site characteristics, accessibility, proximity to centres of population, and the information available; and that the majority of sites provided low value for money.

Countryside Stewardship

Countryside Stewardship (CS) is the other major example of payment-induced voluntary access provision in the UK. It is aimed at conserving a number of target landscapes in England by encouraging positive conservation management (Bishop and Phillips, 1993). It incorporates payments to landowners to create and manage public access on farmland. No evaluation of the scheme has yet been published, so information on the success of its access component is very limited.

There were 2097 agreements under CS in 1991/92, of which around one-third provide for public access mainly in the form of open rather than footpath access, at an annual payment of £50 per hectare. The main source of information on use is derived from a survey by the Ramblers' Association (1993a), who used their members to examine access provision on 42 per cent of the sites on which public access was provided in 1993. No estimates of total usage were made and it is therefore not possible to estimate costs per visitor. Even so, the report indicates that there was considerable difficulty in finding information about the access which had been publicly purchased. In some cases the payments to farmers had not produced any net additions to access over and above that previously available, and elsewhere landowners had taken the opportunity to restrict 'provision' to less than that available prior to the introduction of the scheme. Overall they concluded that 'the scale of the problems in locating the sites, the number of problems encountered once there and the amount of access which already existed before the agreements came into force leads us to question the value for money obtained by the access payments'.

Conclusion

Standardized payment schemes are the only mechanism which has the potential to supply farmland access on a substantial scale at a reasonable administrative cost. In the great majority of cases high transaction costs prohibit farmers from directly engaging in the supply of access to the public, and agency or government intervention provides the only feasible route for greater access provision on farms. Such schemes can be justified on a stand-alone basis if they demonstrate aggregate welfare gains from public expenditure and an acceptable distribution of the access benefits across the population.

The limited evaluation of the two pilot farmland access schemes in the UK casts some doubt over the magnitude of the public benefits achieved in relation to the financial costs involved. This is itself not a major issue since the schemes were experimental and have broken new ground in assessing the potential for greatly increased recreational access on farms. The real interest is in identifying the extent to which more effective discretion in farm selection and more efficient distribution of information can increase· usage rates and benefits without incurring major increase in the transaction costs involved. This implies that sites should be targeted near larger concentrations of residential and tourist demand in areas deficient in access. There is an underlying irony here, however. Focusing on the users as beneficiaries firmly identifies the access provision as a *local* public good. It is only by linking access to other policy objectives with a wider set of beneficiaries (including farm policy and the non-use benefits from nationally significant conservation activity) that public access initiatives are likely to be supported on a *national* or *Community* basis.

Concern with raising the marginal efficiency of access provision should be central to the proposals for access procurement under the agri-environmental measures of CAP Reform. Efficiency, as assessed in terms of net UK exchequer cost rather than agency expenditure, may be easier to achieve. Not only will there be an element of Community financing which will reduce the net financial cost, but any output reductions in supported products would also result in a lower net public investment.

One may question, however, whether either past or proposed access schemes are established solely to obtain greater recreational benefits for the public on a 'value for money' basis, despite definitive statements to this effect (Countryside Commission, 1994a). It may be that the use benefits from access are perceived as complementary to the largely non-use benefits from investment in conservation, in that they provide a more direct and tangible pay-off from the incentive payments to farmers. By facilitating public access the overall benefits from conservation expenditure are then increased. In addition, countryside enhancement schemes that incorporate access fall firmly within the remit of the agency with recreational responsibilities. This permits a wider sphere of countryside and nature conservation activity for that agency than may otherwise be possible, a factor that may be significant in the context of the 'growing competition between agencies for resources and control over the rural environment and the institutional initiatives that drive rural change' (Hodge *et al.*, 1994).

15

Local Countryside = Accessible Countryside? Results from a Countryside Recreation Survey in Wakefield Metropolitan District

MEL JONES AND LYNN CROWE

Introduction

The general features of the patterns of countryside recreation activity in this country are well known. The English countryside was the destination in 1990 of at least one recreational trip by about 76 per cent of the population. In total in that year English people made 1640 million countryside trips (Countryside Commission, 1990a). In the mid-1980s it was estimated that on a typical English summer Sunday, 18 million trips were made into the countryside (Countryside Commission, 1985a). The overwhelming majority of people visit the countryside in order to participate in non-specialist, informal activities such as drives, outings, picnics, walks, visits to friends and relatives and trips to historic buildings. It is also important to note that three times as many people visit the 'ordinary countryside', in which farming or forestry is the main function, than visit managed sites such as country parks or historic buildings (Glyptis, 1991). Finally, it is worth emphasizing that most countryside visiting is done within a short distance of home, with the vast majority of visits taking place in the urban fringe.

What is equally true is that groups within the population as a whole participate in countryside recreation at unequal rates. The Countryside Commission's most recent survey (Countryside Commission, 1990a) has shown that the most frequent visitors (who constitute about 25 per cent of the population but make about 75 per cent of all countryside trips) contain a high proportion of young professional people, who live in or near the countryside, and own at least one and usually two cars. About another 50 per cent of the population are occasional users. A high proportion of these are adults with young children. The adults are in clerical and skilled manual occupations and own a car. The remaining 25 per cent of the population visit the countryside for recreation only rarely or not at all. The adults in this group are most likely to be on low incomes, unskilled, unemployed or of ethnic minority background. They do not own cars and are dependent upon public transport.

It is generally understood that the variations in participation are influenced by a combination of demographic, socio-economic, perceptual and personal factors, although the significance of any one group of factors will vary from individual to individual, from group to group and from place to place. Some writers (Roberts, 1978) have emphasized the strong correlation between participation levels in countryside recreation and income, occupation and social class. Others have demonstrated that countryside sites may have relatively small catchment areas. Elson (1977) and Harrison (1981 and 1983), for example, have shown that urban fringe countryside tends to be used predominantly by local residents rather than by inner city residents. The Countryside Commission, in a range of advisory documents and policy statements, have acknowledged the presence in the population at large of many people who cannot convert their interest in visiting the countryside into reality because the countryside lies 'beyond their familiar territory, beyond their travel horizons, beyond their own experience, and beyond the places where they feel relaxed and at ease' (Countryside Commission, 1989a, p. 5). The Commission has highlighted the need to raise levels of confidence and awareness among such groups and individuals (Countryside Commission, 1989a, 1991c, 1992).

What is of concern is that there has been considerable investment by local authorities in the last 25 years in the development of countryside recreation provision in the urban fringe, particularly of country parks, and a considerable proportion of that provision has taken place opportunistically rather than to meet latent demand in particular places and, apparently, on the basis of a number of untested assumptions. Among these assumptions appear to be that urban fringe recreation sites are accessible to urban residents whatever their residential location and whether or not they are car owners, and that without targeted promotion based on a sound platform of market research, urban residents from all demographic and socio-economic backgrounds will be aware of and confident in using the range of local countryside opportunities available.

In the context of recreation planning in the West Midlands, White and Dunn (1975) concluded that ' ... the principal direction of future research should be in the direction of practice ... research in recreation planning has been fragmentary ... and policy making has therefore had little regard for research results ... ' They went on to say that 'There is a case for pragmatism on the part of the research workers, involving acceptance of the notion that the ultimate objective – verification of such theory that exists, and new theory building – should take second place to that of demonstrating the practical application of research findings.' This sentiment is likely to find only qualified acceptance in the academic community at the present time, but the fact remains that much countryside recreation policy-making and management at the local level, for a variety of reasons, not least lack of resources, often has little regard for general research findings and recreation provision decisions are arrived at, in the absence of supporting empirical evidence, on professional judgements and informed guesswork. It is significant that only within the last few years has the Countryside Commission stressed the importance of data gathering and analysis at the local level in order to inform decisions (Countryside Commission, 1991c).

The purpose of this chapter is to report on a research study undertaken on behalf of the City of Wakefield Metropolitan District Council in order to provide a rational basis on which to evaluate existing provision, which had been developed on an incremental basis over several decades, and to assist future recreation planning and management in what was anticipated would be a period of continued financial constraints (Jones, Crowe and Walsh, 1991).

The Study area, Objectives and Methodology

The City of Wakefield Metropolitan District was created in 1974 as part of West Yorkshire Metropolitan County. It was made up of the former Wakefield County Borough together with a number of municipal boroughs and urban and rural districts formerly under the auspices of the West Riding County Council. In 1986, following the abolition of the metropolitan county councils, the City of Wakefield Metropolitan District became a unitary authority and took on the responsibility for all leisure services provision within its area. Its present countryside recreation provision, therefore, has originated in and been developed by a number of different local authorities, with different resource bases, different outlooks and different priorities. By the beginning of the 1990s it was thought timely to evaluate and review the Countryside Service's provision.

The Metropolitan District is extremely varied with areas of high landscape quality and areas of severe environmental deprivation. The settlement pattern is equally diverse and is composed of multiple nuclei of varying size and socio-economic diversity. There are two main agglomerations, based on the City of Wakefield in the west and a looser spread centred around Pontefract, Featherstone and Castleford in the east. Other small towns, industrial settlements and villages of varying types are also scattered throughout the district (Figure 15.1).

The vast majority of the managed countryside sites in the Metropolitan District occur primarily in the south-western quadrant of the Metropolitan District (Figure 15.1). This pattern is not uncommon in other metropolitan areas, with local authority managed sites often located in the more attractive urban fringe areas. Traditionally these locations have seen the greatest expressed demand for informal countryside recreation, and local authority action has merely followed and reinforced the pattern.

The specific objectives of the study were:

(a) to collect information about:
   (i) levels and types of informal countryside recreation visiting undertaken by residents of Wakefield Metropolitan District within the boundaries of the district;
   (ii) the detailed characteristics of such trips, viz. sites or localities visited, times of visiting, methods of travel, activities undertaken, time spent in the countryside, costs involved besides travel costs, motivation for visiting, and composition of visitor groups;
   (iii) residents' potential future interest in various kinds of countryside recreation activity and the degree of difficulty (if any) perceived in fulfilling interests;
   (iv) any new services (or expansion of existing services) that would increase their likelihood of visiting the countryside more frequently;
   (v) barriers, both real and perceived, discouraging them from going out more frequently into the local countryside;
   (vi) the level of awareness of the Countryside Service;
   (vii) knowledge of sites managed by the Countryside Service;
(b) with regard to the issues explored in (i) to (vii), to investigate variations between residents of different types of settlement and neighbourhood in different parts of the Metropolitan District;
(c) using the information gathered under (a) and (b), to make recommendations about the future development of the Countryside Service and the deployment of its resources.

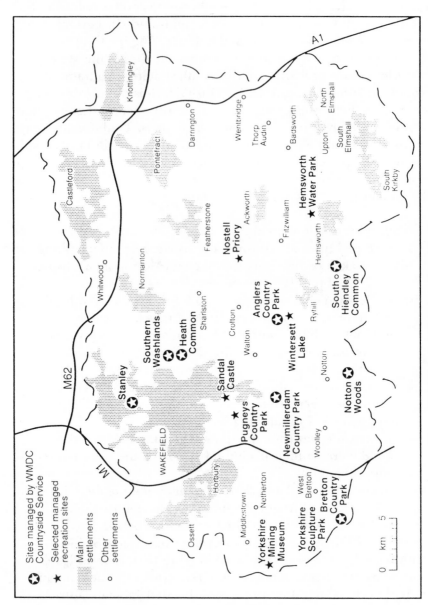

Figure 15.1 Wakefield Metropolitan District

The rationale for the study is summarized in Figure 15.2.

Data were gathered by means of a household questionnaire survey and three small surveys at sites managed by the Countryside Service. The household survey, which involved the completion of 1000 questionnaires, was spread over a number of different settlements to achieve a geographical spread and a variety of different types of settlement. The

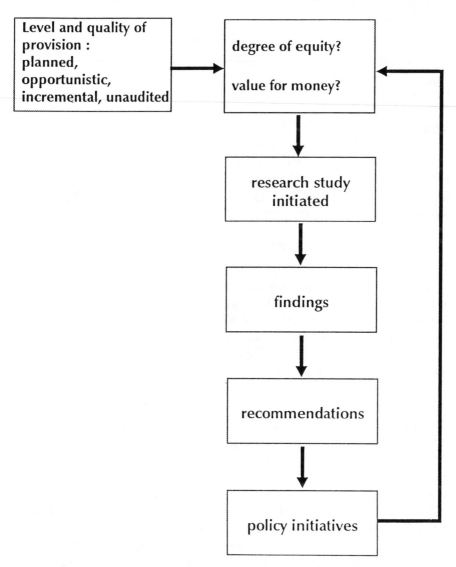

Figure 15.2: The rationale for the Wakefield Metropolitan District countryside recreation study

Table 15.1: Household survey: locations and sample sizes

		Target sample size	Actual sample size
=	Havercroft	200	259
=	South Elmsall	200	141
+	Wakefield – Area A	150	156
•	Wakefield – Area B	150	153
+	Pontefract – Area C	150	174
•	Pontefract – Area D	150	117
Totals		1000	1000

+ *Area dominated by social classes A, B and C1.*
• *Area dominated by social classes C2, D and E.*
= *Socially mixed sample.*

settlements chosen were Wakefield, Pontefract, South Elmsall and Havercroft-Ryhill. In the two large settlements, Wakefield and Pontefract, interviews were carried out in areas of contrasting social status, selected on the basis of known socio-economic characteristics from census statistics (see Table 15.1). The surveys took place in the second half of August and the first week of September, 1991.

Results of the survey

First, it was patently clear from the household and site surveys that informal, non-specialist recreation in the local countryside, such as walking, visiting country parks and going for drives and picnics, is a very popular leisure activity for the majority of people who live in Wakefield Metropolitan District. Two out of every five of the 1000 respondents in the household survey said they went out into Wakefield's countryside at least once a week, and seven out of ten said they visited it at least once a month. Similarly, most of those interviewed at the three managed sites were regular and frequent visitors, summer and winter. At Anglers' Country Park, 60 per cent of the 52 visitors interviewed said they went there once a week in summer; at Newmillerdam, 75 per cent of the return visitors (166 out of 188) said they visited the site at least once a month in summer and 55 per cent said they went there at least once a month during the winter months.

The household survey also showed that there was a strong latent desire among the public to visit Wakefield's countryside more often, with two out of every five respondents stating that they would like to make more countryside trips. This was equally true of respondents in areas where there was already a high level of countryside visiting as it was of those areas where frequent countryside visiting was less common.

However, what was also perfectly plain from both the household and site surveys was that participation rates are uneven across the Metropolitan District. As in other surveys there appears to be a strong relationship between participation in countryside recreation and socio-economic status. The residents of Area A in Wakefield and Area C in Pontefract, predominantly in social classes A, B and C1, had participation rates in most activities well above average; on the other hand, with a few notable exceptions, the residents of Area B in Wakefield and Area D in Pontefract (both dominated by residents in social classes C2, D and E) had participation rates at a noticeably lower level (Table 15.2).

Most countryside visits had been made by car (Table 15.3). Two-thirds of the respondents in the household survey had made their last trip into Wakefield's countryside by car and very little use had been made of public transport (6.3 per cent of 'last trips'). The use of cars among those interviewed during the site surveys was also well above the national average: at Anglers' Country Park, 43 of the 52 interviewees had arrived by car and at Newmillerdam 158 out of 192 had travelled in

Table 15.2 Participation in countryside activities in the Metropolitan District of Wakefield between 1 January and mid-August 1991, by area

	Havercroft	South Elmsall	Wakefield (Area A)	Wakefield (Area B)	Pontefract (Area C)	Pontefract (Area D)
a. Visited park/urban open space	172 (66.4)	72 (51.1)	132 (84.6)	118 (77.1)	129 (74.1)	91 (78.1)
b. Visited historic countryside, gardens, parks etc	90 (34.7)	37 (26.2)	76 (48.7)	57 (37.3)	84 (48.3)	31 (26.7)
c. Visited country parks	148 (57.1)	72 (51.1)	130 (83.3)	96 (68.8)	101 (58.1)	38 (32.8)
d. Visited nature reserves	86 (32.2)	32 (22.7)	68 (43.6)	41 (26.8)	65 (37.4)	35 (30.2)
e. Drives, outings, picnics in c'tryside	125 (48.3)	71 (50.4)	98 (62.8)	81 (52.9)	123 (70.7)	60 (51.7)
f. Long walks or hikes (over 2 miles)	144 (55.6)	53 (37.6)	87 (55.8)	66 (43.1)	87 (50.0)	37 (31.9)
g. Short walks (under 2 miles)	200 (77.2)	94 (66.7)	129 (82.7)	112 (73.2)	142 (81.6)	81 (69.8)
h. Walked dog in countryside	111 (42.9)	47 (33.3)	48 (30.8)	61 (40.0)	45 (25.9)	44 (37.9)
i. Been fishing in countryside	36 (13.9)	10 (7.1)	20 (12.8)	25 (16.3)	19 (10.9)	17 (14.7)
j. Been horse-riding in the countryside	6 (2.3)	5 (3.5)	13 (8.3)	5 (3.3)	7 (4.0)	2 (1.7)
k. Been shooting in the countryside	22 (8.5)	6 (4.3)	6 (3.9)	4 (2.6)	5 (2.9)	7 (6.0)
l. Taken active part in other informal sport in countryside	48 (18.5)	21 (14.9)	50 (32.1)	23 (15.0)	44 (25.3)	21 (18.1)
m. Taken active part in other informal sport in countryside (e.g. kicking ball about/jogging etc.)	106 (40.9)	40 (28.4)	76 (48.7)	67 (43.8)	90 (51.7)	53 (45.7)
n. Watching any organized sport in the countryside	121 (46.7)	44 (31.2)	59 (37.8)	57 (37.3)	77 (44.3)	43 (37.1)
o. Carried out any conservation work or recreation work	18 (6.9)	4 (2.8)	24 (15.4)	14 (9.2)	9 (5.2)	5 (4.3)
p. Picked your own fruit	90 (34.7)	40 (28.4)	81 (51.9)	62 (40.5)	72 (41.4)	42 (36.2)
	259	141	156	153	174	116

n = 1000

Table 15.3: Main method of travel to the site or locality on the last visit – by area (frequency/percentage)

	Havercroft	South Elmsall	Wakefield (Area A)	Wakefield (Area B)	Pontefract (Area C)	Pontefract (Area D)	Aggregates per cent
Car/van	105 (49.5)	76 (69.7)	104 (74.8)	68 (52.7)	130 (82.3)	62 (71.3)	65.3
Walk	85 (40.1)	23 (21.1)	28 (20.1)	41 (31.8)	22 (13.9)	15 (17.2)	25.7
Bus	16 (7.6)	9 (8.3)	2 (1.4)	12 (9.3)	1 (0.6)	7 (8.1)	5.6
Cycle	4 (1.9)	1 (0.9)	2 (1.4)	3 (2.3)	3 (1.9)	3 (3.5)	1.9
Train	0 0	0 0	3 (2.2)	2 (1.6)	1 (0.6)	0 0	0.7
Motor cycle	1 (0.5)	0 0	0 0	1 (0.8)	1 (0.6)	0 0	0.4
Other	1 (0.5)	0 0	0 0	2 (1.6)	0 0	0 0	0.4
Totals	212 100.0	109 100.0	139 100.0	129 100.0	158 100.0	87 100.0	100.0

responses = 834

a car or van. Clearly, lack of access to a car or van as driver or passenger is an important influence on the frequency of countryside visits and on countryside destinations.

The problem of lack of car ownership is exacerbated in Wakefield Metropolitan District because of the concentration of attractive countryside and local authority and other managed countryside sites in the south-west quadrant of the district. Residents in the north-east and south-east quadrants are at a considerable disadvantage when it comes to visiting most of the district's 'flagship' sites. This is shown clearly in the results relating to visits to country parks in Table 15.1. In Wakefield, where there are three country parks within a few miles of those questioned, 83 per cent of those living in Area A said they had visited a country park during the previous eight months, and for those interviewed in Area B of the city the figure was 62 per cent. By contrast, of those interviewees living in Area C in Pontefract, only 58 per cent had visited a country park in the Metropolitan District during the previous eight months, and in Area D in Pontefract the figure dropped to 32 per cent. The nearest country park to both of the Pontefract neighbourhoods is about 12 miles away. Another interesting feature of these findings is the differential effect distance appears to have had on country park visiting among residents of the same types of neighbourhood in different parts of the district, with the visiting rate for Area C in Pontefract 25 per cent below the equivalent Wakefield neighbourhood (Area A). Conversely, the low level of car ownership in Area B in Wakefield appears to have been mitigated by its proximity to Newmillerdam and Pugneys country parks, resulting in visiting rates in the previous eight months being four per cent higher than Area C in Pontefract, even though car ownership levels were much lower (48 per cent as against 83.1 per cent). The friction of distance was also evident in country park visiting patterns in the two smaller settlements. In Havercroft-Ryhill, which lies less than three miles from Anglers' Country Park and about six miles from Newmillerdam, 57.1 per cent of the respondents had visited a country park in the previous eight months; in South Elmsall, which is 11 miles from Anglers' Country Park and 15 miles from Newmillerdam, the corresponding figure was 51 per cent.

The household survey and site surveys also showed that many of Wakefield's local countryside visitors were creatures of habit as far as countryside destinations were concerned, mostly returning to places they had visited before, largely unaware of the Countryside Service and its organized and promotional activities. Only just over one-fifth of the 1000 respondents in the household survey had heard of the Countryside Service prior to the interview and only a tiny minority had been influenced by its advertising: only seven out of more than 823 interviewees had last made a trip into the local countryside as a result of reading a Countryside Service leaflet (Table 15.4) and less than five per cent had previously participated in a Countryside Service event.

Respondents were invited to name up to three sites managed by the Countryside Service. Seven hundred and thirty-two respondents named one site, 607 named two sites and 448 named three sites. Of these 1787 named sites, more than 60 per cent were not in fact managed by the Countryside Service. Of the sites managed by the Countryside Service, the most frequently named was Newmillerdam Country Park, mentioned on 411 occasions, more than twice as many times as the next mentioned site. Other well known sites were Bretton Park (182 mentions) and Anglers' Country Park (113). No other site was mentioned

Table 15.4: How the decision was made regarding where to go on the last trip

	Frequency	Percentage
Been before	341	41
Regular occurrence	276	34
Recommended	68	8
Went with family	65	8
Found by chance	29	4
Went on school/work or other organized trip	20	2
Newspaper	12	2
Leaflet	7	1
Radio	1	0
Television	1	0
Saw on map	1	0
Other	2	0
Totals	823	100.0

Table 15.5: Level of awareness of countryside sites managed by Wakefield Countryside Service (frequency of responses) – by area

	Havercroft	South Elmsall	Wakefield (Area A)	Wakefield (Area B)	Pontefract (Area C)	Pontefract (Area D)
Newmillerdam Country Park	73	48	98	95	65	32
Bretton Country Park	17	13	43	37	24	8
Anglers' Country Park	47	8	18	7	21	12
Woolley Edge	0	0	3	1	2	0
Norton Wood	0	1	0	1	0	2
Seckar Wood	2	0	5	3	0	0
Haw Park Wood	1	0	2	1	0	0
Cold Hiendley Reservoir	2	0	0	0	0	0
Heath Common	0	1	0	6	2	0
Half Moon Pond	0	0	1	0	0	0
Southern Washland	0	0	1	1	0	0
Stanley Marsh	3	0	2	2	1	0
South Hiendley Common	6	0	0	0	0	0
TOTALS	151	71	173	154	115	54

No responses for Sharlston Common, Pothills Marsh and Barnsley Canal

more than ten times. Table 15.5 summarizes the responses from the sampled settlements and shows clearly the variable impact of residential location and socio-economic status on knowledge of Countryside Service managed sites.

Finally, the results indicated a strong latent desire among respondents, no matter where they lived within the Metropolitan District and irrespective of neighbourhood type, to visit the countryside more often. More than half of the household respondents said they were very interested in going on more short walks, and over 45 per cent were very interested in increasing the number of times they went to urban open spaces, visited country parks and went on drives and picnics. When asked what improvements in facilities and services would encourage more frequent countryside visiting, more than two-thirds of household respondents cited better facilities such as benches and toilets as very important, 47 per cent put better parking facilities in this category and nearly 45 per cent said more footpath signs were very important. Guided events attracted the lowest percentage of 'very important' responses. When asked what factors discouraged more frequent countryside visiting, lack of facilities such as toilets and benches was mentioned most (by 55 per cent of respondents) as being very important. Fear of confrontation with landowners, transport difficulties, lack of knowledge of sites and events, and feelings of insecurity were all mentioned as being very important in discouraging visits by between 30 and 40 per cent of the household respondents. A small but significant minority of respondents specifically mentioned the problems of access for the disabled, for those in wheelchairs, and for those with prams and pushchairs.

To summarize, the study showed unequivocally that there was already a high level of participation in informal countryside recreation within the Metropolitan District and a strong latent demand to use the countryside more frequently for recreation purposes. It was equally plain that socio-economic factors and residential location were major influencing factors on participation levels. Two other major constraints were a lack of confidence in using the ordinary countryside – of particular significance for residents living outside the south-western quadrant at some distance from the major managed sites – and a low level of awareness of the existence and functions of the Countryside Service.

Recommendations

With these issues in mind, recommendations were made to Wakefield Countryside Service to assist in the development of initiatives designed to lower barriers to participation among particular groups and individuals. These focused on three areas: creating new countryside opportunities; fostering confidence; and increasing awareness.

Creating new countryside opportunities

• Redress the imbalance between the eastern and western parts of the district by creating a major new countryside site in the east, possibly in partnership with another organization. This is likely to be a long-term objective rather than a practical solution in the short term.

• Create networks of smaller, less formal sites, linked by well managed and promoted rights of way, particularly in the east of the district. Small areas of woodland, common land, canal and river banks and previously derelict or redundant land might be acquired or leased for this purpose. Partnerships with other landowners could be developed for mutual benefit. Such a network would depend on a well-managed public rights of way system as an integral part of the overall network.

• Make more accessible existing sites in the eastern part of the district or beyond the Metropolitan District boundaries managed by other organizations, possibly as partnership projects.

Fostering confidence

• Increase confidence in using the rights of way network by ensuring routes are well signposted.

• The public rights of way network is a fundamental element in the provision of opportunities and in engendering public confidence. Public rights of way should be legally defined and well maintained. Make every effort, in those areas where car ownership is low and managed sites distant, to ensure that public rights of way are clear of obstructions, well surfaced and clear of vegetation. The availability of a specific rights of way team is recommended.

• Develop networks of routes (with explanatory leaflets) linked to settlements; these ought to be a priority in areas of locational disadvantage.

• Publicize existing public transport routes into the countryside and explore new partnerships with public transport operators.

• Liaise with leaders of organizations and agencies such as community centres, old people's clubs, physically and mentally disabled groups, care groups, job clubs, playgroups and youth groups with a view to encouraging countryside visits. Serious consideration should be given to initiating, on an experimental basis, a scheme of the 'Operation Gateway' type, to promote awareness of the local countryside and to facilitate countryside visiting.

Increasing awareness

• Target new and imaginative information about the local countryside in those parts of the district remote from existing well-known and well-used sites. Attractively packaged information needs to be made available where people live, work and congregate socially. A touring 'Countryside Roadshow' in the eastern part of the district is recommended. The emphasis would be on the Countryside service reaching into local communities rather than waiting for people to come to countryside sites.

• Use existing well-used sites as 'gateways' to the rest of Wakefield's countryside, focusing on basic information about facilities and accessibility.

• Develop additional promotional material, including the production of neighbourhood packs and increased liaison with local radio and newspapers, rather than the traditional countryside leaflet approach.

Summary and Conclusions

A number of untested assumptions have formed the basis of country-side recreation policies and plans for the areas surrounding major urban centres in the UK in the period since the end of World War II. Among these assumptions have been that urban fringe countryside is equally accessible to urban populations, whether or not they have access to a car, and that all urban residents are aware of and confident in using the range of countryside recreation opportunities available in the local countryside. Studies published since the 1970s have challenged these assumptions. The bulk of these studies have been site studies concerned with south-east England, particularly with London's urban fringe, and relatively little recent published evidence is available for the provincial conurbations. This chapter has made a modest contribution to the countryside accessibility debate by highlighting the impact of socio-economic status, residential location and knowledge of public sector provision on participation in informal countryside recreation activities in one provincial metropolitan area and by identifying the policy implications of the study's findings.

The study, though making no claims to sophistication – and this is seen as a strength if other local authorities are to be encouraged to follow Wakefield's example and invest in an empirical data gathering exercise – has demonstrated the importance of informal countryside recreation to all residents of Wakefield Metropolitan District, and has identified where opportunities for participation in countryside recreation are restricted and why. In a time of severe financial constraints all public sector services are under review. The study has lent weight to the prioritization of limited funds for schemes which seek to redress the imbalance in recreation provision arising from opportunistic development in the past, and allow all urban residents, whatever their socio-economic circumstances or residential location, to exercise real choice about whether and where to go in the local countryside. The value of studies of this type to local authority departments competing for scarce resources is clear. They are also essential in developing policies and plans to ensure that informal countryside recreation is equally accessible to all sections of the public. Without such information, provision can only be made based on assumptions and speculation.

The survey findings and recommendations were submitted to the District Council's Leisure Services Committee in January 1992. An important element of the submission was an executive summary of the full report, which focused on the financial implications of the recommendations. Politically these were well received. The survey was seen to be a very worthwhile tool with which to identify inequities in access to countryside recreation across the district. Those recommendations having no additional financial implications were approved with immediate effect; the others were noted with a view to implementing them when resources become available.

Figure 15.3: The Walking Women's Network

Subsequent policy initiatives by the Countryside Service have included:

▼ The creation of a dedicated public rights of way maintenance team with an increased budget. This will assist greatly in the development and maintenance of the network of small sites linked by rights of way as advocated in the report.

▼ The production of additional self-guided trail and interpretive leaflets, particularly targeted at groups whose access appeared to be constrained.

▼ The establishment of a Walking Women's Network, aimed at increasing confidence and awareness of opportunities (Figure 15.3).

▼ The running of Countryside roadshows with particular emphasis on the eastern part of the district.

▼ The organization of new events, including a traditional tree dressing held in Pontefract town centre, and walks based on the industrial archaeology of the eastern half of the district.

▼ Greater use of the local media to publicize the local countryside in general and specific events and activities.

▼ The development of a new countryside visitor centre in Anglers' Country Park. The interpretitive facilities promote the 'gateway' concept recommended in the survey report.

Acknowledgements

We wish to thank Wakefield Countryside Service for giving permission to use the findings and other information from the Countryside Recreation Survey undertaken on their behalf, and in particular to Paul Andrews, Countryside Officer (Access and Development), for initiating the survey and for his assistance throughout the survey period and subsequently.

16

Sustaining Enjoyment of the Countryside: The Challenge and Opportunities

KEVIN BISHOP

Introduction

Enjoyment of the countryside, in its totality, has become a mass activity with over 900 million day visits to the UK countryside (including the coast) in 1993 (Walker, 1995) and an estimated 84 per cent of the population participating in at least one countryside activity per annum (Countryside Commission, 1991c). This enjoyment takes many forms: from picnics to power boating; caving to climbing (see Figure 16.1), but the most popular activity is walking or rambling, which accounted for 19 per cent of trips in the 1990 survey of countryside recreation in England and 363 million day trips in the 1993 UK Day Visits Survey (Walker, 1995).

There has always been concern about the potential and actual impact of leisure use of the countryside. In the 1960s, Michael Dower wrote about the challenge of the 'fourth wave' (Dower, 1965). He predicted that industrialization, railway construction and the sprawl of car-based suburbs would be followed by a new wave of pressures arising from increasing leisure demands facilitated by the growth in car ownership. The Council for Nature (1965) also warned of threats to conservation from the increased popularity of countryside recreation: 'almost complete destruction of vegetation is taking place where the public congregate at weekends in large numbers ... some control is necessary unless the places that they wish to visit are to be destroyed' (p. 24). In the 1970s the Department of the Environment warned that the greatest impact of countryside recreation was yet to be witnessed.

These traditional concerns have been given new and additional emphasis by recent research which has spoken of a cultural crisis

Table 16.1 Main Purpose of Leisure Day visits from home as recorded in the 1993 UK day visits survey

Purpose of day trip	per cent	Number (millions)
Eat and/or drink out	18	376.1
Walk/ramble/hill walk	18	363.1
Visit friends/relatives in their home	15	301.0
For entertainment	7	141.7
Leisure shopping	6	129.0
Outdoor sport	6	115.6
Indoor sport	5	97.7
Drive/picnic/sightseeing/pleasure boating	4	72.4
Pursue a hobby/special interest	3	71.9
Visit a tourist/leisure attraction	3	68.5
Swimming – indoors	3	62.1
Countryside sport	3	55.1
Watch sport	3	52.0
Cycling/mountain biking	2	48.3
Informal sport/children's games/sunbathing/relaxing	2	46.4
Visit the beach/seaside	1	16.0

Source: Walker, 1995

crystallizing in the countryside (Clark *et al.*, 1994). Clark *et al.* argue that we have entered a new era in which conflicts about leisure use of the countryside are assuming increased significance due to a number of reasons. With the prospect of surplus agricultural land, leisure uses are seen as a viable alternative or supplement to farm incomes. The language is no longer about recreation as a threat to agricultural viability (House of Lords Select Committee on Sport and Leisure, 1973) but of recreation as an important means of farm diversification (MAFF, 1991). Clark *et al.* argue that leisure and tourism developments are likely to consume thousands of acres of undeveloped land in the English countryside over the coming decade. They also argue that the current institutional infrastructure is failing to acknowledge and address adequately the cultural conflicts now emerging through leisure use of the countryside and that this could have adverse impacts. They suggest that new public mechanisms are needed urgently, to understand and explore ways of guiding new leisure and tourism activity with greater environmental and cultural sensitivity. The *Leisure Landscapes* (Clark *et al.*, 1994) report was one of the factors that prompted the House of Commons Environment Select Committee to undertake its recent investigation into the environmental impact of leisure activities.

Against this backdrop of renewed concern about the environmental and cultural impacts of countryside leisure, there has been almost universal acceptance of the notion of sustainable development as a guiding principle for the management of human interaction with the environment. There is concern from some that sustainability will become a byword or justification for restricting access in the name of conservation but, as this chapter outlines, this is a misinterpretation of what sustainability means in terms of enjoyment of the countryside.

Sustainability

Since 1987 and the publication of the Brundtland report *Our Common Future* and, more significantly, the agreements reached at the 1992 United Nation's Conference on Environment and Development, the notion of sustainable development has been widely accepted as an overarching principle for policy formulation and implementation. At the global level Agenda 21, agreed at the Earth Summit, attempts to provide a comprehensive and far-reaching programme for sustainable development. At the European Union level the fifth environmental action programme aims to provide a framework 'towards sustainability' (CEC, 1992). At the national level, sustainability is now embedded, at least in rhetoric, close to the centre of political discourse, with the Secretary of State for the Environment stating that the UK is 'determined to make sustainable development the touchstone of its policies' (H.M. Government, 1994).

The development of the sustainability paradigm has led to a re-modelling of leisure policies. *Sustainable Development: The UK Strategy* (H.M. Government 1994) outlines a framework for sustainable leisure, which identifies three objectives:

- to maintain the quality of the environment in which leisure takes place for future generations to enjoy
- to contribute to the health, well-being and quality of life of those taking part in leisure activities without destroying the natural resources upon which leisure depends
- to ensure that leisure activities are a major means of creating awareness of, and appreciation for, the environment. (p.178)

All of the main agencies with a remit that includes countryside recreation have begun to re-couch their long term strategies to incorporate the concept of sustainability (see Figure 16.1).

The concept of sustainability is important because it is centred on the notion of environmental limits – the environment's capacity to support or absorb the effects of human activity is finite and this consideration

We believe that countryside activities should generally be promoted in ways which allow increases in participation to be sustainable with respect to the natural resources in question.
(Sports Council, 1992)

The enjoyment of the Welsh countryside should help to protect and enhance the natural and cultural qualities and values of the land, the sea and their resources; it should enrich the quality of human experience amongst those visiting the countryside and deepen their understanding of it; and it should both bring sustainable economic and social benefits to those living and working in the countryside and enable the active participation of those communities in the developments that bring such benefits.
(Countryside Council for Wales, forthcoming)

Scottish Natural Heritage's vision is of an accessible and welcoming countryside, but one in which access is arranged so as not to place unreasonable burdens on rural land or on those who live and work in the countryside. Nor should improved access impair the qualities of the natural heritage on which so much of the recreational value of Scotland's outdoors rests. To this end we lay great emphasis on the importance of our five guiding principles of sustainability to inform any decisions made in this field, and on the role of environmental education in catering for people's growing concern about the protection, the care, the use and the management of the natural heritage.
(Scottish Natural Heritage, 1994)

A prime purpose in sustaining a beautiful countryside is to enable people to enjoy it: but they should be encouraged to do so in sustainable ways.
(Countryside Commission, 1993e).

Figure 16.1 The Policy Interpretations of Sustainability by British Countryside Agencies

should determine policy and practice in all spheres. In theory at least it should be possible to identify thresholds beyond which continued activity will cause irreparable damage. An automatic consequence of the existence of capacity constraints is that human activity (and the aspirations that drive them) need to be undertaken so that they remain within these limits. However, sustainability is not just about the maintenance and enhancement of environmental quality; it incorporates a concern for the social and economic well-being of people through the principle of development not being at the expense of future generations (inter-generational equity) nor other groups (intra-generational equity). Enjoyment of the countryside involves two human communities: the visitor, and those who live and work in the countryside. Thus, policies for sustainable enjoyment of the countryside must be concerned with the needs of both groups as well as with the condition of the environment – a triangular and dynamic relationship as illustrated in Figure 16.2.

Sustainability has implications for policy formulation, the nature of those policies and methods of policy delivery. Some of the implications of the sustainability agenda are considered below.

Bringing Sustainability Principles into Recreation Policy Development

Various authors have started to identify the principles involved in formulating policies which are aimed at ensuring sustainable development or use. However, most of this work has been related to land-use

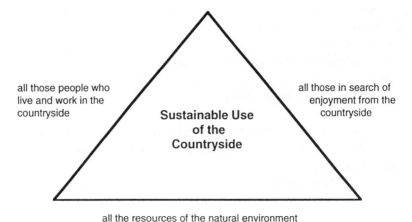

Figure 16.2 Dimensions of Sustainable Enjoyment

planning (see, for example, Jacobs, 1993; Land Use Consultants, 1993). The Sports Council (1990) was one of the first agencies to attempt to operationalize the concept of sustainability as applied to countryside recreation. Their consultation document *A Countryside for Sport: Towards a Policy for Sport and Recreation in the Countryside* (Sports Council, 1990) outlined a proposed system of sporting land-use categories as a mechanism to indicate the level of use for countryside sport and recreation which might be expected to be sustainable for different natural environments. The aim was for the four tier classification (see Figure 16.3) to

---

Category 1 – Robust Areas
Areas where use by most countryside activities can be increased whilst simultaneously improving the quality of the environment.

Category 2 – Resilient Areas
Areas where the development of the majority of countryside activities would be environmentally sustainable; where development of certain activities such as noisy sports might be dependent upon careful site location, design and good management. Long-term effects upon the natural environment would be minimal. In these areas, problems which are likely to arise are between other users of the countryside or other sports activities, rather than with nature conservation interests.

Category 3 – Stable Areas
Areas where it is possible to maintain or gradually increase current levels of use by most activities through improved management or well-designed new facilities; where other uses of the countryside including agriculture, are not usually intensive, so conservation of the natural environment becomes one of the primary interests.

Category 4 – Sensitive Areas
Areas where the current level of use by particular activities exceeds the carrying capacity of an area or site which has exceptional conservation, landscape or other value, and serious damage or major conflicts are occurring. Where a series of different management techniques has been tried, but the conflicts with the conservation of the natural resource or other established interests have been shown to be incapable of resolution at the current levels of use and there is a need to provide for and promote the activity elsewhere to reduce the pressure on the area.

Figure 16.3 Sporting Land Use Categories (Sports Council, 1990)

be used as a basis of an assessment of an area's suitability for use by different countryside activities. The categories would then be used as a guide for planning the provision for countryside sport and recreation at all levels through the identification of such areas within the land-use planning system.

This system of land use categories was abandoned in the final policy paper *A Countryside for Sport: A Policy for Sport and Recreation* (Sports Council, 1992) because of concerns about whether the categories would be upheld through the planning system. Instead, a more general commitment to 'encourage the sustainable use of natural resources by countryside activities' through a particular emphasis on the development of voluntary codes of practice was inserted.

If enjoyment of the countryside is to be sustainable, then human use of the natural and cultural resources that the countryside provides must not in overall terms erode or destroy them. In theory it should be possible to develop a more systematic approach to recreation planning and management based on the identification of environmental capacities (the capacity of an area to sustain a particular level of use or activity), with policies aimed at ensuring that thresholds (the point beyond which irreparable or unacceptable change occurs) are not exceeded. The carrying capacity concept is not new; it was first explored as a management tool in the 1960s and 1970s, but has recently gained renewed support. The chapter on leisure in *Sustainable Development: The UK Strategy* endorses the capacity approach: 'Determining capacity is, therefore, the first step in sustainable management' (H.M. Government, 1994, p. 181) and Magnus Magnusson, the Chairman of Scottish Natural Heritage, in his foreword to their policy paper *Enjoying the Outdoors* (Scottish Natural Heritage, 1994), describes the question of carrying capacity as one of the major strategic issues to be tackled.

Despite the apparent simplicity of the carrying capacity concept and its obvious appeal as a possible method of reconciling conflicts between recreation and conservation; between different recreational users; and recreational users and landowners and managers, it is not an easy concept to define and operationalize. There is no single recreational carrying capacity but a complex mosaic of ecological, perceptual, physical, social and economic capacities. Physical capacity is normally defined as the maximum number of visitors a site or facility can physically accommodate for a given activity (Patmore, 1983). For informal recreation, physical capacity can often be determined by support facilities such as car parks. Ecological capacity refers to the level of use an area can sustain prior to irreversible ecological damage occurring. Perceptual capacity refers to the user's own perception of the site: for some a walk is a group activity, for others it is a means of seeking solitude and the 'wilderness' experience. As such it is extremely difficult to define as it will vary between sites; between different activities at the same site; and between different participants. Economic capacity is applicable when a charge is made for entry or other form of use and refers to the level of use required to yield a specified financial return. Social capacity refers to the impact of visitors on the host community and the cultural and social tensions that can arise between visitor and host. The principal problems associated with the carrying capacity approach are fundamental and relate to the assessment of capacity and identification of critical thresholds (Bruton, 1974; Green, 1985; Glyptis, 1991).

More recently, attention has focused on the Limits to Acceptable Change (LAC) approach that was developed by the US Forest Service in the mid-1980s as an alternative to assessing the carrying capacity of wilderness areas (Stankey *et al.*, 1985). LAC is now being applied in the UK on an experimental basis (Sidaway, 1994a). It represents a shift away from what some have described as the negative concept of carrying capacity to a more positive management for environmental quality (Sidaway, 1994a). It also represents a consensus approach which seeks to incorporate views of recreationists, conservationists and resource managers in the identification of desirable or acceptable patterns of change and the definition of quality standards against which change and management can be monitored.

The LAC approach has been adopted by an Access Consultative Group established by the Peak District National Planning Board to assess concerns about potential recreational disturbance of ground-nesting birds on grouse moors; the aim is to identify indicative capacities and management thresholds for open land (Sidaway, 1993). A modified form of LAC was used to monitor the environmental of skiing development at Anach Mor in Scotland, where the main benefit was found to be the forum for discussion which the LAC approach requires. The disadvantages associated with LAC are: costs, difficulties associated with the definition and monitoring of environmental qualities and problems associated with public involvement (Sidaway, 1994a).

The Recreation Opportunity Spectrum (ROS) is another management tool aimed at integrating recreation opportunities with other management objectives such as the protection of sensitive environments. The ROS was first developed in the USA but has been most widely adopted in New Zealand (Hilary Commission and Department of Conservation, 1993). The ROS is based around a recreational experience continuum with management policy largely determined by the experiences of participants. Its strengths are in its ability to analyse recreation experiences from a supply aspect and then use this information to shape management prescriptions.

Carrying capacity, LAC and, to a certain extent, ROS, are essentially site or area based approaches which must be implemented through appropriate management strategies. In more general terms there is a need for a systematic consideration of the potential and actual environmental impact of policies facilitating enjoyment of the countryside – an environmental assessment of all policies and programmes to ensure that the impacts of various options are made explicit and the chosen option is the one with least environmental consequence and maximum social benefit. The need for strategic environmental assessment is demonstrated by the car-based nature of much recreation provision. Our dependency on the private motor car to access the countryside may be increased further by the fact that most recreation policies have been designed to cater for the car-borne visitor. As a result, most recreation provision in the countryside – including visitor centres, guided and self-guided walks, countryside activity programmes – is linked to the use of the car. For example, walks start at car parks rather than railway stations. Even a rudimentary environmental appraisal would illustrate that such policies are potentially contributing to car-based enjoyment of the countryside and suggest that we should be linking recreation provision to public transport networks, safe cycle routes and public rights of way that connect to areas of demand. This need for strategic environmental assessment is recognized by the Countryside Commission, which has committed itself to conducting a 'policy impact analysis' of its 'Enjoying the Countryside' policies as part of its aim to work towards a sustainable countryside (Countryside Commission, 1993e)

The assessment of environmental impacts and evaluation of differing policy options is made more difficult by the lack of reliable data on both recreation trends and environmental impacts. There is often an implicit assumption that recreational use of the countryside is increasing apace, yet overall demand seems to be relatively stable. More important are the trends that the gross figures hide: the diversification and fragmentation of rural leisure pursuits and the extension of the 'recreation season'. The biggest growth areas are the formal and more active forms of countryside recreation, which bring with them the potential for both environmental impact and social conflict with more informal forms of recreation (witness the debates about mountain biking and the notion of 'quiet enjoyment'). The paucity of information on the impact of recreation on the natural heritage is even more severe. Existing research tends to focus on specific activities and areas and covers only a limited range of impacts (Sidaway, 1994b). This leads to a situation where isolated examples (for example, footpath erosion on the Pennine Way) can be used to present emotive arguments about the impact of 'hordes of recreationists', when the true picture may be an isolated example of overuse.

Policy Principles for Sustaining Enjoyment of the Countryside

The concept of sustainability will obviously have implications for the nature of individual policies as well as methods of policy generation; whilst we struggle with systematic methods of generating sustainable policies and ensuring sustainable use, these implications can be assessed under a number of guiding themes or principles:

- linking enjoyment and conservation
- linking enjoyment and understanding
- linking enjoyment and the local economy
- promoting opportunities for all sectors of society to enjoy the countryside.

Linking Enjoyment and Conservation

Whilst our national parks were given twin aims of 'preserving and enhancing the natural beauty of the areas' and 'promoting their enjoyment by the public' (Section 5, National Parks and Access to the Countryside Act, 1949) and the Countryside Commission describes its role in terms of conserving and enhancing the beauty of the English countryside and helping people enjoy it (Countryside Commission, 1994d), in the past recreation and conservation have often been treated separately. Thus country parks and picnic sites were regarded as about recreation in the countryside, and nature reserves about protecting wildlife. In the last few years these separate trends have become much closer as conservation bodies have seen the advantages of building public support and understanding by improving access to conservation sites; and as the techniques for managing potentially damaging visitor pressures are more widely understood. As a result, for example, the Royal Society for Nature Conservation has a policy to encourage public access to County Wildlife Trust reserves, and country park design and management now puts more emphasis on safeguarding and creating habitat and wildlife assets.

This trend has been reinforced in recent years by 'institutional integration' of 'scientific' conservation and recreation with the formation of the Countryside Council for Wales in 1991 and Scottish Natural Heritage in 1992 (the first UK agency to have a remit that specifically refers to sustainability). There are two schools of thought as to the impacts, real and potential, of institutional integration. One school of thought espoused by the Ramblers' Association and Grove-White (1994) is that countryside recreation issues have been marginalized by institutional integration. They cite as evidence the experience of Scottish Natural Heritage. In February 1994 a leading member of the Scottish Natural Heritage internal task force on access, Bob Aitken, resigned in apparent protest over the Board's reluctance to promote innovative access policies in the countryside in fear that such recommendations would damage relationships with landowners. Grove-White (1994) argues that such evidence illustrates limited scope for integrated agencies to pursue new opportunities for increased leisure provision in the countryside, with implementation of the Government's biodiversity obligations always the first call on limited resources.

The second school of thought argues that there is considerable scope for synergy in uniting the two strands both in terms of skills (natural science plus social science) and approach (advisory/promotional and regulatory/land management). Proponents of this viewpoint to the experience of the Countryside Council for Wales. Within months of establishment, the Chairman of the Council had committed the organization to 'strive to ensure that a public right-of-way network throughout Wales was in good order by 1995' – five years earlier than the Countryside Commission's target. Although the target was subsequently modified, it demonstrates the Council's willingness to set hard targets in the sphere of countryside recreation – the antithesis of criticisms of Scottish Natural Heritage. The Council has also pursued policies aimed at integrating its functions in practice: for example, a programme of encouraging access to the National Nature Reserves that it owns and manages, provided that such access does not significantly compromise nature conservation objectives (Roberts, 1993).

The experience of the Countryside Council for Wales illustrates the potential for synergy between conservation and recreation, a potential that is also demonstrated in recent innovations in agri-environment policy. The Countryside Stewardship scheme in England and Tir Cymen in Wales, both experiments in a new 'market-based' approach

(Bishop and Phillips, 1993), demonstrate the potential to integrate scientific conservation, landscape protection and enhancement, heritage conservation and access provision. They are based on voluntary management agreements with farmers and landowners and offer financial incentives to farmers for creating new facilities for informal recreation. This integration of all forms of conservation (scientific, landscape and heritage) with public access opportunities is also witnessed in Environmentally Sensitive Areas (ESA) where, as part of the UK Government's agri-environment package, new payments for public access have been offered to participants in the scheme.

Visitors to the countryside can provide: an important source of income for those managing conservation sites; a new use for neglected countryside resources (e.g. the conservation of traditional, redundant stone barns by their conversion into bunkhouses); an additional rationale for justifying environmental expenditure; a wider constituency for conservation (e.g. by encouraging visitors to reserves or other sites to join a conservation body and/or participate in practical conservation work) and, as demonstrated by the Countryside Stewardship, Tir Cymen and ESA schemes, a source of income for farmers even when a formal market does not exist (see Chapter 14). This is not to say that enjoyment of the countryside is environmentally benign. In certain cases visitors to the countryside, often unwittingly and unknowingly, damage the very environment which they seek to appreciate and enjoy.

Two basic forms of environmental impact can be identified. First, the impact of individual activities on the host environment, for example the erosion of path surfaces due to over-use, disturbance of wildlife and damage to habitats. Secondly, the impact of recreational travel.

The direct impacts of visitors upon the host environment have provided the impetus for recent initiatives on carrying capacity, LAC and ROS, which are seen as tools for developing sustainable management policies for destination areas/sites. There has traditionally been a consensus amongst public agencies and authorities that the interests of conservation and recreation can be balanced and conflicts resolved by the adoption of appropriate management techniques such as zoning and charging. We are relatively well versed in techniques for managing demand at a site level, but the notion of sustainability may also require a wider management of leisure demands in order to influence the desire for certain activities or destination areas, through the creation of new leisure landscapes or the more sensitive marketing of existing ones.

The impacts of recreational travel are primarily linked to our love affair with the motor car. The private motor car is the dominant means by which people reach the countryside – 77 per cent of all visits to the Welsh countryside are made by persons travelling in a car (Survey Research Associates, 1993). Whilst the creation of a comprehensive road network and increased car ownership has 'opened' up the countryside for recreation, the true costs of this dependence on the private car are only now beginning to be recognized in official policy circles. Congestion can create serious difficulties for local people and for visitors themselves, in certain places and at certain times of the year. Tailbacks along even minor roads in National Parks, indiscriminate roadside parking blocking access points and congested village streets are now familiar problems in many areas of the countryside. Cars often cause serious visual intrusion in otherwise unspoiled areas of countryside. Traffic noise can destroy any sense of peace and tranquillity. The danger posed to other road users is such that pedestrians, horse riders and cyclists may no longer feel safe on minor roads, which were once freely and safely available to them. A longer-term problem is the impact of car exhaust emissions which, although not fully understood, is now known to be a threat to human health and wildlife, a cause of acid rain contributing to the acidification of lakes and streams, and a contributor to the greenhouse effect. It could be stated with some truth that the traffic generated by recreational use of the countryside is now the single greatest adverse impact associated with the pursuit of such activities.

The notion of sustainability has helped focus attention on the need to reduce the use of the car and related car dependency among visitors to the countryside. The Countryside Commission (1993e) has stated that it will concentrate its own resources on recreational opportunities nearer where people live in order to reduce trip distances, but there is no guarantee that people will use such facilities. Evidence from empirical studies questions assumptions regarding the accessibility of urban fringe sites and their appeal as surrogates for the 'wider' countryside (refer to Harrison, 1991 for a review and Chapter 15).

Other bodies are using a mix of regulation and persuasion to urge people to leave their cars at home or use them less when they reach their destination. The voluntary approach has been adopted in West Wales where the 'Greenways in South Pembrokeshire' project is aimed at reducing dependency on the private motor car to access the countryside by more effective marketing of existing rail services, provision of new bus services linking railway stations and recreation destinations, provision of information on inland walking trails and cycle routes and an initiative to allow and encourage people to spend a short break or longer activity holiday in South Pembrokeshire, without needing to use a car. The Lake District Traffic Management Initiative proposes a mix of measures to combat traffic congestion in the National Park including: 'access only' classification for small roads; lower speed limits on distributor roads within the park to discourage 'rat-running'; and, traffic management measures for local distributor roads to reduce traffic flows to appropriate levels.

Linking Enjoyment and Understanding

Conservation of the countryside depends, in part, upon public resources. A policy that attempts to conserve through exclusion is unlikely to be 'sustainable' in political or practical terms as it divorces those who are paying for conservation (taxpayers) from the benefits of their investment. Rather, enjoyment of the countryside should be seen as a means of deepening understanding and appreciation of natural resources, and in so doing should further the cause of conservation. Linking enjoyment and understanding can bring: a deeper sense of enjoyment by the visitor; a greater public sensitivity to environmental issues and an awareness of the link between human actions and environmental degradation; more support for conservation of the countryside; and more sensitive use of the countryside through greater awareness.

Such a philosophy is more readily applied to the 'quiet' forms of enjoyment than the more active pursuits such as motor sports, but this does not mean that it is not applicable to the more active pursuits.

Linking Enjoyment to the Local Economy

Whilst visitors to the countryside can cause social and cultural tensions (Bouquet and Winter, 1987), there is a growing awareness, through various 'green tourism' initiatives, that visitors to the countryside can also play an important role in sustaining the rural economy. The Countryside Commission (1991c) estimate that visitor spending in the English countryside amounted to £12,432m in 1990; £1764m of this is in the form of wages, profits and rents to rural communities supporting some 530,000 full-time, part-time and temporary jobs. A more specific study into the economic value of the Pennine Way National Trail (Walker and Vaughan, 1992) found that walkers on the Pennine Way spent a total of £1.9m during the survey period (April to October 1990). This spending resulted in £423,000 of income to residents of the counties through which the Pennine Way passes and created or sustained 155 jobs (95 of which were all-year full-time equivalents).

If enjoyment of the countryside is to be sustainable then policies need to recognize the importance of generating local economic benefits. Visitors to the countryside can: help maintain the viability of rural services (from village shops to public infrastructure); support jobs and local crafts and customs; and, provide opportunities for farm diversification. Even when a formal market does not exist, the demand for new recreational opportunities can provide landowners and managers with a source of additional income through their participation in schemes such as Tir Cymen, Countryside Stewardship and Environmentally Sensitive Areas (see above).

Promoting Opportunities for All Sectors of Society to Enjoy the Countryside

Not everyone has equal opportunity to exercise their rights of access to the countryside. Research has shown that approximately 25 per cent of British people are 'frequent' visitors to the countryside, who may visit their chosen areas of countryside several times per annum; these people are typically relatively affluent with one or more cars in their household. Approximately 50 per cent of the population are occasional visitors. The remaining 25 per cent or so go rarely, or not at all (Countryside Commission, 1991c). The infrequent visitors to the countryside include: those with poor access to private transport; ethnic minorities and those from deprived areas; those lacking the ability to use the countryside easily (especially the physically disabled); and visitors from outside Britain (Survey Research Associates, 1993).

Policies should aim to serve all who can derive enjoyment from visiting the countryside. This might include confidence building (for example, the Countryside Commission's 'Stepping Stones' project); removing barriers to countryside access for people with disabilities or handicap, those with young children or older people; improving awareness of opportunities; addressing issues of personal safety; linking opportunities to public transport networks; and researching the reasons for non-participation by ethnic minority groups (is it because they lack opportunities/confidence or a function of different cultural values and beliefs? see Chapter 10.)

Delivering Sustainable Policies

In recent years we have witnessed a move away from corporate provision to community empowerment, whereby public agencies set the strategic framework and local communities are enabled to make provision for the care and enjoyment of their countryside. The concept of sustainability is likely to increase this emphasis on community involvement: one of the key principles of *Caring for the Earth* (IUCN, UNEP and WWF, 1991) and Agenda 21 is enabling local communities to care for their own environments.

A number of the public agencies involved in countryside recreation have already adopted policies which encourage people to take action to sustain their local countryside and improve opportunities for enjoyment of that countryside. For example, the Countryside Commission's Parish Paths Partnership initiative, launched in 1992, aims to enable local people to improve the condition of their rights of way and to keep them open and in use as part of the Commission's wider efforts to ensure that the entire rights-of-way network in England is legally defined, properly maintained and well publicized by the year 2000. The Countryside Council for Wales, through its Public Paths Campaign for Wales, is pursuing a similar policy of inviting local communities to help survey public rights of way as part of a process of ensuring that they are all open and fit for use. Many local authorities have also developed schemes to encourage communities and other local interests to join in rights-of-way improvements, pond clearances and the creation of pocket parks. For example, Devon County Council's Adopt-a-Path Scheme aims to enable local people to keep a regular check on the condition of public rights of way and Northamptonshire County Council's Pocket Park initiative empowers local communities to establish small, natural green areas for nature and informal recreation.

Community action is seen as more sustainable than the imposition of projects by public agencies or authorities, as people who have been involved in planning or creating a facility are more likely to be willing to manage the site. It is viewed as being more democratic and avoids the problem of imposing fixed solutions – 'local solutions for local problems' – and there are other benefits: local environmental action is often cheaper than other forms of management as labour and even materials are normally provided free of charge, and it improves awareness of environmental issues through direct action (BDOR, 1991).

This move towards community empowerment and local environmental action is reinforced by prevailing political ideologies, be they Conservative concepts of 'active citizenship', Labour's experiments with decentralization or Liberal Democrat empowerment and community government initiatives.

A parallel development is the emergence of a partnership approach in tackling all aspects of countryside recreation and conservation. Although public sector bodies may have key roles, increasingly they achieve their ends through a complex of mutually-supportive arrangements. Examples include: partnerships between local authorities and local wildlife trusts for survey work and the management of nature reserves; partnerships involving Groundwork, itself a partnership-based organization, and local authorities; and, partnerships between the NRA, local community groups and local authorities. In many such partnership arrangements, a key role is played by a funding agency, for example Shell Better Britain Campaign, The Prince of Wales Committee or the Countryside Commission. Funds made available in this way unlock resources from many other quarters, so enabling new initiatives to go ahead.

Conclusions

To argue that sustainability could become a byword for restricting access in the interests of nature conservation is to misinterpret what sustainability means in terms of enjoying the countryside. Sustainability combines respect for environmental capacity with social considerations relating to equality and equity of opportunity. Recreational use of the countryside has a close relationship with the environment as the former is in part a function of the latter – people visit the countryside because of its natural beauty and other spiritual and cultural values.

All of the UK countryside agencies are revising their long-term strategies in terms of sustainability. Whilst this has focused attention on the environmental impacts associated with leisure use of the countryside (witness the House of Commons Select Committee investigation into the environmental impacts of leisure), the social dimension of sustainability, coupled with the development of a socially and economically differentiated countryside, provides an equally stern challenge. There is a risk of a growing divide between those with the resources and time for leisure pursuits and those who do not, especially if the trend towards a commoditized countryside where leisure experiences are purchased continues. The diversification of countryside recreation activities also raises the spectre of increased conflict. The recent inquiry into power boating on Windermere and debates about mountain biking in national parks reflect a growing intolerance of different leisure pursuits and the potential for conflict between different recreational users of the countryside. The debate about 'quiet enjoyment' that surrounded the Environment Act of 1995 also reflects the way in which leisure is becoming a focus for social conflict. This trend raises the spectre of agencies, such as the Countryside Commission and the Sports Council (in its reincarnated form), becoming social wardens refereeing conflicts between different leisure users of the countryside, rather than just advocates and enablers.

Some of the issues raised by sustainability pose profound questions for agencies charged with facilitating enjoyment of the countryside and conserving our natural heritage. For example, should bodies such as the Countryside Commission, Countryside Council for Wales and Scottish Natural Heritage accept ever greater dependence on the private motor car as an implicit assumption of strategies for enjoying the countryside? Should such agencies urge curbs in forms of recreation which damage the environment, even if this appears to threaten freedom of choice? What role do they adopt in social conflicts between different recreational users of the countryside? A fundamental tenet of sustainability is that demands for finite resources, such as land, should be managed. In the future it may be necessary to consider whether the demand for certain countryside activities should be managed, rather than automatically planning for an expansion in the supply of that activity. Can the view that a conserved countryside is there to be enjoyed by everyone be 'sustained' when increasingly free, informal forms of rural leisure are being replaced by a commoditized countryside in which you pay for your 'countryside experience'?

Bibliography

Adams, R. (1983) Planning a microcosm, *The Geographical Magazine*, **4**, 139–41.

Agyeman, J. (1989a) A snail's pace, *New Statesman and Society*, **35**, 30–31.

Agyeman, J. (1989b) Black people, white landscape, *Town and Country Planning*, **58**, 336–8.

Agyeman, J. (1990a) Black people in a white landscape: social and environmental justice, *Built Environment*, **16**, 232–6.

Agyeman, J. (1990b) A positive image, *Countryside Commission News*, **45**, 3.

Agyeman, J. and Hare, T. (1988) Towards a cultural ecology, *Urban Wildlife*, June, 39–40.

Agyeman, J., Warburton, D. and Wong, J.L. (1991) *The Black Environment Network Report: Working for Ethnic Minority Participation in the Environment*. London: BEN.

Ahlström, I. (1993) Allemansrätten – ett hotat kulturarv (The Right of Public Access – a threatened Cultural Heritage), *Bygd och natur, Årsbok*, 80–92.

Allison, L. (1975) *Environmental Planning. A Political and Philosophical Analysis*. London: Allen & Unwin.

Anderson, B. (1983) *Imagined Communities: Reflections on the Origins and Spread of Nationalism*. London: Verso.

Archbishops' Commission on Rural Areas (1990) *Faith in the Countryside*. Worthing: Churchman Publishing Ltd.

Atkinson, I. (1973) Geology shapes dam for giant lake, *Contract Journal*, 24 May 1973, 32–3.

Balibar, E. (1991) Racism and nationalism. In I.E. Balibar and I. Wallerstein (eds) *Race, Nation, Class: Ambiguous Identities*. London: Verso.

Banton, M. (1977) *The Idea of Race*. London: Tavistock.

Banton, M. (1983) *Racial and Ethnic Competition*. Cambridge: Cambridge University Press.

Barkan, E. (1992) *The Retreat of Scientific Racism: Changing Concepts of Race in Britain and the United States between the World Wars.* Cambridge: Cambridge University Press.

Bateman, I., Willis, K. and Garrod, G. (1994) Consistency between contingent valuation estimates: a comparison of two studies of UK National Parks, *Regional Studies,* **28,** 457–76.

Batie, S.S. and Sappington, A.G. (1986) Cross-compliance as a soil conservation strategy, *American Journal of Agricultural Economics,* **68,** 880–85.

Baudrillard, J. (1981) *For a Critique of the Political Economy of the Sign* (trans C. Levin). St. Louis: Telos Press.

Baudrillard, J. (1983) *In the Shadow of the Silent Majorities.* New York: Semiotext(e).

Bauman, Z. (1992) *Intimations of Postmodernity.* London: Routledge.

BDOR (1991) *Countryside Community Action.* Cheltenham: Countryside Commission.

Becker, L. (1977) *Property Rights: Philosophic Foundations.* London: Routledge.

Beddington, J. (1938) Patronage in art to-day. In R.S. Lambert (ed.) *Art in England,* pp. 82–7. Harmondsworth: Penguin.

Benson, J.F. and Willis, K.G. (1990) *The Aggregate Value of the Non-priced Recreation Benefits of the Forestry Commission Estate.* A Report to the Forestry Commission. University of Newcastle-upon-Tyne: Environmental Research Consultants.

Bergeron, J.H. (1993) From property to contract: political economy and the transformation of value in English common law, *Social and Legal Studies,* **2,** 5–23.

Berman, M. (1983) *All That's Solid Melts to Air.* London: Verso.

Bishop, K.D. (1991) Community Forests: implementing the concept, *The Planner,* **77** (18), 6–10.

Bishop, K.D. and Phillips, A.C. (1993) Seven steps to market – the development of the market-led approach to countryside conservation and recreation, *Journal of Rural Studies,* **9,** 315–38.

Bishop, K.D. and Stabler, M.J. (1991) *The Concept of Community Forests in the UK: The Assessment of their Benefits.* Paper presented at a meeting of the European Association of Environmental and Resource Economists, Stockholm School of Economics, 10–14 June.

Blackstone's Commentaries (1809), Volume III, 15th edn London.

Blunden, J. and Curry, N. (eds.) (1988) *A Future for our Countryside.* Oxford: Basil Blackwell.

Blunden, J. and Curry, N. (eds.) (1990) *A People's Charter?* London: HMSO.

Bonyhady, T. (1987) *The Law of the Countryside: The Rights of the Public.* Abingdon: Professional Books.

Boumphrey, G. (ed) (1963) *The Shilling Guides: Berkshire.* London: George Rainbird.

Boumphrey, G. (ed.) (1964) *The Shell and BP Guide to Britain*. London: Ebury Press.

Bouquet, M. and Winter, M. (1987) *Who from their Labours Rest? Conflict and Practice in Rural Tourism*. Aldershot: Avebury.

Bovaird, T., Tricker, M. and Stoakes, R. (1984) *Recreation Management and Pricing*. Aldershot: Gower.

Boverket (1993) *Kust och hav i översiktsplaneringen* (Coast and Sea in General Planning). Karlskrona: National Board of Housing, Building and Planning.

British Mountaineering Council (1991) *BMC News*, **5**, Autumn 1991.

British Mountaineering Council (1992) *BMC News*, **6**, Spring 1992.

Bromley, D. (1991) *Environment and Economy: Property Rights and Public Policy*. Oxford: Blackwell.

Burgess, J. (1994) Woods must not become no-go, *Countryside*, July/August 1994, 68. Cheltenham: Countryside Commission.

Burton, R.J.C. (1974) *The Recreational Carrying Capacity of the Countryside*. Keele University Library Occasional Paper No. 11. Keele: University of Keele.

Byrne, P. and Ravenscroft, N. (1989) *The Land Report. Diversification and Alternative Land Uses for the Landowner and Farmer*. London: Humberts, Chartered Surveyors.

Byron, R. (1964) Unreferenced quotation in the catalogue of the *Art in Advertising* exhibition, sponsored by Shell-Mex and BP Ltd at Worthing Art Gallery (7 March–3 April 1964).

Chambers, J. and Mingay, G. (1966) *The Agricultural Revolution 1750–1880*. London: Batsford.

Cherry, G. (1975) *History of Environmental Planning, Volume II*. London: HMSO.

Cherry, G. (1975) *History of Environmental Planning, Volume III*. London: HMSO.

Clark, G., Darall, J., Grove-White, R., McNaughton, P. and Urry, J. (1994) *Leisure Landscapes: Main Report*. London: Council for the Protection of Rural England.

Clarke, R. (1992) Access and recreation. Paper presented at a seminar conducted by the Council for Awards of Royal Agricultural Societies. *RICS Rural Practice Bulletin*, March/April 1993, 17.

Clifton-Brown, A. (1992) Woodlands. In K. Bishop (ed) (1992) *Off the beaten track: Access to Open Land in the UK*. Proceedings of the 1992 Countryside Recreation Conference. Cardiff: Countryside Recreation Network, 42–50.

Cloke, P. (1989) Rural geography and political economy. In R. Peet and N. Thrift (ed) *New Models in Geography*. London: Unwin Hyman.

Cloke, P. (1990) *Analysis of Responses to 'Training for Tomorrow's Countryside': Results of the Consultation on the Countryside Staff Training Advisory Group's Report*. CCP 313. Cheltenham: Countryside Commission.

Cloke, P. and Goodwin, M. (1992) Conceptualising countryside change: from post-Fordism to rural structured coherence. *Transactions of the Institute of British Geographers*, **17**, 321–36.

Cloke, P. and McLaughlin, B. (1989) Politics of the alternative land use and rural economy (ALURE) proposals in the UK. *Land Use Policy*, July, 235–48.

Coalter, F. with Long, J. and Duffield, B. (1986) *Rationale for Public Sector Investment in Leisure*. London: The Sports Council and Economic and Social Research Council.

Colman, D.R., Crabtree, J.R., Froud, J. and O'Carroll, L. (1991) *Comparative Effectiveness of Conservation Mechanisms*. University of Manchester, Department of Agricultural Economics.

Colvin, B. (1970) *Land and Landscape: Evolution, Design and Control*. London: John Murray.

Commission of the European Communities (1991) *The Development and Future of the CAP*. COM(91) 100. Brussels: Commission of the European Communities.

Commission of the European Communities (1992) *Towards Sustainability: A European Community Programme of Policy and Action in Relation to the Environment and Sustainable Development*. Com (92)33, Vol. II. Brussels: Commission of the European Communities.

Cosgrove, D.E. (1995) Nature and national identity: the dialectic of access and enclosure. Paper given to *Nature, Environment, Landscape: European Attitudes (1920–1970)*, IBG 1995 conference session, Northumbria University, Newcastle-upon-Tyne.

Cosgrove, D.E., Roscoe, B. and Rycroft, S.P. (eds) (1994) *Nature, Environment and Landscape: European Attitudes and Discourses in the Modern Period (1920–1970)*. Report to the European Commission (Contract No. EV5V-CT92–0151). Egham: Department of Geography, Royal Holloway.

Council for National Parks (1990) *A Vision for National Parks*. London: CNP.

Council for Nature (1965) *Outdoor Recreation, Active and Passive*. Countryside in 1970 Conference, Report of Study Group 6. London: Royal Society of Arts.

Country Landowners' Association (1991) *Recreation and Access in the Countryside: A Better Way Forward*. London: CLA.

Country Landowners' Association (1994a) *Focus on Woodlands: a CLA Policy Review*. London: CLA.

Country Landowners' Association, National Farmers Union and Countryside Commission (1994b) *Managing Public Access*. Cheltenham: Countryside Commission.

Countryside Commission (1985a) *National Countryside Recreation Survey 1984*. CCP 201. Cheltenham: Countryside Commission.

Countryside Commission (1985b) The Access Charter, *Countryside Commission News*, January.

Countryside Commission (1986) *Report of the Common Land Forum.* CCP 215. Cheltenham: Countryside Commission.

Countryside Commission (1987a) *Policies for Enjoying the Countryside.* CCP 234. Cheltenham: Countryside Commission.

Countryside Commission (1987b) *Enjoying the Countryside: Priorities for Action.* CCP 235. Cheltenham: Countryside Commission.

Countryside Commission (1987c) *New Opportunities for the Countryside.* Countryside Commission, Cheltenham.

Countryside Commission (1987d) *Forestry in the Countryside.* CCP 245. Cheltenham: Countryside Commission.

Countryside Commission (1989a) *A Countryside for Everyone: An Advisory Booklet.* CCP 265. Cheltenham: Countryside Commission.

Countryside Commission (1989b) *Forests for the Community.* CCP 270. Cheltenham: Countryside Commission.

Countryside Commission (1989c) *Countryside Commission News,* 39, September/October. Cheltenham: Countryside Commission.

Countryside Commission (1989d) *Training for Tomorrow's Countryside: The Report of the Countryside Staff Training Advisory Group (CSTAG).* CCP 269. Cheltenham: Countryside Commission.

Countryside Commission (1990a) *National Survey of Countryside Recreation (England).* Cheltenham: Countryside Commission.

Countryside Commission (1990b) *Capital Tax Relief for Outstanding Scenic Land.* CCP 204. Cheltenham: Countryside Commission.

Countryside Commission (1991a) *An Agenda for the Countryside.* CCP 336. Cheltenham: Countryside Commission.

Countryside Commission (1991b) *Countryside Stewardship: An Outline.* CCP 346. Cheltenham: Countryside Commission.

Countryside Commission (1991c) *Visitors to the Countryside.* CCP 341. Cheltenham: Countryside Commission.

Countryside Commission (1991d) *Countryside Stewardship Application Pack.* CCP 345. Cheltenham: Countryside Commission.

Countryside Commission (1992) *Enjoying the Countryside: Policies for People.* CCP 371. Cheltenham: Countryside Commission.

Countryside Commission (1993a) *Grants and Payment Schemes.* Cheltenham: Countryside Commission.

Countryside Commission (1993b) *Paying for a Beautiful Countryside.* Cheltenham: Countryside Commission.

Countryside Commission (1993c) *Countryside Premium for Set-Aside Land, Monitoring and Evaluation 1989–1992.* Cheltenham: Countryside Commission.

Countryside Commission (1993d) *1990/91 Survey of Local Authority Public Expenditure on Public Rights of Way.* Cheltenham: Countryside Commission.

Countryside Commission (1993e) *Sustainability and the English Countryside – A Position Statement.* Cheltenham: Countryside Commission.

Countryside Commission (1994a) *Access Payment Schemes.* CCP 443. Cheltenham: Countryside Commission.

Countryside Commission (1994b) *Countryside Stewardship: Handbook and Application Form.* Cheltenham: Countryside Commission.

Countryside Commission (1994c) *Countryside,* 67, May/June, p. 1.

Countryside Commission (1994d) *Annual Report 1993–1994.* Cheltenham: Countryside Commission.

Countryside Commission (1995) *Growing in Confidence: Understanding People's Perceptions of Urban Fringe Woodlands.* Cheltenham: Countryside Commission.

Countryside Council for Wales (forthcoming) *Enjoying the Welsh Countryside: Consultation Paper.* Bangor: Countryside Council for Wales.

Countryside Recreation Network Newsletter (1994) *The 1993 UK Leisure Day Visits Survey.* CRN, April/May. Cardiff: University of Wales.

Cox, A. (1984) *Adversary Politics and Land.* Cambridge: Cambridge University Press.

Cox, G. (1993) Shooting a line?: field sports and access struggles in Britain, *Journal of Rural Studies,* 9, 267–76.

Cox, G., Hallett, J. and Winter, M. (1994) Hunting the wild red deer: the social organization and ritual of a 'rural' institution, *Sociologia Ruralis.* 34, 190–205.

Cox, G., Lowe, P., and Winter, M. (1988) Private rights and public responsibilities: the prospects for agricultural and environmental controls, *Journal of Rural Studies,* 4, 323–37.

Cox, G., Lowe, P. and Winter, M. (1990) *The Voluntary Principle in Conservation.* Chichester: Packard.

Cox, G., Watkins, C. and Winter, M. (1996) *Game Management in England.* Cheltenham: Countryside and Community Press.

Crabtree, J.R., Appleton, Z.E.D., Thomson, K.J., Slee, W., Chalmers, N. and Copus, A. (1992) *The Economics of Countryside Access in Scotland.* SAC Economics Report 37. Aberdeen: Scottish Agricultural College.

Crabtree, J.R., and Chalmers, N.A. (1993) Economic evaluation of standard payments and capital grants as conservation instruments, *Land Use Policy,* 11, 94–106.

Cresswell, T. (1994) Putting women in their place: the carnival at Greenham Common, *Antipode,* 26, 35–58.

Crouch, D. (1992) *Land in common.* Paper presented at the Labour land campaign seminar of the Conference of Socialist Economists, Polytechnic of Central London, 11–12 July 1992.

Crowe, S. (1974) Empingham Reservoir: a brand new lake with recreation facilities, *Water Space,* Autumn, 11–13.

Crowe, S. (1978) *The Landscape of Forests and Woods.* Forestry Commission Booklet 44. London: HMSO.

Crowe, S. (1982) The landscape of Rutland Water, *Hydrobiologia,* 88, 44–50.

Crowson, D. (1978) *Rambles with John Clare.* CE Cutforth.

CRRU (1992) *A Survey of the Rights of Way Network in the Marston Vale.* A report for Bedfordshire County Council's Leisure Services Department, Conservation and Recreation Research Unit, Bedford College of Higher Education.

CRRU (1993a) *The Marston Vale Community Forest Draft Plan Public Consultation, Report No 1: Questionnaire Survey.* A report for the Marston Vale Community Forest Project, Conservation and Recreation Research Unit, Bedford College of Higher Education.

CRRU (1993b) *The Marston Vale Community Forest Draft Plan Public Consultation, Report No 2: Panel Meetings.* A report for the Marston Vale Community Forest Project, Conservation and Recreation Research Unit, Bedford College of Higher Education.

CRRU/MVA (1992) *The Marston Vale Community Forest: Community Survey.* A report for the Marston Vale Community Forest Project, Conservation and Recreation Research Unit, Bedford College of Higher Education.

Curry, N.R. (1993) Deals for a better countryside, *Countryside,* **63**, November/December.

Curry, N.R. (1994) *Countryside Recreation, Access and Land Use Planning.* London: Spon.

Cushing, S. (1994) Personal Communication, Senior Press Officer, National Farmers Union.

Cutter, S.L., Renwick, H.L. and Renwick, W.H. (1991) *Exploitation Conservation Preservation – A Geographic Perspective on Natural Resource Use.* New York: John Wiley.

Dahrendorf, R. (1979) *Life Chances.* Chicago: University of Chicago Press.

Daily Telegraph (1992) *Under Wraps: Your Right to Roam,* August 1.

Dalton, S. (1993) You can't beat the system! *New Musical Express,* 9 January.

Daniels, S. (1993) *Fields of Vision: Landscape Imagery and National Identity in England and the United States.* Cambridge: Polity Press.

Daniels, S. and Watkins, C. (1991) Picturesque landscaping and estate management: Uvedale Price at Foxley, 1770–1829, *Rural History,* **2**, 141–70.

Danish Government (1937) *Lov (Nr. 140–1937) om Naturfredning* (The Danish Nature Conservation Act, No 140–1937). Copenhagen.

Deaville, J (1995) *A Database of Public Access to Agricultural Land in England and Wales.* Worcester: Department of Geography, Worcester College of Higher Education (Working Paper 3).

Deleuze, G. and Guattari, F. (1987) *A Thousand Plateaus.* Minneapolis: University of Minnesota Press.

Denman, D. (1978) *The Place of Property.* Berkhamstead: Geo Publications.

Department of the Environment (1992a) *Sport and Recreation.* Planning Policy Guidance Note 17. London: HMSO.

Department of the Environment (1992b) *Tourism.* Planning Policy Guidance Note 21. London: HMSO.

Department of the Environment (1992c) *Action for the Countryside*. London: HMSO.

Dixon, D. (1987) Protest and disorder: the Public Order Act 1986, *Critical Social Policy*, **7**, 90–98.

Donnelly, P. (1986) The paradox of parks: politics of recreational land use, *Leisure Studies*, **5**, 211–31.

Donzelot, J. (1980) *The Policing of Families*. London: Hutchinson.

Dower, J. (1945) *National Parks in England and Wales*. London: HMSO.

Dower, M. (1965) The fourth wave: the challenge of leisure. A Civic Trust survey, *Architects Journal*.

Earle, F., Dearling, A., Whittle, H., Glasse, R. and Gubby (1994) *A Time to Travel? An Introduction to Britain's Newer Travellers*. Lyme Regis: Enabler Publications.

Eder, K. (1990) The rise of counter-culture movements against modernity: nature as a new field of class struggle, *Theory, Culture and Society*, **7**, 21–47.

Edlin, H.L. (1953) Britain's new forest villages, *Canadian Forestry Gazette*, 151–59.

Edlin, H.L. (1963) Amenity values in British forestry, *Forestry*, **36**, 65–89.

Edlin, H.L. (1969) Fifty years of Forest Parks, *Commonwealth Forestry Review*, **48**, 113–26.

Eliason, B., Hellström, A. and Johansson, R. (1987) *Plan- och bygglagen – Naturresurslagen* (The Planning and Building Act – The Natural Resource Act). Stockholm: LTs Förlag.

Elson, M.J. (1977) *A Review and Evaluation of Countryside Recreation Site Surveys*. Cheltenham: Countryside Commission.

Fairlie, S. (1993) Tunnel vision. The lessons from Twyford Down, *The Ecologist*, **23**, 2–4.

Fairlie, S. (1994a) Them that trespass against us, *The Ecologist*, **24**, 5–7.

Fairlie, S. (1994b) On the march, *The Guardian*, Section 2, 21 January 1994, 14–15.

Featherstone, M. (1991) *Consumer Culture and Postmodernism*. London: Sage.

Fitton, M. (1978) The reality: for whom are we actually providing? In: *Countryside for All? A Review of the Use People Make of the Countryside for Recreation*. Countryside Recreation Research Advisory Group annual conference. CCP 117. Cheltenham: Countryside Commission.

Forestry Commission (1935) *Report of the National Forest Park Committee 1935*. London: HMSO.

Forestry Commission (1937) *State Forests*. London: HMSO.

Forestry Commission (1938) *Report of the National Forest Park Committee (Forest of Dean) 1938*. London: HMSO.

Forestry Commission (1940) *Twentieth Annual Report of the Forestry Commissioners for the Year ending 30th September 1939*. London: HMSO.

Forestry Commission (1948) *Britain's Forests: Forest of Ae*. London: HMSO.

Forestry Commission (1950) *Thirtieth Annual Report of the Forestry Commissioners for the Year ending 30th September 1949.* London: HMSO.

Forestry Commission (1951a) *Thirty-first Annual Report of the Forestry Commissioners for the Year ending 30th September 1950.* London: HMSO.

Forestry Commission (1951b) *Britain's Forests: Strathyre.* London: HMSO.

Forestry Commission (1952) *Thirty-second Annual Report of the Forestry Commissioners for the Year ending 30th September 1951.* London: HMSO.

Forestry Commission (1962) *The Border.* London: HMSO.

Forestry Commission (1963) *North Yorkshire Forests.* London: HMSO.

Forestry Commission (1969) *Britain's Forest Parks.* London: HMSO.

Forsberg, H. (1992a) Central-local relations in Swedish Acts on physical planning – a historical review, *Scandinavian Housing and Planning Research*, **9**, 19–28.

Forsberg, H. (1992b) *En politisk nödvändighet – En studie av den fysiska riksplaneringens introduktion och tillämpning* (A political necessity – a study of the genesis and implementation of National Land-use Planning). Linkoping: Linkoping University.

Foucault, M. (1980) *Power/knowledge: Selected Interviews and Other Writings 1972–1977.* (ed C. Gordon). London: Harvester Press.

Foucault, M. (1984) *The Foucault Reader*, ed P. Rabinow. London: Penguin Books.

Fudge, J. and Glasbeek, H. (1992) The politics of rights: a politics with little class, *Social and Legal Studies*, **1**, 45–70.

Gallie, W.B. (1962) Essentially contested concepts. In M. Black (ed.) *The Importance of Language.* Englewood Cliffs: Prentice-Hall, 121–46.

Garner, R. (1993) Political animals: a survey of the animal protection movement in Britain, *Parliamentary Affairs*, **46**, 333–52.

Gale, C.J. (1972) *Gale on Easements*, 14 edn. London: Sweet and Maxwell.

Ghodiwala, A., Gough, A., Johnson, O. and Samat, B. (1993) *The Bolton Initiative.* Bolton: Bolton College.

Giddens, A. (1985) *The Nation State and Violence.* London: Macmillan.

Giddens, A. (1990) *The Consequences of Modernity.* Cambridge: Polity Press.

Giddens, A. (1991) *Modernity and Self-Identity.* Cambridge: Polity Press.

Gilroy, P. (1987) *'There ain't no Black in the Union Jack': the Cultural Politics of Race and Nation.* London: Hutchinson.

Glyptis, S. (1991) *Countryside Recreation.* London: Longman.

Glyptis, S. (1992) Setting the scene. In K. Bishop (ed.) *Off the Beaten Track: Access to Open Land in the UK.* Proceedings of the 1992 Countryside Recreation Conference. Cardiff: Countryside Recreation Network, 4–18.

Gratton, C. and Taylor, P. (1985) *Sport and Recreation: An Economic Analysis.* London: Spon.

Green, B. (1985) *Countryside Conservation.* London: Allen and Unwin.

Gregory, M. (1994) *Conservation Law in the Countryside.* Croydon: Tolley.

Grigson, G. and Fisher, J. (1964) *The Shell Nature Book.* London: Phoenix House.

Grove-White, R. (1994) *England's Green Horizon: A Conservation and Countryside Access Agency for the post-Rio World.* Newbury: British Association of Nature Conservationists.

The Guardian (1993) Twyford showdown on motorway trail, 5 July.

The Guardian (1994) It was a May Day rally a few beats removed from tradition ..., 2 May.

The Guardian (1994) Mounted officers break up assault on Downing Street, 25 July.

The Guardian (1994) Protest against justice bill leads to violence, 10 October.

Gyford, J. (1991) *Citizens, Consumers and Councils.* Basingstoke: Macmillan.

Hadfield, M. (1967) *Landscape with Trees.* London: Country Life.

Halfacree, K. (1993) Locality and social representation: space, discourse and alternative definitions of the rural, *Journal of Rural Studies,* 23–37.

Halfacree, K. (1995) Talking about rurality: social representations of the rural as expressed by residents of six English parishes, *Journal of Rural Studies,* **11**, 1–20.

Halfacree, K. (forthcoming) Out of place in the country: travellers and the 'rural idyll', *Antipode.*

Hall, S. and Jacques, M. (eds) (1989) *New Times. The Changing Face of Politics in the 1990s.* London: Laurence & Wishart.

Hansard (08/02/1994) *Standing Committee B, Criminal Justice and Public Order Bill 1993, House of Commons, Proceedings of 12th Sitting.* London: HMSO.

Haraldsson, D. (1987) *Skydda vår natur! – Svenska Naturskyddsföreningens framväxt och tidiga utveckling* (Protect Our Environment! – The early expansion and development of the Swedish Society for the Conservation of Nature). Lund: Lund University Press.

Harley, D.C. and Hanley, N.D. (1989) *Economic Benefit Estimates for Nature Reserves: Methods and Results.* University of Stirling: Department of Economics.

Harrison, C.M. (1981) *Preliminary results of a Survey of Site Use in the South London Green Belt.* Working Paper No 9, University College London.

Harrison, C.M. (1983) Countryside recreation and London's urban fringe, *Transactions Institute of British Geographers,* **8**, 295–313.

Harrison, C.M. (1991) *Countryside Recreation in a Changing Society.* London: The TMS Partnership.

Harrison, M.L. (1987) Property rights, philosophies, and the justification of planning control. In M.L. Harrison and R. Mordey (eds) *Planning Control: Philosophies, Prospects and Practice.* Beckenham: Croom Helm, 32–58.

Harvey, D. (1989) *The Condition of Postmodernity.* Oxford: Blackwell.

Hay, D. (1975) Property, authority and the criminal law. In D. Hay, P. Linebaugh, J.G. Rule, E.P. Thompson, and C. Winslow (eds) *Albion's Fatal*

Tree. Crime and Society in Eighteenth Century England. London: Allen Lane, 17–63.

Heater, D. (1990) *Citizenship: the Civic Ideal.* New York: Longman.

Held, D. (1989) *Political Theory and the Modern State.* Cambridge: Polity Press.

H.M. Government (1994) *Sustainable Development: the UK Strategy.* London: HMSO.

Hetherington, K. (1992) Stonehenge and its festival. In R. Shields (ed) *Lifestyle Shopping. The Subject of Consumption.* London: Routledge, 83–98.

Hilary Commission and Department of Conservation (1993) *The New Zealand Recreation Opportunity Spectrum: Guidelines for Users.* Wellington: Department of Conservation.

Hill, H. (1980) *Freedom to Roam. The Struggle for Access to Britain's Moors and Mountains.* Ashbourne: Moorland Publishing.

Hillmo, T. and Lohm, U. (1990) Naturens ombudsmän (The Ombudsmen of Nature), reprinted from S. Beckman, (ed) *Miljö Media Makt* (Environment Media Power). Helsingborg: Carlssons.

Hobhouse, Sir A. (1947a) *Report of the National Park Committee (England and Wales).* London: HMSO.

Hobhouse, Sir A. (1947b) *Report of the Special Committee on Footpaths and Access to the Countryside.* London: HMSO.

Hodge, I.D. (1988) Property Institutions and Environmental Improvement, *Journal of Agricultural Economics,* **39**, 369–75.

Hodge, I.D., Adams, W.M. and Bourn, N.A.D. (1994) Conservation Policies in the Wider Countryside: Agency Competition and Innovation, *Journal of Environmental Planning and Management,* **37**, 199–213.

Hoggart, K. (1990) Let's do away with rural, *Journal of Rural Studies,* **6**, 245–57.

Holt, A. (1990) *A Charter For Whom? The Access Provision of the National Parks and Access to the Countryside Act 1949.* London: Ramblers' Association.

Hopkins, H. (1985) *The Long Affray.* London: Secker and Warburg.

Hoskins, W.G. (1963) *Rutland: A Shell Guide.* London: Faber and Faber.

Hoskins, W.G. (1976) *The Age of Plunder: the England of Henry VIII, 1500–1547.* London: Longmans.

House of Commons, *Hansard,* 13 April 1994. London: HMSO, Col. 367.

House of Lords Select Committee on Sport and Leisure (1973) *Second Report of the Select Committee on Sport and Leisure.* HL, 193, I–III, London: HMSO.

House of Lords, *Hansard,* 24 May 1994. London: HMSO, Col. 712.

Ilbery, B. (1992) From Scott to ALURE – and back again?, *Land Use Policy,* April 1992, 131–42.

Ingrams, R. and Piper, J. (1983) *Piper's Places.* London: Chatto and Windus, The Hogarth Press, 47.

IUCN, UNEP and WWF (1991) *Caring for the Earth.* Gland, Switzerland; IUCN.

Jackson, R. (1947) 'Hands off' says Rutland, *Illustrated,* 1 November, 19–23.

Jacobs, M. (1993) *Sense and Sustainability*. London: Council for the Protection of Rural England.

Jameson, F. (1991) *The Cultural Logic of Late Capitalism*. London: Verso.

Jeffcote, M. and Kearney, D. (1994) *The Asian Community and the Environment: Towards a Communications Strategy*. Leicester: Environ.

Joad, C.E.M. (1945) *The Untutored Townsman's Invasion of the Country*. London: Faber and Faber.

Jones, M., Crowe, L. and Walsh, B.E. (1991) *Countryside Recreation Survey on behalf of Wakefield Metropolitan District Council, Final Report*. Sheffield City Polytechnic: School of Leisure and Food Management.

Jones, N. (1993) *Living in Rural Wales*. Llandysul: Gomer.

Kempe, P. (1992) Maps of open country. *Rights of Way Law Review*, September.

Kinsbury, J. (1994) Personal Communication, Countryside Officer, Youth Hostels Association.

Kinsman, P. (1995) Landscapes, race and national identity: The photography of Ingrid Pollard, *Area*, **27**, 300–10.

Kirk, E.M. (1990) *Freedom to Roam*. Discussion Paper to NYMA, Unpublished Ramblers' Association Material.

Knight, E.A. (1982) Rutland Water: from conception to operation, *Hydrobiologia*, **88**, 7–17.

Knightbridge, R. and Swanwick, C. (1993) A scheme under scrutiny, *RICS Rural Practice Bulletin*, November/December 1993, 12–15.

Lagerqvist, M. and Lundberg, E. (1993) Allemansrätten – en tillgång i fara? (The Right of Public Access – an Asset in Danger?), *Lantmäteritidskriften*, **1**, 22–7.

Land Use Consultants (1993) *Conservation Issues in Strategic Plans*. Cheltenham: English Nature, Countryside Commission and English Heritage.

Lash, S. and Urry, J. (1987) *The End of Organised Capitalism*. Cambridge: Polity Press.

Lawson, P. (1982) A 'regrettable necessity': the decision to construct, *Hydrobiologia*, **88**, 19–30.

Lefebvre, H. (1991) *The Production of Space*. Oxford: Blackwell.

LeGrand, J. (1991) *Equity and Choice*. London: HarperCollins.

Leonard, P. (1982) Management agreements: a tool for conservation, *Journal of Agricultural Economics*, **33**, 351–60.

Lewis, R. (1993) Rights or agreements? Paper presented at the Byways and Bridleways Trust symposium, *Public access and conservation*, Church House, London, 7 April 1993.

Lindman, G. and Påhlman, G. (1936) Skärgårdsproblemet (The Archipelago Problem), *Byggmästaren*, **20**, 251–58.

Livingstone, D.N. (1992a) 'Never shall ye make the crab walk straight': an inquiry into the scientific sources of racial geography, in F. Driver and G.

Rose (eds) *Nature and Science: Essays in the History of Geographical Knowledge.* Cheltenham: Historical Geography Study Group, 37–48.

Livingstone, D.N. (1992b) *The Geographical Tradition.* Oxford: Blackwell.

Lloyd, L. (1993) Proposed reform of the 1968 Caravan Sites Act: producing a problem to suit a solution?, *Critical Social Policy,* **38,** 77–85.

Lorrain-Smith, R. (1992) *The Forestry and Economic Potential of the Great North Forest.* Cheltenham: Countryside Commission.

Lowe, P., Clark, J. and Cox, G. (1993) Reasonable creatures: rights and rationalities in valuing the countryside. *Journal of Environmental Planning and Management,* **36,** 101–15.

Lowe, P. and Goyder, J. (1983) *Environmental Groups in Politics.* London: Allen and Unwin.

Lowe, R. and Shaw, W. (1993) *Travellers.* London: Fourth Estate.

Lowenthal, D. (1985) *The Past is a Foreign Country.* Cambridge: Cambridge University Press.

Lowenthal, D. (1991) British national identity and the English landscape, *Rural History,* 2, 205–30.

MacDougall, H.A. (1982) *Racial Myth in English History: Trojans, Teutons and Anglo-Saxons.* Montreal: Harvest House.

MacEwen A. and MacEwen, M. (1982) *National Parks: Conservation or Cosmetics?* London: Allen and Unwin.

Maffesoli, M. (1991) The ethic of aesthetics, *Theory, Culture and Society,* **8,** 7–20.

Maffesoli, M. (1988) *Le Temps des Tribus.* Paris: Méridiens Klincksieck.

Malcolmson, R. (1973) *Popular Recreations in English Society 1700–1850.* Cambridge: Cambridge University Press.

Malik, S. (1992) Colours of the countryside: a whiter shade of pale, *ECOS,* **13,** 33–40.

Marsden, T., Murdoch, J., Lowe, P., Munton, R., and Flynn, A. (1993) *Constructing the Countryside.* London: UCL Press.

Marshall, T. and Bottomore, T. (1992) *Citizenship and Social Class.* London: Pluto Press.

Marston Vale Community Forest Project (1993) *The Draft Plan for the Marston Vale Community Forest.* Bedford: MVCFP.

Matless, D. (1990) Definitions of England 1928–89: preservation, modernism and the nature of the nation, *Built Environment,* **16,** 179–91.

Matless, D. (1994) Doing the English village, 1945–1990: An essay in imaginative geography, in P. Cloke, M. Doel, D. Matless, M. Phillips and N. Thrift *Writing the Rural: Five Cultural Geographies.* London: Paul Chapman Publishing.

McCallum, I.R.M. (ed) (1945) *Physical Planning.* London: The Architectural Press.

McCallum, J.D. and Adams, J.G.L. (1980) Charging for countryside recreation, *Transactions of the Institute of British Geographers,* **5,** 350–68.

McEachern, C. (1992) Farmers and conservation: conflict and accommodation in farming politics, *Journal of Rural Studies*, **8**, 159–71.

McInnes, H. (1993) *Trends in Sports Participation*. Sports Council Facilities Factfile 2; Planning and Provision for Sport. London: Sports Council.

Melucci, A. (1989) *Nomads of the Present*. London: Radius.

Merrifield, A. (1993) Place and space: a Lefebvrian reconciliation, *Transactions of the Institute of British Geographers*, **18**, 516–31.

Miles, R. (1989) *Racism*. London: Routledge.

Miljöaktuellt (1989–91) (Environment news). Publication of the National Environmental Protection Board.

Ministry of Agriculture, Fisheries and Food (1991) *Our Farming Future*. London: MAFF.

Ministry of Agriculture, Fisheries and Food (1993a) *Agriculture and England's Environment*. London: MAFF.

Ministry of Agriculture, Fisheries and Food (1993b) *Agriculture and England's Environment*. News Release 266/93. London: MAFF.

Ministry of Agriculture, Fisheries and Food (1993c) *Agriculture and England's Environment. Provision of New Public Access in ESAs: a Consultation Document*. London: MAFF.

Ministry of Agriculture, Fisheries and Food (1993d) *Agriculture and England's Environment. Set-aside Management: a Consultation Document*. London: MAFF.

Ministry of Agriculture, Fisheries and Food (1993e) *CAP Reform: Proposed Countryside Access Scheme*. Leaflet AR 15. London: MAFF.

Ministry of Agriculture, Fisheries and Food (1994) *The Somerset Levels and Moors Guidelines for Farmers*. London: MAFF, SLM/ESA/2, 6–7.

Moore, D. and Driver, A. (1989) The conservation value of water supply reservoirs, *Regulated Rivers Research and Management*, 4, 202–12.

Moore, T. (1991) Countryside 'must welcome blacks', *The Daily Telegraph*, 26 April.

Moore-Colyer, R.J. (1992) (ed) *A Land of Pure Delight. Selections from the Letters of Thomas Johnes of Hafod 1748–1816*. Llandysul: Gomer.

Moscovici, S. (1984) The phenomenon of social representations. In R. Farr and S. Moscovici (eds) *Social Representations*. Cambridge: Cambridge University Press, 3–69.

Mouffe, C. (1993) Liberal socialism and pluralism: which citizenship? In J. Squires (ed) *Principled Positions*. London: Lawrence and Wishart.

Murdoch, J. and Pratt, A.C. (1993) Rural studies: modernism, postmodernism and the 'post-rural', *Journal of Rural Studies*, **9**, 411–27.

Murdoch, J. and Pratt, A.C. (1994) Rural studies of power and the power of rural studies: a reply to Philo, *Journal of Rural Studies*, **10**, 83–7.

Musgrave, R.A. and Musgrave, P.B. (1976) *Public Finance in Theory and Practice*. Tokyo: McGraw-Hill.

Mutch, W.E.S. (1968) *Public Recreation in National Forests: a Factual Survey*. London: HMSO.

Naish, D. (1993) Reform CAP, *Countryside*, **59**, 7.

Nash, R. (1982) *Wilderness and the American Mind.* Yale: Yale University Press.

National Council for Civil Liberties (1986) *Stonehenge.* London: NCCL.

National Parks (England and Wales) (1947). Report of Committee: Chairman Sir Arthur Hobhouse. London: HMSO, Cmd 7121.

National Parks in England and Wales (1945). A report by John Dower for the Ministry of Town and Country Planning. London: HMSO, Cmd 6628.

Newby, H. (1985) (2nd Edition) *Green and Pleasant Land?* London: Wildwood.

Newby, H. (1986) Towards a new understanding of access and accessibility (1), Values, attitudes and ideology. In H. Talbot-Ponsonby (ed) *New Approaches to Access in the Countryside.* Proceedings of the 1986 Countryside Recreation Conference, Bristol, Countryside Recreation Research Advisory Group, 14–24.

Newby, H., Bell, H., Rose, D., and Saunders, P. (1978) *Property, Paternalism and Power.* London: Hutchinson.

New Musical Express (8 May/1993) Features on the 'Convoy Clampdown'.

Norton-Taylor, R. (1982) *Whose Land is it Anyway?* Wellingborough: Turnstone Press.

Nuffield Commission (1986) *Town and Country Planning* (the Flowers report), Commission of enquiry report. Oxford: Nuffield Foundation.

Ödmann, E., Bucht, E. and Nordström, M. (1982) *Vildmarken och välfärden – Om naturskyddslagstiftningens tillkomst* (The wilderness and welfare – The Creation of the Nature Conservation Act). Stockholm: Liber.

Olsson, G. (1984) Towards a sermon of modernity. In D. Gregory and R. Martin (eds) *Recollections of a Revolution.* London: Macmillan, 73–85.

Open Spaces Society (undated) *AGM Resolutions on the Countryside.* OSS.

PA Cambridge Economic Consultants (1990) *Tourism in Scotland. Visitor Externalities and Displacement,* Industry Department for Scotland, ESU Research Paper 19.

Passmore, J. (1974) *Man's Responsibility for Nature.* New York: Charles Scribner's Sons.

Patmore, A. (1983) *Recreation and Resources.* Oxford: Basil Blackwell.

Pearlman, J.J. (1992) *Give us some Quo for our Quid.* London: Ramblers' Association.

Pepper, D. (1984) *The Roots of Modern Environmentalism.* London: Routledge.

Peppin, B. and Micklethwaite L. (1983) *A Dictionary of British Book Illustrators: The Twentieth Century.* London: John Murray.

Phillips, M. (1994) Father of Tony Blair's big idea, *The Observer*, 24 July 1994, 27.

Philo, C. (1992) Neglected rural geographies: a review, *Journal of Rural Studies*, **8**, 193–207.

Philo, C. (1994) Postmodern rural geography? A reply to Murdoch and Pratt, *Journal of Rural Studies*, **9**, 429–36.

Piddington, H. (1981) *Land Management for Shooting and Fishing.* Cambridge: Department of Land Economy.

Planning Week (1994) Labour pledges right to roam, *Planning Week,* **2**, No. 39, 29 September 1994, 4.

Plowden, W. (1971) *The Motor Car and Politics in Britain.* Harmondsworth: Penguin (1973 edn).

Poliakov, L. (1974) *The Aryan Myth: A History of Racist and Nationalist Ideas in Europe.* London: Chatto & Windus.

Pollard, I. (1989) Pastoral interludes. *Third Text: Third World Perspectives on Contemporary Art and Culture,* **7**, 41–6.

Pond, P. (1993) Are we simply being led up the footpath?, *Weekend Telegraph,* 30 October 1993, 3.

Power in the Land, London Weekend Television for Channel 4, 1987.

Pratt, A. (forthcoming) Rurality: loose talk or social struggle?, *Journal of Rural Studies.*

Prendergast, S. (1993) *Access to the Countryside by Agreement.* MMU.

Price, U. (1810) *Essays on the Picturesque, as compared with the Sublime and the Beautiful; and on the Use of Studying Pictures for the Purpose of Improving Real Landscape.* London: Mawman.

Pye-Smith, C. and Hall, C. (eds) (1987) *The Countryside We Want: a Manifesto for the Year 2000.* Bideford: Green Books.

Ramblers' Association (1992a) *Access to the Countryside Bill.* EC Papers: Ramblers' Association unpublished material.

Ramblers' Association (1992b) *Access to the Countryside in Europe for Walkers.* Proceedings of a Ramblers' Association Seminar, November 1992.

Ramblers' Association (1993a) *Harmony in the Hills.* London: Ramblers' Association.

Ramblers' Association (1993b) *Launch of Harmony in the Hills.* EC Papers: Ramblers' Association unpublished material.

Ramblers' Association (1993c) *Countryside Stewardship Scheme – Survey of RA of Public Access Sites.* Ramblers' Association.

Ramblers' Association (1993d) *Response to Countryside Stewardship.* Ramblers' Association unpublished material.

Ramblers' Association (1993e) *Public Access to Woodland Sold off by the Forestry Commission.* Ramblers' Association.

Ratcliffe, D. (1992) Rambling and nature conservation, *Rambling Today,* **No. 4**, Spring 1992, 7–8.

Ravenscroft, N. (1992) *Recreation Planning and Development.* Basingstoke: Macmillan.

Ravenscroft, N. (1993) Public leisure provision and the good citizen, *Leisure Studies,* **12**, 33–44.

Reiling, S.D, Anderson, M.W, and Gibbs, K.C. (1983) Measuring the costs of publicly supplied outdoor recreational facilities: a methodological note, *Journal of Leisure Research,* **15**.

Reynolds, F. (1992) Lowland countryside. In K. Bishop (ed) *Off the Beaten Track: Access to Open Land in the UK*, Proceedings of the 1992 Countryside Recreation Conference, Cardiff, Countryside Recreation Network, 33–7.

Roberts, G. (1993) Access to national nature reserves in Wales, *Countryside Recreation Network News*, 3, 7.

Roberts, K. (1979) *Countryside Recreation and Social Class*, unpublished report to the Countryside Commission, Cheltenham.

Robertson Gould (1992) *Summary of the Report of Monitoring on the Meadowland Option of the Countryside Premium Scheme*, Robertson Gould Consultants.

Roche, M. (1992) *Rethinking Citizenship*. Oxford: Polity Press.

Rojek, C. (1988) The convoy of pollution, *Leisure Studies*, 7, 21–31.

Romell, L.G. (1936) 'Kronjuveler på auktion – Stockholms skärgård blir villastad' (Crown jewels for sale – The Stockholm archipelago will become a garden suburb), *Sveriges natur*, 123–35.

Rossiter, J.P. (1972) *An Analytical Study of the Public Use of Private Land for Outdoor Recreation in England 1949–1968*. Unpublished PhD thesis, University of Cambridge.

Rothman, B. (1982) *The 1932 Kinder Trespass: A Personal View of the Kinder Scout Mass Trespass*. Willow.

Royal Institution of Chartered Surveyors (1989) *Managing the Countryside: Access, Recreation and Tourism*. London: Royal Institution of Chartered Surveyors.

Royal Society for the Protection of Birds (1990). Unpublished letter to the Ramblers' Association.

Rycroft, S. and Cosgrove, D.E. (1994) The stamp of an idealist, *The Geographical Magazine*, 66(10), 36–9.

Sack, R. (1986) *Human Territoriality*. Cambridge: Cambridge University Press.

Sagoff, M. (1988) *The Economy of the Earth*. Cambridge: Cambridge University Press.

Sandell, K. (1991) Outdoor Recreation – Re-creation or Creation?, *Nordisk Samhällsgeografisk Tidskrift*, 14, 35–46.

Scott, P. (1991) *Countryside Access in Europe: A Review of Access Rights, Legislation and Provision in Selected European Countries*. Edinburgh: Countryside Commission for Scotland.

Scottish Natural Heritage (1994) *Enjoying the Outdoors: A Programme for Action*. Edinburgh: Scottish Natural Heritage.

Segrell, B. (1993) Moderaterna och strandskyddet – Moderata samlingspartiets agerande i riksdagen angående strandskyddslagstiftningen (The Swedish Conservative Party and the Riparian Law), *Geografiska Notiser*, 1, 50–55; 2, 112–17.

Segrell, B. (1994) 'Nationell Naturvårdspolicy i lokal kontext – den planerade nationalparken i S:t Anna yttre skärgård' (National nature conservation policy in local context – the planned national park in the S:t Anna archipelago), *Forskning om livsstil och miljö*, FRN Rapport, 6, 105–15. Stockholm: The Swedish Council for Planning and Coordination of Research.

Segrell, B and Lundqvist, J. (1993) The attractive coast – context for development of coastal management in Sweden 1930–90, *Scandinavian Housing and Planning Research*, **10**, 159–76.

Sheail, J. (1981) *Rural Conservation in Inter-war Britain*. Oxford: Clarendon Press.

Shell-Mex and BP Ltd (June 1961) Britain's network of motorways is taking shape, *Shell–BP News*, **No. 166**, 3–5.

Shell-Mex and BP Ltd (1964a). Catalogue of the Art in Advertising exhibition, held at Worthing Art Gallery (7 March–3 April 1964).

Shell-Mex and BP Ltd (October 1964b) *Shell-BP News*, **No. 206**, 16.

Shell-Mex and BP Co Ltd (November 1964c) *Shell-BP News*, **No. 207**, 8.

Shields, R. (1991a) *Places on the Margin*. London: Routledge.

Shields, R. (1991b) Introduction to 'The ethics of aesthetics', *Theory, Culture and Society*, **8**, 1–5.

Shivji, I.G. (1989) *The Concept of Human Rights in Africa*. London: Codesria Book Series.

Shoard, M. (1978) Access: can present opportunities be widened? *Countryside for All? A Review of the Use People Make of the Countryside for Recreation*. Countryside Recreation Research Advisory Group annual conference, CCP 117. Cheltenham: Countryside Commission.

Shoard, M. (1980) *The Theft of the Countryside*. London: Maurice Temple Smith.

Shoard, M. (1982) The people's countryside, *New Statesman*, **103**, no. 2666, 23 April.

Shoard, M. (1987) *This Land is Our Land*. London: Grafton Books.

Shoard, M. (1989) Turnstiles on the trails, *The Times*, 4 February, 12.

Shoard, M. (1991) The German Way, *Rambling Today*, **No. 3**, Winter, 19.

Shoard, M. (1992a) Getting Back to the Land, *The Times*, 18 April, 12.

Shoard, M. (1992b) Walkers' rights in Switzerland, *Rambling Today*, no. 4, Spring, 36.

Shoard, M. (1992c) Access to the Danish way, *Rambling Today*, no. 6, Autumn, 40–1.

Shoard, M. (1995) Harmony in Sweden, *Rambling Today*, no. 19, Winter, 21–3.

Shonfield, A. (1965) *Modern Capitalism. The Balance of Public and Private Power*. Oxford: Oxford University Press.

Short, J. (1991) *Imagined Country*. London: Routledge.

Sibley, D. (1981) *Outsiders in Urban Societies*. Oxford: Blackwell.

Sibley, D. (1988) Purification of space, *Environment and Planning D. Society and Space*, **6**, 409–21.

Sidaway, R. (1988) *Sport, Recreation and Nature Conservation*. London: The Sports Council.

Sidaway, R. (1990) *Birds and Walkers: A Review of Existing Research on Access to the Countryside and Disturbance to Birds*. London: Ramblers' Association.

Sidaway, R. (1993) *The Limits of Acceptable Change: an Assessment of the Technique and its Potential Relevance to the Management of Public Access on Open Land.* Unpublished briefing paper for the Countryside Commission.

Sidaway, R. (1994a) Limits of acceptable change in practice, *ECOS*, **15**, 42–9.

Sidaway, R. (1994b) *Recreation and the Natural Heritage: A Research Review.* Edinburgh: Scottish Natural Heritage.

Smart, B. (1993) *Postmodernity.* London: Routledge.

Smith, N. (1984) *Uneven Development.* Oxford: Blackwell.

Smith, S. (1989) Society, space and citizenship: a human geography for the 'new times'?, *Transactions of the Institute of British Geographers*, **14**, 144–56.

Söderköpings Kommun (1991) Översiktsplan 1991–06–13 (General plan for land and water use in Soderkoping district authority).

Soja, E. (1985) The spatiality of social life: towards a transformative retheorisation. In D. Gregory and J. Urry (eds) *Social Relations and Spatial Structures.* Basingstoke: Macmillan, 90–127.

Spalding, F. (1986) *British Art Since 1900.* London: Thames and Hudson.

Sports Council (1990) *A Countryside for Sport: Consultation Paper.* London: Sports Council.

Sports Council (1992) *A Countryside for Sport: A Policy for Sport and Recreation.* London: Sports Council.

Squires, J. (ed) (1993) *Principled Positions.* London: Lawrence and Wishart.

Stamp, L.D. (1946) *Britain's Structure and Scenery.* London: Collins New Naturalist.

Stamp, L.D. (1960) *Applied Geography.* Harmondsworth: Penguin.

Stamp, L.D. (1948) *The Land of Britain: Its Use and Misuse.* London: Longmans, Green and Co. Ltd.

Stankey, G.H., Cloe, D.N., Lucas, R.C., Petersen, M.E. and Frissell, S.J. (1985) *The Limits of Acceptable Change of Wilderness Planning.* Washington DC: US Forest Service.

Stephenson, T. (1989) *Forbidden Land.* Manchester: MUP.

Stevenson, G.G. (1991) *Common Property Economics.* Cambridge: Cambridge University Press.

Survey Research Associates (1993) *1993 UK Day Visits Survey.* Unpublished report to the Countryside Council for Wales.

Swedish Code of Statutes (SFS) (1952:382) *Strandlagen* (The Riparian Law); (1964:822) *Naturvårdslagen* (The Nature Conservation Act); (1974:1025) *Lag om ändring i naturvårdslagen* (Changes of the Nature Conservation Act); (1987:12) *Naturresurslagen* (The Natural Resource Act).

Swedish Commission Report (1938) *Reglering av strandbebyggelse m.m.* (Regulation of near-beach buildings). Stockholm: Ministry of Health and Social Affairs, SOU 1938, 45.

Swedish Commission Report (1940) *Inrättande av fritidsreservat* (Establishing of recreation areas). Stockholm: Ministry of Health and Social Affairs, SOU 1940, 12.

Swedish Commission Report (1951) *Lagstiftning om förbud mot bebyggelse m.m. inom vissa strandområden* (Restriction laws for buildings in certain beach areas). Stockholm: Ministry of Justice, SOU 1951, 40.

Swedish Commission Report (1952) *Kristidspolitik och kristidshushållning i Sverige under och efter andra världskriget* (Policy and economy in Sweden during and after the Second World War). Stockholm: Ministry for Foreign Affairs Trade Department, SOU 1952, 50.

Swedish Commission Report (1962) *Naturen och samhället* (Nature and society). Stockholm: Ministry of Agriculture, SOU 1962, 36.

Swedish Commission Report (1979) *Hushållning med mark & vetten 2 – Del I Övervaganden* (Economizing on land and water resources 2 – Part I Considerations). Stockholm: Ministry of Housing, SOU 1979, 54.

Swedish Commission Report (1990) *Översyn av naturvårdslagen m.m.* (Views on the Nature Conservation Act). Stockholm: Ministry of Environment and Energy, SOU 1990, 38.

Swedish Commission Report (1993) *Miljöbalk* (Environmental Code). Stockholm: Ministry of Environment and National Resources, SOU 1993, 27.

Swedish Commission Report (1994) *Levande skärgårdar* (Living archipelagos). Stockholm: Ministry of Agriculture, SOU 1994, 93.

Swedish Government Bill (1990/91:90) *Bilaga A: Hur mår Sverige?* (Appendix A: How is Sweden getting on?). Stockholm: Ministry of Environment.

Swedish Ministry of Housing (1988) *Mark ach vatten år 2010 – Framtidsbedömningar om kulturlandskapets utveckling* (Land and water in year 2010). Stockholm: Ministry of Housing, Ds 1988, 35.

Swedish National Environmental Protection Board (SNV) (1989) *Nationalparksplan för Sverige* (National Park Plan for Sweden). Solna: SNV Publications.

Swedish National Environmental Protection Board (SNV) (1990a) *Strandskydd* (Beach protection). Stockholm: SNV, 90, 5.

Swedish National Environmental Protection Board (SNV) (1990b) *Miljötagarna i korthet* (The environmental laws in brief). Solna: SNV Publications.

Swedish National Environmental Protection Board (SNV) (1991a) *Naturresursavdelningen: överklagade strandskyddsdispenser 1975–90* (Department for Natural Resources: beach protection exemptions and appeals 1975–90).

Swedish National Environmental Protection Board (SNV) (1991b) *Naturvårdsplan för Sverige – En strategi for säkerställandearbetet* (Nature Conservation Plan for Sweden – a Strategy for Implementation). Solna: SNV Publications.

Swedish Official Parliamentary Publications (1936–94) (Motions, bills, records of proceedings, reports and official letters).

Symonds, H.H. (1936) *Afforestation in the Lake District: A reply to the Forestry Commission's White Paper of 26th August 1936.* London: Dent.

Tapper, S. (1992) *Game Heritage.* Fordingbridge: Game Conservancy.

Taylor, D.E. (1993) Minority environmental activisim in Britain: from Brixton to the Lake District, *Qualitative Sociology*, **16**, 263–95.

Taylor, G. (1989) *The National Community Forests Programme and the South Tyne and Wear/North East Durham Community Forest.* Newcastle-upon-Tyne: Countryside Commission.

Taylor, W.L. (1939) Forestry, foresters, and forest policy in Great Britain, *Forestry,* **13**, 99–104.

Thakrar, N. (1994) *Ethnic Minority Participation in Community Forest Activities.* Cheltenham: Countryside Commission.

Thomsen, P. (1934) *National Parks. A paper read to Delegates of the Corresponding Societies of the British Association at Aberdeen, September,* 59 Promenade, Portobello, Edinburgh (PRO).

Thompson, E.P. (1975) *Whigs and Hunters.* London: Allen Lane.

Thompson, E.P. (1993) *Customs in Common.* Harmondsworth: Penguin.

Tiffin, R. (1993) *Community Forests: Conflicting Aims or Common Purpose.* Unpublished M.Phil. thesis, University of London.

Traylen, A.R. (1977) *Dialect in Rutland.*

Van Gunsteren, H. (1994) Four conceptions of citizenship. In B. Van Steenbergen (ed) *The Condition of Citizenship.* London: Sage, 36–48.

Vidal, J. (1992) The Battle of Camelot, *The Guardian,* 15 December.

Vidal, J. (1993) Explode a condom, save the world, *The Guardian,* 10 July.

Vidal, J. (1994a) Long live Wanstonia, *The Guardian,* 17 February.

Vidal, J. (1994b) Raving rebels with a cause, *The Guardian,* 7 May.

Waites, B. (1972) Rutland: human conservancy?, *Leicester-Rutland Topic,* June 1972, 49–50.

Waites, B. (1973) Rutland: lake district of the East Midlands?, *Leicester-Rutland Topic,* September.

Waites, B. (1980) Rutland Water: vision of the future, *The Great Outdoors,* June, 18–20.

Waites, B. (1983) Rutland does exist, *The Geographical Magazine,* lv(3), 133–4.

Walker, S. (1995) *UK Day Visits Survey 1993 – Main Report.* Cardiff: Countryside Recreation Network.

Walker, S. and Vaughan, N. (1992) *Pennine Way Survey, 1990 – the Economic Impact of Walker Spending.* Cheltenham: Countryside Commission.

Watkins, C. (1987) The future of woodlands in the rural landscape, in D.G. Lockhart and B. Ilbery (eds) *The Future of the British Rural Landscape.* Norwich: Geo Books, 71–96.

Watson, A. (1991) *Critique of the Report 'Moorland Recreation and Wildlife in the Peak District'* by P. Anderson, PPJPB, 1990. London: Ramblers' Association.

Westerlund, S. (1991) *EG:s miljöregler ur svenskt perspektiv* (Environmental laws in the European Common Market from a Swedish perspective). Stockholm: Swedish Society for the Conservation of Nature.

Whatmore, S., Munton, R. and Marsden, T. (1990) The rural restructuring process: emerging divisions of agricultural property rights, *Regional Studies,* **24**, 235–45.

White, J. and Dunn, M.C. (1975) *Countryside Recreation Planning: Problems and Prospects in the West Midlands.* Occasional Paper No. 23. University of Birmingham: Centre for Urban and Regional Studies.

Williams, D. (1987) Processions, assemblies and the freedom of the individual, *Criminal Law Review,* March, 167–79.

Williams, D., Lloyd, T. and Watkins, C. (1994) *Farmers not Foresters: Constraints on the Planting of New Farm Woodland.* University of Nottingham: Department of Geography, Working Paper 27.

Williamson, R. (1992) Opportunities and constraints for landowners. In K. Bishop (ed.) *Off the Beaten Track: Access to Open Land in the UK.* Proceedings of the 1992 Countryside Recreational Conference, Cardiff, Countryside Recreation Network, 86–90.

Willis, K.G. and Benson, J.F. (1988) Valuation of wildlife: a case study on the Upper Teesdale Site of Special Scientific Interest and comparison of methods on environmental economics. In R.K. Turner (ed.) *Sustainable Environmental Management.* Colorado: Westview Press.

Willis, K.G. and Benson, J.F. (1989a) Recreational Value of Forests, *Forestry,* **62,** 93–110.

Willis, K.G. and Benson, J.F. (1989b) Option value and non-user benefits of wildlife conservation, *Journal of Rural Studies,* **5,** 245–56.

Willis, K.G. and Benson, J.F. (1989c) *Values of User Benefits of Forest Recreation: Some Further Site Studies.* Report to the Forestry Commission. Edinburgh: Forestry Commission.

Wordsworth, C. (1891) *Rutland Words.* Compiled for the English Dialect Society. London: Kegan Paul.

Wordsworth, William (1835) A Guide through the District of the Lakes. In J Hayden (ed) (1988) *William Wordsworth. Selected Prose.* Harmondsworth: Penguin.

Wright, P. (1993) Olde England outfoxed, *The Guardian,* 3 December.

Yorke, M. (1988) *The Spirit of Place: Nine Neo-Romantic Artists and their Times.* London: Constable.

Index

AA 128
Aberdeen 101
abstract space 179–93
access
  agreements 2, 11, 27, 55–6, 59, 64–5, 71, 82, 199, 225, 232
  conditional 38
  de facto 25, 38, 52, 55–8, 77, 82–3, 85, 198–9
  laws 50, 64, 72
  liaison groups 33
  management 3, 7, 31–2, 34, 36, 233
  payment schemes 31–2, 219
  policy 2–3, 24–5, 32, 34, 66, 84, 112, 122–6, 264
  restrictions on 16, 65
  rights of 1–4, 16, 20–2, 25–6, 31–4, 37–9, 45, 47, 57–8, 64, 66, 77, 79, 82, 129, 148–9, 156, 158, 160, 207, 230, 268
  state subsidised 30, 33, 232–4, 237
Access Charter, The 25
Access Payment Schemes 71, 81–5
Access to Commons and Open Country Bill 25
Access to Mountains Act (1937) 45, 53–4
Access to Mountains (Scotland) Bill (1884) 26, 53
acid rain 266
Acland, Sir Francis 103
Addison Committee 100
afforestation 4, 100, 102–3, 109–10, 116–19
agricultural policy 43–4
agricultural revolution 71
Agriculture Act (1947) 37
Agriculture Act (1986) 71, 82
Agyeman, Julian 163–78
Aitken, Bob 264
allemansrätten 2, 4, 22, 52, 148–50, 158–9, 229
Allerston Forest 124

Anach Mor 261
Andrews, Paul 253
Anglers' Country Park 244–7, 253
animal rights campaigns 191
Area of Outstanding Natural Beauty 183
Argyll 102, 117
  National Forest Park 103–5, 119, 123
art 92
Arundel estate 12
Ashcroft, Peter 169–70, 174, 177
Attlee, Clement 54
Aysgarth Upper Falls 56

Badmin, S.R. 90, 99
Bakewell tart 91
Baltic Sea 150
Baudrillard, J. 39, 190
Bawden, Edward 89
Beddington, Jack 91–2
Bedford 216, 219
Bedford, Duke of 11
Bedfordshire County Council 11
Bedlam 183, 190
Berkhamsted Common 52, 57
Berkshire 95–6
Berry Farm 224
Betjeman, Sir John 95, 97, 99
Birkett KC, Sir Norman 104
Birmingham 90
Birmingham Corporation Water Works Act (1892) 57
Birthrights 171, 175
Black Act, The (1723) 14, 197
Black Environment Network 4, 162–78
Black Forest 118
Bledisloe, Lord 101
Blenheim estate 12
bloodsports 14, 21, 142, 153, 156, 182, 191, 203

Bolton Abbey 54
Bolton Countryside Initiative 175
Boumphrey, Geoffrey 97
Boundary Commission 133, 140
bourgeoisie 49
Boy Scouts 128
Bradford-on-Avon 89, 99
Bretton Park 247
bridleways 6, 29–30, 50, 201, 207–11
British Association 101
British Broadcasting Corporation 109
British Horse Society 29
British Mountaineering Council 64
British Society of Foresters 108, 110
British Transport Commission 106
British Trust for Conservation Volunteers 175
Brocket, Lord 15
Bryce, James 26, 53, 85
Buckinghamshire 199–200, 203–4, 208
Burgess, Dr Jaquie 175
Burghley estate 12
Byron, Robert 92, 99

Cairngorms Forest Park 126
Cambridgeshire 93
Camping Club of Great Britain 102
capitalism 40, 46, 69, 74, 84, 132, 180, 184–6, 189, 192
Caravan Club 128
Caravan Sites Act (1968) 181–2
Caravan Sites Office 181
Castleford 241
Castlemorton 182–3, 188, 190
Central Office of Information 110
China 13
Churchill, Sir Winston 54
citizenship 3, 26, 35, 37–8, 44–7, 69–85, 129, 170, 176, 270
civil war 131
Clare, John 52
class
  conflict 37, 76
  fragmentation 69, 78–9, 184
  middle 124
  system 45–7, 80, 173, 239
  working 49, 53, 104, 172
class war 184
Colvin, Brenda 140
Common Land Forum 25–6, 58, 64, 66–7
Commons Open Spaces and Footpath Preservation Society 52, 128
Community Forests 5, 26, 28, 83, 175, 213–4, 218–9, 221, 223–4, 233
Community Woodland Supplement 214
compensation 29, 42, 63, 67, 147–8, 150–1, 198
conservation 2, 6, 12, 22, 41–3, 45, 58, 61–3, 67, 82, 101, 109, 130, 134, 137–9, 145–7, 151, 153, 156, 158, 164, 167, 176, 192,

197, 218, 224, 230–7, 254–5, 259–60, 263–5
Conservation, Amenity and Recreation Trusts 228
Conservative Party 63, 73, 84–5, 138, 270
Conservative Party (Sweden) (*Högerpartiet*) 151–2
co-operatives 13
Corby 130
Cotteswold Naturalists' Trust 105
Cotton, Charles 90–1
Council for National Parks 64
Council for Nature 254
Council for the Protection of Rural England 65–6, 100, 104–5, 128, 137–8
County Wildlife Trusts 6, 263
Country Code 209
Countryfile 170–1, 175
Country Landowners' Association 24, 26, 32–3, 60, 65, 134, 199–200, 203
country parks 7, 71, 238–9, 244, 246, 248, 263
Countryside Access Scheme 2, 6, 43
Countryside Act (1968) 28, 56, 66, 167
Countryside Commission 2–4, 24–5, 28, 31–2, 37–8, 42–3, 45, 58–60, 82, 90, 162–78, 211, 213–14, 235, 237–40, 262–71
Countryside Council for Wales 264, 269, 271
Countryside Premium Scheme 2, 27, 42, 82, 226, 233–4
Countryside Recreation Network 39
Countryside Stewardship Scheme 3, 6, 20, 27, 42–3, 57–8, 70, 77, 80, 82, 85, 235, 264
Courthope, Sir George 101–2, 105, 108
Criminal Justice and Public Order Act (1994) 4, 17–19, 45, 70, 77–8, 85, 179–83, 188, 190, 192
Crowe, Dame Sylvia and Associates 134–41
Culbin Forest, Morayshire 110
Cumbria 199
Cyclists' Touring Club 128

Daily Telegraph 131, 170
Daventry 130
Definitive Map Modification Bill 25
democracy 15, 50, 75, 78, 114, 124, 147, 269
Denmark 12, 22, 150, 159
Department of the Environment 24, 41, 166, 254
Derby 91
Derbyshire 90–91
deviancy 41, 72, 79–80
Devon 199, 202, 208–9, 269
Diggers 14
discrimination 39, 75, 177
Doncaster Metropolitan Borough Council 52, 68
Donga Tribe 184, 188, 191
Dudmaston (Shropshire) 110
Dukeries of Nottinghamshire 116

Earth First! 184
Earth Summit 256
East Midlands 132–3, 138, 139
Economic and Social Research Council 199
Ecstasy 190
Edlin, Herbert 106–10, 112, 117–9, 124, 126
Egypt 13
Elan Valley 57
elitism 47–8, 108, 167
Ellis v. Loftus Iron Company (1874) 51
Ely Cathedral 93
Empingham reservoir – *see* Rutland Water
English Nature 26
Environmental Land Management Services 33
environmental protesters 5, 61, 64, 179–93,
    197
Environmentally Sensitive Areas 2–3, 20, 27,
    42, 82, 226, 233, 265, 268
equal opportunities 166
ethnic minorities 162–78, 239, 268
Ethnic Minority Awards Scheme 167–8
European Commission 41, 129
European Common Agricultural Policy 20, 41,
    43, 73, 226, 237
European Union 81, 158, 256
Evans, Estwick 49
exclusion 19–21, 23, 164–5, 179, 186, 267

Fagan, Michael 17
Farm Diversification Grant Scheme 41
Farm Woodland Premium Scheme 44, 82, 214
Farmers' Party (Sweden) (*Bondeforbundet*) 151
farming 5, 12–13, 21, 27–9, 31–4, 36–7, 39–45,
    56, 60, 62–3, 69–74, 82–4, 112, 142, 144,
    147, 150–1, 153, 156, 197–215, 219–21,
    224, 226–37, 255, 259, 265
Featherstone 241
Ferrers, Earl 18
Festival of Britain (1951) 110
Finance Act (1975) 28
Finland 154
food surpluses 41
footpaths 6, 50, 59–60, 106, 122, 129, 201,
    203–11, 223, 229, 235, 263, 265
Forbidden Britain 61
Fordism 70
Forest Law (1975) 21
Forest of Ae 106, 114–15
Forest of Bowland 55
Forest of Dean 105, 107, 112, 122
Forest Park Guides 100, 105–6, 109–10, 114,
    117, 121, 123–4, 126
Forest Villages 110–11, 114
Forestry Authority 32
Forestry Commission 2, 4, 56–7, 100–26, 141,
    175, 213
Forestry Fund 103
Foucault, Michel 39–40
France 13

Freedom Network 180
freehold 15
Friends of the Lake District 104

Gainsborough, Lord 131
game
    laws 14, 108
    management 62, 108, 197, 200, 203–4, 209
Game Management Project 5, 199, 204, 211
General Development Order 30
Geographical Information Systems 7
Germany 13, 22, 119, 150, 158–9, 229
Girl Guides 128
Gloucestershire 199–200, 202, 204
Green Belt 215
greenhouse effect 266
Greensand Ridge 223
Greenways in South Pembrokeshire 266
Greenwood Community Forest 214
Groundwork Trust 29, 270
gymkhana 170

Haddon Hall 91
Hafod, Aberystwyth 116
Hambleton Peninsula 135
Hanson Trust 219
Hardknott Forest Park 121
Harwell 96
Havercroft-Ryall 243, 246
Highlands, the 127
Highway Creation Order 67
Hilder, Rowland 90, 92, 97
Hobson Moor Quarry 28
Holiday Act (Sweden 1938) 147
Home Office 182
Hoskins, W.G. 130–1, 139
House of Commons Environment Select
    Committee 255, 270
Howard, Michael 180
Hudson, R.S. 104
Hulcot Wood 224
hunt saboteurs 17, 79, 179, 182, 191

Illustrated magazine 131
industrialization 3, 35, 107, 131, 147, 158–9,
    254
Industrial Revolution 35, 49, 132
inheritance tax 13, 28, 57, 60, 230
Inheritance Tax Act (1984) 59
Inland Revenue 231
Institute of Contemporary Arts 97

Jackson, Peter 137
Japan 13
John Smith Memorial Bill 85
Johnes, Thomas 116
Joint Standing Committee for National Parks
    104

Jones, Barbara 95
jostle rights 77–8
jus spatiandi 52, 68

Kant, Immanuel 198
Keilder Forest village 110, 112
Kempston 216
Kinder Scout 197
King's College Chapel, Cambridge 93

Labour Party 53–4, 63–4, 66, 85, 104, 137, 270
laissez-faire 84
Lake District 55, 57, 100, 109, 116–7, 164, 267
Lamont, Norman 59
land
    nationalization 73–4
    ownership 12–27, 29, 31–4, 36–40, 42–5,
        52–6, 58, 60, 62–3, 66–73, 77, 81–2, 84–5,
        149–53, 156, 159, 197–219, 223–4,
        226–37, 248–9, 260, 264–5, 268
    reform 13
    tax 13
Land Utilisation Surveys 93
law
    common 38, 52, 198
    English 51–2, 67
Law of Property Act (1925) 52, 55–7
Lefebvre, Henri 184–5, 188, 192
Leicestershire 130, 133
leisure – *see* recreation
Levellers, The 190
Liberal Democrat Party 63–4, 66, 270
Liberal Party 53
Liberty 180
Limits to Acceptable Change 261–2, 265
Lloyd George 13
Llwyn-y-Gog (North Wales) 110
Local Government Boundary Commission Act
    (1945) 131
Local Government Planning and Land Act
    (1980) 181–2
Loch Achray 125
Loch Lubnaig 114
Loch Voil 115
Locke, John 198
London 90, 164, 170, 175, 180, 183–4, 204,
    213, 250
Lowenthal, David 99

McKenna, Conrad 126
Macley, George 107
Magnusson, Magnus 260
Malham Cove 58
Manchester Corporation Water Works Act
    (1878) 57
Marston Vale Community Forest Project 5,
    213–25
Marxism 15, 39

Mattingly, Alan 50
Mereworth Castle (Kent) 97
Metropolitan Commons Act (1866–1898) 57
Mexico 13
Mill, J.S. 77
Ministry of Agriculture, Fisheries and Food
    2–3, 32, 82, 234
Ministry of Health 104
Ministry of Justice (Sweden) 150
Modernism 99, 187–8
Moorland Association 60, 66
motor touring 89–90, 95, 97, 99, 122, 130,
    248, 262, 266, 271
motorways 89–90
Mumford, Lewis 131, 139–40
Mutch, W.E.S. 123, 126, 128

Nash, John 90, 93
Nash, Paul 112
National Advisory Council for Physical
    Training 128
National Benzole 90
National Conservancy Council for England
    176
National Environment Protection Board
    (Sweden) 156–60
National Farmers' Union 26, 60, 65, 134
National Forest Parks 4, 100, 103–4, 107–12,
    118, 121, 123, 128
    Committee 102–3, 105
national identity 4, 93, 99, 132–3, 147, 162,
    171, 178
National Nature Reserves 264
National Parks 64, 67, 101–2, 105, 108–9, 229,
    263, 266–7, 271
    Commission 109, 119
National Parks and Access to the Countryside
    Act (1949) 25, 27–8, 45, 54–6, 66–7, 77
National Park Authorities 56
National Parks Committee 101
National Playing Fields Association 128
National Trust 6, 57, 104, 128
National Trust Act (1907) 57
National Trust Act (1971) 57
Natural Resource Act (Sweden)
    (*Naturresurslagen*) 143–6, 153, 156
Nature Conservation Act (Germany 1987) 22
Nature Conservation Act (Sweden) 151–2
Nature Protection Act (Denmark 1992) 22
Nature Protection Act (Sweden 1937) 147,
    150
nature trails 218, 232
neo-tribalism 184, 187–8, 192
New Age 182–3, 188
New Deal 109
New Forest, The 107, 112
New Forest Act (1871) 58
New Left 78
Newmillerdam 244–7

New National Forest 26
New Right 179
New Town Corporations 106
New Towns Act (1965) 130
New Zealand 261
Non-Rotational Set-Aside 20
Norman rule 107–8
Northampton 130, 269
North Sea 150
North Yorkshire Forest Guides 112
Norway 13, 22, 229
Nottinghamshire 199, 208
nuclear family 114
nuclear power plants 144

Oakham 138
Office of Population Censuses and Surveys
    General Household Survey 60
Office of Woods 107
Old Testament 49
Open Spaces Society 52, 64
Ordnance Survey Maps 57
Outdoor Recreation Act (Norway 1957) 22

Parish Paths Partnership Scheme 33, 223, 269
Parliament 38, 53, 66, 102–5, 180
paternalism 75
patriarchy 128
Patterson, Lennox 107
Peak District 27, 55
Peak Planning Board 11, 55, 261
Pennine Way 263, 268
Peterborough 130
Piddington, Helen 199–200
Piper, John 97
poaching 17, 201, 208–9
police 85, 181, 183
Pollard, Ingrid 164–5
Pontefract 241, 243, 245–6, 252
post-Fordism 69, 73
post-modernism 69, 73, 186–92
power relations 39
Price, Uvedale 116
privilege 13, 17, 44
property rights 3, 35, 37–9, 47–8, 51, 60, 64,
    70–3, 79–85, 197–8, 227–8
public enquiry 53–4
Public Order Act (1986) 79, 181–3
Public Path Orders 25
public transport 239, 245, 249, 262, 268

Queen, the 12
Queen Elizabeth Forest Park 125

railways 90, 262, 266
Ramblers' Association 3, 24, 26–8, 44, 50, 55,
    58, 60–8, 104–6, 128, 137, 173, 209, 235,
    264

rambling 5, 18–20, 35, 39, 53–4, 60, 63, 102,
    110, 112, 121, 123, 126, 138, 149, 204,
    209, 218, 223, 228, 238, 244, 248, 254,
    261–2, 266–8
ravers 5, 179–93
recreation 1, 5, 24, 30, 32, 35–6, 38–9, 41–6,
    51–3, 58, 60–1, 63, 65, 91, 100, 116, 119,
    122, 124–5, 137, 142–62, 167–9, 172–4,
    185, 209–10, 213–21, 227–51, 254–71
    facilities 7, 101–2, 107, 135–6
    policy 6, 82–3, 240, 250, 256, 258
Recreation Opportunity Spectrum 261–2, 265
regional water companies 136
reindeer breeding 152
religion 49–50
right to roam 3, 16, 38, 47, 49–50, 52, 57,
    60–1, 63–5, 67, 85, 211, 215, 229–30
right to silence 180
rights of way 15, 32, 34, 52, 56, 59, 65, 179,
    192, 200–1, 207–11, 218, 223, 249, 251,
    262, 264, 269
riksentressen 145–6, 153, 156
Riparian Law (Sweden) 143, 145, 149, 151,
    160
Robinson, Sir Roy 101–5, 108, 123
Romantic Movement 49, 172–3
Ropner, Colonel 103
Rotary Club 109
Royal Forests 108
Royal Society for Nature Conservation 263
Royal Society for the Protection of Birds 6,
    60–2, 64–5
Ruddle, Kenneth 131
rural idyll 5, 179–80, 184, 185, 187–92
Russia 13
Rutland 4, 129–41
Rutland Water 4, 129–41
Rye 102

Sankt Anna Archipelago 153–7
Savernake Forest 182–3
Scandinavia 138
Scotland 228
Scottish Association of Boys' Clubs 102
Scottish Natural Heritage 257, 260, 264, 271
Scruton, Roger 191
Secretary of State for the Environment 256
semiotics 129
Set-aside 41, 43
Shanks and McEwan 219
Sharp, Thomas 114
Sheffield 91
Shell 4, 89–99, 270
Shell-Mex and BP Ltd 89–91, 95, 97, 99
Sherwood 117
Shilling Guides 95–7
shooting 5, 12–14, 16, 19, 22, 27, 62, 197,
    199–211, 227
Sites of Special Scientific Interest 41, 136

Snowdonia 105–6, 117–18, 121
  National Forest Park 110
Social Democrat Party (Sweden) 147, 150–1
socialism 15, 78
social theory 70
Society for the Preservation of Fauna of the
  Empire 128
Southampton 183
South Elmsall 243, 247
Soviet Realism 109
Spiral Tribe 183
Sports Council 24, 35, 259, 271
Staffordshire 213
state 4, 36–7, 39–40, 51, 70, 73–6, 83, 92, 115,
  148–9, 179, 188, 192
State Forests 108, 112
state subsidies 40, 42, 70, 84
Stirling-Maxwell Bart, Sir John 101
Stockholm 149, 158, 160
Stourhead (Wiltshire) 97
Strathfyre Forest 114
Sweden 12, 22, 142–61, 229
Swedish National Environment Protection
  Board (*Statens Naturvardsverk*) 152
Swedish National Land-Use Planning system
  (*Fysisk riksplanering*) 144
Swedish Planning and Building Act 144
Swedish Society for the Conservation of
  Nature (*Naturskyddsforeningen*) 145
Switzerland 138

Tamesdown Metropolitan Borough 28
tax concessions 28, 57
Taylor, Dorceta 168
Taylor, W.L. 108–10
technology 36
Thatcher, Mrs 17
Thompsen, Peter 101
timber production 104, 106
Tir Cymen 6, 20, 264–5, 268
Tory Party 53
tourism 92–3, 110, 116, 122, 154, 157–9, 255,
  267
travellers 5, 179–93
Treasury, the 28, 32, 59, 63, 128
trespass 15–20, 26, 28, 30, 34, 38, 45, 47, 51,
  53–5, 60, 62–3, 67, 71, 85, 102, 179–84,
  190–2, 197
Trumpington, Sir Roger de 93
Tunnicliffe, C.F. 107

Twyford Down 182–4, 188, 192

Unionist Party 102
United Nations Conference on Environment
  and Development (1992) 256
U.S.A. 103, 261

venison 108
Victorians 89

Waites, Bryan 131–2, 139–41
Wakefield Metropolitan District Council
  238–53
Wales 264, 266
Walkers (Access to the Countryside) Bill 25
walking – *see* rambling
Wanstead 191
water purification 137
welfare provision 75, 108, 114, 124, 132, 229
Welland and Nene River Authority 134
Wellingborough 130
West Midlands 239
Wheeler, Dr 105
White Horse, Uffington 97
wilderness 49, 100, 119, 121, 123–5, 261
Wildlife and Countryside Act (1981) 27, 41,
  56, 67
Wilson, Maurice 97
Wilson, Norman 125
Windermere, Lake 271
Windermere Urban District Council 55
Windsor Castle 96
Woburn Estate 11
Women's Walking Network 251–2
Wong, Judy Ling 170
Woodland Grant Schemes 27
Woodland Trusts 6, 224
Wordsworth, William 116
World War II 40, 54, 95, 108, 121, 150, 250
Worth, Jeremy 171
Worthing Art Gallery 92
Wright, Joseph 91
Wye, River 122

Yellow Pages 199
Yorkshire Dales 55
  National Park 56, 58
Young Farmers Club 109–10
Youth Hostel Association 64, 106, 122–3, 128
youth hostelling 102–4, 121